James Joyce: *The Centennial Symposium*

James Joyce
The Centennial Symposium

Edited by Morris Beja, Phillip Herring, Maurice Harmon,
David Norris

UNIVERSITY OF ILLINOIS PRESS · Urbana and Chicago

Acknowledgments

The editors would like to thank Lynn Childress, Deborah Fleming, and Elizabeth O'Neill for their assistance in preparing these essays for publication.

LIBRARY OF CONGRESS CATALOGING-IN-PUBLICATION DATA

Main entry under title:

James Joyce : the centennial symposium.

Papers presented at the Eighth International James Joyce Symposium, Dublin, Ireland, 1982.
1. Joyce, James, 1882–1941—Criticism and interpretation—Congresses.   I. Beja, Morris.
II. International James Joyce Symposium (8th : 1982 : Dublin, Dublin)
PR6019.09Z644   1986   823'.912   85-24591
ISBN 0-252-01291-7

For Lucia Joyce, 1907–1982

Contents

Preface, *Phillip Herring*   XI

Abbreviations   XVII

1. ## The Joyce Connection

   Joyce and the Professors   3
   William Chace

   "Masked with Matthew Arnold's Face":   9
   Joyce and Liberalism
   Seamus Deane

   Yeats and Joyce (Papers by A. Walton Litz, Giorgio   21
   Melchiori, and Richard Ellmann)
   Ellen Carol Jones, Moderator

   Gender and Narrative Voice in *Jacob's Room* and   31
   A Portrait of the Artist as a Young Man
   Karen Lawrence

   Virginia Woolf Reads James Joyce: 39
   The *Ulysses* Notebook
   Suzette A. Henke

   What Joyce after Pynchon?   43
   Richard Pearce

   Naming in Pynchon and Joyce   47
   David Seed

2. ## Sirens Without Music

   Joyce's Lipspeech: Syntax and the Subject in "Sirens"   59
   Derek Attridge

   To Sing or to Sign   66
   Maud Ellmann

Echo or Narcissus?   70
    Daniel Ferrer

"Sirens": The Emblematic Vibration   76
    André Topia

The Silence of the Sirens   82
    Jean-Michel Rabaté

The Language of Flow   89
    Robert Young

3. Aspects of *Finnegans Wake*

Beyond Explication: The Twice-Told Tales in   95
    Finnegans Wake
    Bernard Benstock

Finnegans Wake as a History of the Book   109
    Carol Shloss

Finnegans Wake: The Passage toward Pentecost   123
    Beryl Schlossman

"Mixing Memory and Desire": The "Tristan and   132
    Iseult" Chapter in *Finnegans Wake*
    Margot Norris

Narratology and the Subject of *Finnegans Wake*   137
    Jean-Michel Rabaté

4. Joyce's Consubstantiality

Joyce's Consubstantiality   149
    Sheldon Brivic

Joyce's Goddess of Generation   158
    Elliott B. Gose, Jr.

5. Biographical Studies

"Thrust Syphilis Down to Hell"   173
    J. B. Lyons, M.D.

Joyce's Early Publishing History in America   184
    Ann McCullough, O.P.

Shadow of His Mind: The Papers of Lucia Joyce   193
   David Hayman

6.   Major Addresses
     Signs on a White Field   209
        Hugh Kenner

     Ulysses and Its Audience   220
        A. Walton Litz

Notes on Contributors   231

Preface

Phillip Herring

Here came everybody, some five hundred and fifty Joyceans, from countries far and near, and from around the corner of Grafton Street, to celebrate the centennial of James Joyce's birth (2 February 1882), on Bloomsday, 16 June 1982, in Dublin. The Eighth International James Joyce Symposium took place in Joyce's birthplace at a fascinating historical moment. His native land seemed either to have forgiven him his exile, apostasy, and bitter rebukes, or to have decided that his infamy is good for tourist revenue. Whatever the motive, Dublin's red carpet was spread for Joyce and Joyceans as never before.

During the symposium Patrick Hillery, the president of Ireland, remarked that "It is time to repay the honor and fame he has brought his native city." Dublin seemed to agree. The national Irish radio broadcast a reading of *Ulysses* for upwards of thirty-one hours and featured many parts expertly done. At the time of day in *Ulysses* when the "Wandering Rocks" episode occurs, the episode was reenacted as street theater by some one hundred players in period costume, with a viceregal procession complete with horses and coaches wending its way through Dublin. Dubliners were surely surprised to see their Lord Mayor Alexis FitzGerald, newly wed, playing the Viceroy, while a throwaway boat filled with odd-looking people, including a ranting preacher in black, floated merrily down the Liffey. And some of us will never forget the look of horrified disgust on a nun's face when she saw Joyce scholar Clive Hart dressed as Father Conmee in black cassock and biretta, yoyoing a rosary in his left hand. When the word got out that the viceregal procession might go by the Ormond Hotel, and that for a short time it would be selling stout at 1904 prices, there was a mob scene that vividly illustrated how thirsty a Dubliner—or a European or American visitor, for that matter—can get when they're "givin' the stuff away."

The Chapelizod Bridge near Phoenix Park was renamed the Anna Livia Bridge after Joyce's female principle in *Finnegans Wake,* although the Irish stopped short of actually renaming the Liffey River. Presumably it was thought wise to save something for 2082. Lest *Ulysses* enthusiasts feel slighted, a plaque was unveiled by Hugh Kenner at 52 Upper Clanbrassil Street which read, "Here in Joyce's imagination was born in May 1866 Leopold Bloom, citizen, husband, father, wanderer." Some of the neighbors seemed to remember the Blooms as quite decent folks, but they believed that the correct address was more likely Lower Clanbrassil Street, nearer the center of the old Jewish neighborhood. One Dubliner whose house Kenner photographed remembered Joyce well: "used to fly over here on weekends," he said. (It was Kenner who coined the term "Irish facts.")

An Irish postage stamp was issued with Joyce's face on it for the occasion of the symposium; one Dubliner was heard grumbling over how the Irish would feel about licking the reverse side of such a dirty author. Joyce's face also appeared on a bust unveiled on St. Stephen's Green during symposium week, dim eyes peering across the street at his alma mater, University College. The artist, Marjorie Fitzgibbon, was commissioned by American Express. Dublin had nothing to do with the financing, and rumor had it that it was for that reason that Joyce's grandson Stephen decided to stay at home in Paris.

Actually, Ireland has probably never before displayed more generosity toward any writer. There was a state reception in Dublin Castle, and although the Irish president was cordial and accessible throughout, he was in danger of being upstaged by numerous other dignitaries, including at least two American pop singers and a television actor. During the week there was an exhibition called "James Joyce in Trieste" opened by the Italian ambassador, a reception in the National Gallery, and exhibitions in Newman House, the Douglas Hyde Gallery, Oriel II Gallery, the National Library, the James Joyce Tower, the Peacock Theatre, and the Ormond Hotel. Other exhibitions were held in Cork. The highlight of the symposium may well have been the moving tribute to Joyce by blind Argentine writer Jorge Luis Borges at the Bloomsday Banquet.

If the extracurricular festivities at the Centennial James Joyce Symposium seemed overwhelming, the variety and number of academic events made the intellectual side of the conference simply awesome. The success of this complex undertaking is due to the efforts of many people who cannot all be named here, but special thanks are owed to David Norris, chairman of the Joyce Centennial Committee; to the director, Patrick J. Long; the secretary, Robert Nicholson; and G. P. Malone, the public relations officer. Credit for the academic program goes to Maurice Harmon, Morris Beja, and the Centennial Committee.

The volume of essays which follows represents a fair sampling of the best that was thought and said at the Centennial James Joyce Symposium. It is the result of a considerable amount of deliberation on the part of the four editors. Roughly half the submissions were declined for one reason or another; many valuable ones did not fit the editors' collective vision of what the volume should be: a selection of the best contributions, but only those which lent themselves to thematic cohesion.

Several of the addresses were unavailable for inclusion: Anthony Burgess spoke brilliantly without notes for precisely one hour. The acoustics at Mansion House were unfortunately so awful that the recording of his talk was untranscribable. Richard Ellmann's address had previously been promised elsewhere. Burgess, Sir William Empson, Jorge Luis Borges, and Dennis Potter were guests of the Irish government and were not required to perform, but rather to honor Joyce with their presence. For varying reasons their remarks would not make publishable manuscripts.

The first section of essays in this volume concerns Joyce, the critics, and other writers. Most Joyce critics are professors, but before William Chace's contribution here, probably nobody had adequately focused on Joyce's attitude toward us academics, as reflected in his works. The section continues with Seamus Deane's thesis that Joyce rejected not only his Irish Catholic heritage, but the British liberal tradition as well, especially as represented by Matthew Arnold. For Arnold, Ireland was more fiction than fact, a counterpoint to his theory of poetry and morality.

At the symposium Ellen Carol Jones chaired a panel on Joyce and Yeats. In her introduction here she gives the general contours of their relationship, mentioning Joyce's early contentiousness with the older poet who eventually helped him so much. Walton Litz singles out Yeats's poetry of the 1890s as the phase that most attracted Joyce. Apparently he could cite most of it from memory, and did so during sentimental moods. When they first met in 1903, Yeats was most interested in local issues that bored Joyce. The result was that they met on nearly equal terms, and Joyce was thus able to avoid feelings of envy. Giorgio Melchiori compares the two writers' interest in towers and finds political implications worth reflecting upon. Richard Ellmann compares Joyce with Yeats and finds each metaphysical in his own way.

Two critics in the "Joyce Connection" section place Joyce and Woolf side by side with interesting results. In comparing the narrative strategies in *A Portrait of the Artist* and *Jacob's Room*, Karen Lawrence illuminates the respective attitudes of Joyce and Woolf toward patriarchal authority. Suzette Henke looks at the connection from a different perspective. She examines Woolf's unpublished notebook on modern novels in the New York Public Library and finds Woolf's attitude toward Joyce's work to be less negative, more cognizant of its importance, than the standard quotations on the subject would indicate. Indeed, Henke believes that Woolf saw Joyce as a kind of artistic double "in the modernist battle for psychological reality in fiction."

Joyce and Thomas Pynchon are considered by the two final contributors to the first section of essays. Richard Pearce believes that reading the novels of Pynchon gives us new perspectives on Joyce, while David Seed explores the meaning of names and naming in the works of Joyce and Pynchon.

The "Sirens Without Music" section derives from a panel on the "Sirens" episode of *Ulysses* which examined linguistic patterns. All contributors agree that too much attention has been paid to the chapter's musical qualities and too little to its language. Derek Attridge's contribution is about the way organs of the body in "Sirens" seem to have lives of their own, many actions being attributed to them rather than to specific persons. Bipolar modalities of time-space, the audible and the visible, reading and writing, all become part of Maud Ellmann's often hilarious reading of Bloom's farted "ee." Daniel Ferrer's interest is in the misleading nature of Joyce's schema and much previous commentary on "Sirens." André Topia focuses on typical sentence patterns, while Jean-Michel Rabaté discusses silence and the advantages of classical rhetorical terms in reading this episode. Finally, Robert Young studies the language of flow in "Sirens."

The next section deals with various aspects of *Finnegans Wake*. Bernard Benstock tracks narrative flux, and listens to tone in "The Mookse and the Gripes" tale, especially the Nuvoletta portion, and "Burrus and Caseous." Carol Shloss reminds us of Joyce's battles with printers and errata, and how his interest in printing generally is communicated in *Finnegans Wake*. Some interesting illustrations accompany her essay. The intricacies of Pentecostal language in *Finnegans Wake* are examined from a Judaic perspective by Beryl Schlossman, while Margot Norris looks at the themes of memory, desire, and growing old as they explain the four old men in the "Tristan and Iseult" chapter. In his second contribution, Jean-Michel Rabaté takes us gracefully through complexities of narration in "Narratology and the Subject of *Finnegans Wake*."

Sheldon Brivic examines an original thesis: that in *Finnegans Wake* "the structure of God is the structure of the family, and both of these are the structure of the mind." A separate exposition of this thesis appears in his book *Joyce the Creator* (University of Wisconsin Press). Also in the section entitled "Joyce's Consubstantiality," Elliott B. Gose, Jr., illuminates the many female forms of *Ulysses,* "goddesses of generation" animated by a Joyce aware of his own feminine urges.

In the next section of our book are two biographical studies and one on Joyce's publishing history. In response to rumors, Dr. J. B. Lyons, an eminent Dublin physician, examines Joyce for symptoms of syphilis and gives him a clean bill of health. Sister Ann McCullough provides new information on a topic of which Joyceans are largely ignorant: Joyce's business relationship with his American publisher Benjamin W. Huebsch, who "was the first publisher of *Dubliners* in the United States, and the first to publish *A Portrait of the Artist as a Young Man* anywhere." He could have been the first to publish *Ulysses,* but wasn't.

Joyceans will also be largely unaware of the existence of certain relevant documents written by Joyce's schizophrenic daughter Lucia, recently deceased, which provide insight into her troubled mind and interesting imagination. These fascinating documents have been described and evaluated by David Hayman.

In the final section are two of the major addresses, by a pair of the most respected authorities on modern literature in English. Hugh Kenner starts by examining the relationship between the *Dubliners* stories and Biblical paradigms, then moves on to the story of Rory-Roderick O'Connor in *Finnegans Wake,* to curious dictionary meanings and unintentional puns. One thesis is that Joyce felt that people reenacted paradigms; another is that words conceal identities, some of which may be false.

A. Walton Litz explores the way in which a great writer like Joyce creates his own audience, tastes, and critical tradition, but Litz focuses as well on the modernist audience of 1922 who were the first readers of *Ulysses.* He writes of Eliot's concern about influence and Pound's lack of it, and how the critical tradition about *Ulysses* has evolved since the 1950s. A major point is that all works are more hospitable to some approaches than to others, and that this congeniality is historically determined.

All in all, the collection is not only a record of the symposium which celebrated the centennial of James Joyce's birth; it also contains essays which will be continual reference points in the years to come. This volume presents a representative cross-section of contemporary theoretical approaches and current research with regard to the works of one of the century's greatest writers.

Abbreviations

The following abbreviations—those also used in the *James Joyce Quarterly*—have been used throughout this volume to indicate standard editions of Joyce's works and important secondary texts. No additional references to these works have been given in individual bibliographies.

CP Joyce, James. *Collected Poems*. New York: Viking Press, 1957.

CW Joyce, James. *The Critical Writings of James Joyce*. Ed. Ellsworth Mason and Richard Ellmann. New York: Viking Press, 1959.

D Joyce, James. *Dubliners*. Ed. Robert Scholes in consultation with Richard Ellmann. New York: Viking Press, 1967.
Joyce, James. *"Dubliners": Text, Criticism, and Notes*. Ed. Robert Scholes and A. Walton Litz. New York: Viking Press, 1969.

E Joyce, James. *Exiles*. New York: Viking Press, 1951.

FW Joyce, James. *Finnegans Wake*. New York: Viking Press, 1939; London: Faber and Faber, 1939.

GJ Joyce, James. *Giacomo Joyce*. Ed. Richard Ellmann. New York: Viking Press, 1968.

JJI Ellmann, Richard. *James Joyce*. New York: Oxford University Press, 1959.

JJII Ellmann, Richard. *James Joyce*. New York: Oxford University Press, 1982.

Letters I, II, III Joyce, James. *Letters of James Joyce*. Vol. I. Ed. Stuart Gilbert. New York: Viking Press, 1957; reissued with corrections 1966. Vols. II and III. Ed. Richard Ellmann. New York: Viking Press, 1966.

P Joyce, James. *A Portrait of the Artist as a Young Man*. The definitive text corrected from Dublin Holograph by Chester G. Anderson and edited by Richard Ellmann. New York: Viking Press, 1964.
Joyce, James. *"A Portrait of the Artist as a Young Man": Text, Criticism, and Notes*. Ed. Chester G. Anderson. New York: Viking Press, 1968.

SH Joyce, James. *Stephen Hero*. Ed. John J. Slocum and Herbert Cahoon. New York: New Directions, 1944, 1963.

SL Joyce, James. *Selected Letters of James Joyce*. Ed. Richard Ellmann. New York: Viking Press, 1975.

U Joyce, James. *Ulysses*. New York: Random House, 1934 ed., reset and corrected 1961.

1. The Joyce Connection

Joyce and the Professors

William Chace

In *Joyce's Voices* the most influential Joycean of all, Hugh Kenner, observes that an understanding of *Ulysses* was first enabled by Joyce himself acting through the helpful persons of Valéry Larbaud, Stuart Gilbert, and Frank Budgen: "It is behind (them) that the artist disappears, nail-file in hand. It was they, at (Joyce's) behest, who equipped the great affirmation of meaninglessness with meaning" (Kenner 63). Without necessarily being right about the meaninglessness of the book, Kenner is surely right about the ventriloquial process by which Joyce *saw to it* that readers would learn about such matters as the Homeric analogues, the *monologue intérieur,* and the intricate means by which hours, organs, and the various arts systematize each episode. After Larbaud, Gilbert, and Budgen came, of course, Edmund Wilson; he was followed by legions of scholars, mostly American, mostly professional academics, mostly faithful to the sober imperatives of explication and interpretation. The words of Joyce continue to generate the professorial words in whose dense complexity and sophistication we today thrive.

The Joyce who adroitly provided—through Larbaud, Gilbert, and Budgen—the fundamental patterns within which our energies are still to be deployed might now cast a sardonic eye on the professorial guild encamped around his achievement. It was Joyce, after all, who sensed where the entire business might have been heading; it was he who said, as early as the mid-1920s, "I've put in so many enigmas and puzzles that it will keep the professors busy for centuries, arguing over what I meant . . ." (*JJII* 521). But it was also Joyce who, in speaking to Arthur Power, apparently sensed that where it was heading might be into an academic cul-de-sac, and said that ". . . *Ulysses* is fundamentally a humorous work, and when all this present critical confusion about it has died down, people will see it for what it is" (Power 89). But even what it is—a book about love, about paternity, about words, about fidelity, about Ireland, about itself—seems at times never to have been fixed rigidly in Joyce's mind, much less in the minds of his most learned and clever interpreters. "Though people may read more into *Ulysses* than I ever intended," Joyce also said to Power, "who is to say that they are wrong: do any of us know what we are creating?" (89). In the presence of the implacable energies of the interpreting professors, we are thus reminded of at least three opinions on Joyce's part about the merits of interpreting *Ulysses:* one, that such interpretation is merely of "puzzles"; two, that the book obviates interpretation because it is plainly humorous; and three, that the book might very well be, à la currently fashionable critical discourse, no more or less than what its various readers, in their interpretations, can ingeniously claim it to be.

Out of such authorial ambivalence, and into such a codified world of professorial discourse as we today maintain, comes *Ulysses*. Even with his doubts about interpretation, Joyce could have only dimly imagined just how organized, how industrious, how systematic professorial interpretation could have become. That the English departments of American universities would ultimately comprise the home for his books would, of course, have been dismaying to him, but more powerful than his dismay would have been his total surprise, a surprise mixed with roguish satisfaction. The source of that satisfaction would have been the knowledge that he and his great cunning had set the academic machine in motion. Combine such dismay with such surprise and such satisfaction, then, and reflect on how Joyce might have viewed things when authority of understanding passed from Larbaud and Gilbert to Wilson and Harry Levin and then to all of us.

But Joyce's work does not come into our hands unarmed and defenseless against the pressures of interpretation we apply to it. It has its own ways of resisting our professional solicitude. In fact, as I shall here contend, its way of talking about professors as professors talk about it is one of its many means of self-preservation. Without knowing what English departments in modern universities would turn out to be, Joyce clearly had his eye on professors.

Consider, if you will, one of the first professorial references we encounter in *Ulysses*. In "Calypso," it is to "Professor Goodwin," or rather, in Bloom's words, to "poor, old Professor Goodwin. Dreadful old case" (63:5). He had, we learn, accompanied Molly in a concert in 1893 or 1894 and had, as she was to discover, kept a small mirror in his silk hat. Later, in "Lestrygonians," the concert is again mentioned and Professor Goodwin is once more the object of Bloom's pity and condescension: "Shaky on his pins, poor old sot" (156:16). His later appearance in "Circe" emphasizes his effete uselessness and incompetence: "Professor Goodwin, in a bowknotted periwig, in court dress, wearing a stained inverness cape, bent in two from incredible age, totters across the room, his hands fluttering. He sits tinily on the piano stool and lifts and beats handless sticks of arms on the keyboard, nodding with damsel's grace, his bowknot bobbing" (575:1–6). He retires at last from the book as if dismissed by Molly herself, whose lover he is unaccountably held to be in "Ithaca" (along with other unlikelies such as Julius Mastiansky, Father Corrigan, and Pisser Burke); of him she speaks disdainfully in "Penelope," comparing him to Stephen. Against the latter's promise is held Goodwin's alcoholic fecklessness: "I hope hes not a professor like Goodwin was he was a patent professor of John Jameson" (775:20–22).

The next professor we are offered is Professor MacHugh. Appearing in "Aeolus," he is at once cynical, pompous, unshaven, and defeated. Modeled by Joyce after Hugh McNeill, who had once taught Romance languages at Maynooth, and whose title as "Professor" was unfortunately spurious, MacHugh is an unhappy toady both to Latin and to British colonialism: "—We were always loyal to lost causes, the professor said. Success is for us the death of the intellect and of the imagination. We were never loyal to the successful. We serve them. I teach the blatant Latin language. I speak the tongue of a race the acme of whose mentality is the maxim: time is money. . . . I ought to profess Greek, the language of the mind" (133:10–14, 23–24). When MacHugh later appears in the book, it is in "Circe," where he high-handedly speaks on behalf of all those who have been subjecting Bloom to the ordeal of a cross-examination involving the affair of the plasterer's bucket. He coughs and calls to Bloom from the press-table: "Cough it up, man. Get it out in bits" (462:28–29). As a professor, MacHugh is thus seen as a man who, defeated himself, derives his pleasure from entangling others in defeat. Opinionated, officious, and only slightly less useless than "Professor" Goodwin, "Professor" MacHugh figures in *Ulysses* as another means of obliquely indicting the world of established learning.

This indictment is reinforced by the appearance, in "Wandering Rocks," of "Mr Denis J. Maginni, professor of dancing, &c., in silk hat, slate frockcoat with silk facings, white kerchief tie, tight lavender trousers, canary gloves and pointed patent boots, walking with grave deportment" (220:24–27). This startling fop, who preserves his elegant pointlessness through the episode, reappears, dancing like a bee, in "Circe." A "professor" by courtesy only, he is based on a real eccentric and minor fraud of the time who, born Maginnis, renamed himself Maginni. So much, then, for yet another Joycean professor.

Professors cited in the book, but who do not appear in it, include most prominently the various late-nineteenth-century Shakespearean critics and scholars, such as Gerald Massey, Edward Dowden, George Brandes, Sidney Lee, and Frank Harris. Their tidbits of biographical information, synthesized by Joyce, provide the "local color" and convincing detail which lubricates Stephen's theory of *Hamlet*. And just as Stephen's theory meets opposition owing to its extreme implausibility, so Joyce himself was attracted to one of the most improbable of the theories promulgated by a professor of Joyce's time. Karl Bleibtreu (mentioned at 214:9) published in 1907 a book asserting that Shakespeare's plays had been written by the Fifth Earl of Rutland (Roger Manners). As a testimonial to the affinity which Joyce felt for Bleibtreu and his assertions, he met and questioned the professor when both of them were living in Zurich. Joyce's interest in theories of Shakespearean authorship seems to have been in direct proportion to their implausibility. Their implausibility, moreover, seems to have been all the more inviting to him in direct proportion to their having been advanced by professors.

To move now from real professors and their eccentric reputations and questionable notions, we return to Bloom. For it is in the narrative deformations to which his character is vulnerable that we find another reflection of Joyce's attitude towards the profession of professor. In "Cyclops," Bloom's fortunes sink and fail, at least in the perspective of those who surround and dislike him. As he is made to look weak and as he ineptly tries to defend himself against his overbearing countrymen, he twists, squirms, and at last starts speaking like . . . a professor:

> So they started talking about capital punishment and of course Bloom comes out with the why and wherefore and all the codology of the business. . . .
>
> And then he starts with his jawbreakers about phenomenon and science and this phenomenon and the other phenomenon.
>
> The distinguished scientist Herr Professor Luitpold Blumenduft tendered medical evidence to the effect that the instantaneous fracture of the cervical vertebrae and consequent scission of the spinal cord would, . . . (304:19–21, 37–42)

As Bloom toils ineffectually on under the weight of his polysyllables, we are obliged to take the obvious point: to be seen as a professor of science, in a world of crass violence, is to be seen, unfortunately, as a fool. The Joycean phrase given to all the otiose talk that Professor Blumenduft and his ilk spout is "pornosophical philotheology" (432:22).

It is to "Circe" that we turn at last to find the Joycean valediction offered to professors in *Ulysses*. Given that the prejudicial treatment accorded to Bloom in "Cyclops" is nothing compared to what he, his character, and his reputation are forced to undergo in "Circe," it is worth noting that among the last of the indignities he suffers in that episode, an indignity preceded by his being diagnosed as bisexually abnormal, demented, epileptic, bald, exhibitionistic, ambidextrous, idealistic, and virginal, is that he is a *professor*. One of the presiding doctors cries out: "Professor Bloom is a finished example of the new womanly man" (493:29–30). And being that kind of professor, we are told, is to be simple, lovable, quaint, coy, and, the doctor adds, capable of writing "a really beautiful letter, a poem in itself" (494:1–2). No surer sense of the affinity presumed to exist between the professorial and the effetely harmless is to be found in *Ulysses*. And finding it there should lead us to imagine it turning up in *Finnegans Wake*. There, transmogrified, it does, in fact, appear—in the section exposing us to the arguments, such as they are, of Shaun (now called Jones) about his brother Shem. Jones is a professor, and so asks questions of unresponsive students, possesses an abundance of learning in the form of digressions, wars with other scholars, and gets nowhere. His style can be described as quack mandarin:

> (I am purposely refraining from expounding the obvious fallacy as to the specific gravitates of the two deglutables implied nor to the lapses lequou asousiated with the royal gorge through students of mixed hydrostatics and pneumodipsics will after some difficulties grapple away with my meinungs). (151)
>
> As my explanations here are probably above your understandings, lattlebrattons, though as augmentatively uncomparisoned as Cadwan, Cadwallon, and Cadwalloner, I shall revert to a more expletive method which I frequently use when I have to sermo with muddlecrass pupils. (152)

Jones, like most Joycean professors, is pledged to the notion that the use of rationality, learning, and consciousness is preferable to their abdication. The space-oriented man is more practical than the time-oriented man. With the writings of Lucien Lévy-Bruhl somewhere in his mind, Professor Jones declares in favor of objectivity, the outward and the real. He who lives, as Shem lives, brooding on time and his inward subjectivity, is a beggar. But he who lives in clear relationship to the actualities of the day will be victorious. In short, Professor Jones serves as one of the instruments within *Finnegans Wake* by which arguments against *Finnegans Wake* may be mounted. The Professor tries to discredit the Night World so that the World of Day may be validated.

He fails, of course. He is meant to fail. In representing the professorial world and in being incapable of arresting—by the force of his intentional rationality—the contrary and alogical motions of mind on which the *Wake* is founded, Professor Jones speaks for a Joyce who had long before conceded the inadequacies of wholly systematic discourse. In *Ulysses,* the professorial cast of mind is a fit subject for comic ridicule. In the *Wake,* that cast of mind is larger and more imposing. But in both works, it is humbled by forces of life that are blind, nameless, and larger than any argument.

Robert Martin Adams is right, then, in saying that Joyce's "extraordinary view of life grew out of a defeat for, and disillusion with, the conscious, rational mind . . ." (171). The blackness at the end of "Ithaca" is the telltale mark of a sleeping energy so powerful that it can generate, first, Molly's soliloquy and, later, the whole of the *Wake.* It is the nuclear energy that can explosively repudiate the punier energies of applied rationality. For reasons wholly familiar to us all, however, it is with these lower levels of rationality that we professors do our work. There is obviously nothing else for us to work with. But, in so working, we would do well to remind ourselves of the other professors—Goodwin, MacHugh, Maginni, Bleibtreu, Blumenduft, and Jones—in whose professional company Joyce might well have been satisfied to see us labor away. As with most things, he had a place for us too.

Works Cited

Adams, Robert Martin. "The Bent Knife Blade: Joyce in the 1960's." *Partisan Review* (1960). As reprinted in *James Joyce: A Collection of Critical Essays,* ed. William M. Chace. Englewood Cliffs, N.J.: Prentice-Hall, 1974.

Kenner, Hugh. *Joyce's Voices*. London: George Allen and Unwin, 1980.

Power, Arthur. *Conversations with James Joyce*. New York: Barnes and Noble, 1974.

"Masked with Matthew Arnold's Face": Joyce and Liberalism

Seamus Deane

Let us begin in randomness. Joyce and De Valera share their birth year with Franklin Delano Roosevelt, Igor Stravinsky, Georges Braque, Virginia Woolf, and that memorable Malaprop, Samuel Goldwyn. It was also the year of *Treasure Island,* of the performance of Wagner's *Parsifal* at Bayreuth, of the posthumous publication of Bakunin's *God and the State.* In that year the Maxim machine gun was patented, Edison designed the first hydroelectric plant, in Wisconsin, and Joseph B. Breuer began to use hypnosis in the treatment of hysteria. In Dublin, the Kilmainham Treaty and the Phoenix Park murders took the headlines. In County Galway, the Maamtrasna murders, involving a number of Joyces, both as perpetrators and victims, took place. Ibsen's *An Enemy of the People* and Nietzche's *The Gay Science* also appeared, the latter announcing the death of God and providing for him a memorable obituary. One of the types of the new men to emerge from this Godless world, men who would be "a part of a higher history than all history hitherto," was the renouncer: "What does the renouncer do? He strives after a higher world, he wants to fly farther and longer and higher than all men of affirmation—*he throws many things away* that would hinder him in his flight, and among them several things that are not valueless, not unpleasant to him: he sacrifices them to his desire for the heights . . ." (*The Gay Science* Book I, Section 27).

Joyce, it may be said, was one of the embodiments of this sketch of the renouncer, although we are more likely to attend to those aspects of his Irish Catholic heritage which he repudiated—its religion, provincialism, and nationalism—than to those elements of British culture which he also renounced. In particular, he rejected the British liberal tradition, represented at its best in the nineteenth century by men like John Morley, the Stephens brothers, Leslie and Fitzjames, and, most of all, by Matthew Arnold. Here again, the birth year helps us, for it was in 1882 that Arnold's *Irish Essays* appeared. Joyce was nineteen days old on the date of their publication. A popular edition of the *Essays* appeared in 1891, the year of Parnell's death. About the time Joyce was conceived, in June 1881, Arnold had published his selection of Burke's *Letters, Speeches and Tracts on Irish Affairs.* Arnold died in 1888, the year of T. S. Eliot's birth, when the young Joyce was a student at Clongowes and the young Padraic Pearse was a student in a private school in Dublin. George Moore's *Confessions of a Young Man,* Wordsworth's *The Recluse* (published twenty-eight years after his death), Samuel Butler's idiosyncratic *Ex Voto,* Hardy's *Wessex Tales,* and Gissing's *A Life's Morning* all appeared then, the last two disfigured by having their conclusions altered to suit the demand of the publisher. In all, the decade of the 1880s seems now, in a century's retrospect, to provide us with an inventory of the forces which were to influence the work of Joyce. They may be listed as (a) Irish nationalism; (b) British liberalism; (c) the emergence of a specifically modern literature from the Romantic-Victorian climate; (d) the emergence of a mass audience; (e) the salience of modern Irish writing, led by Wilde, Shaw, Moore, and Yeats. All of the things mentioned here have a bearing on Joyce. Most of them are included in his work. We are concerned, however, only with a particular area of contact— that between Joyce and liberalism and the general implications that may be drawn from that.

Arnoldian liberalism can be seen now, without too great a distortion, as an attempt to preserve an idea of "culture" for a society which was undergoing one of the earliest experiments in mass education. Arnold Toynbee pointed out, in *A Study of History,* that "universal compulsory gratuitous public instruction was inaugurated in this country in A.D. 1870; the Yellow Press was invented some twenty years later . . ." (vol. 4, 193). In other words, as Toynbee goes on to say, the first generation of children educated under this scheme had a new kind of reading matter provided for them. The Philistines thus won a great victory by seizing the minds of the populace and making a profit from doing so. Although the intervention of the state in educational policy in 1870 (and later in 1902 and 1922) did represent a success of a kind for Arnold's beseechings, the separation indicated by the audience which read the *Yellow Book* and that which read the Yellow Press was ominously deep. William Morris's words of 1882, in his *Hopes and Fears for Art,* sound hopelessly naive in the light of future developments: "If art which is now sick is to live and not die, it must in the future be of the people, for the people, by the people; it must understand all and be understood by all" (189). As far as the general audience was concerned, that meant that art must be more like *Robert Elsmere* than like *Tess.*

Arnold, like many of his best-known contemporaries, wished to create a new national vision for an England which had become, in his view, stupefied by commercial advancement and success and, at the same time, dislocated by the disappearance of the shared certainties of religious faith. In his efforts to forge this new collectivity, he sought to find a counterbalance to the predominant "Hebraic" mentality. "The friends of culture," by enlarging and enriching the minds of the Hebraic "believers in action" were to bring about the conclusion Arnold spoke of in *Culture and Anarchy*

(1868): "And thus man's two great natural forces, Hebraism and Hellenism, should no longer be dissociated and rival, but should be a joint force of right thinking and strong doing to carry him on towards perfection. This is what the lovers of culture may perhaps dare to augur for such a nation as ours" (264).

The Hellenist, who sees the true law of things, who, for instance, would advocate birth control for the poor of the East End of London rather than belated schemes of philanthropy for their endless immiseration, is as much a figure of the Enlightenment as he is a Greek. The Hebraist is inclined to a fixity of opinions and a fetishistic belief in phrases, particularly Biblical phrases, which make him as provincial as they make him purposeful. George Eliot had given wonderful expression to this view in *Middlemarch* (1871–72), in the characters of Dorothea (a Hebraist) and Ladislaw (a Hellenist) and also in *Daniel Deronda* (1876), in which Zionism becomes the great project for the establishment of a new and harmonious community. Yet Arnold could see that the failure of English polity at home was nothing compared to its failure in Ireland. The Irish question, therefore, demanded the exercise of the Hellenist intelligence, for it was a good deal more worrying and violent than the Hyde Park Riots of 1866 or the anti-Catholic riots of 1867 and 1868 in Birmingham, Manchester, and elsewhere. Although Arnold could dismiss the Fenians in 1867, the year of their worst attacks in England, he was less sanguine by the 1880s. The Irish Celt had been recruited for literature and the imagination in the famous Oxford lecture of 1867; but the Irish Fenian, the Irish University Question, the Irish Home Rule Bill, and many other issues concerning the whole vexed problem of Ireland had accumulated such a force in his thought in the succeeding years that Arnold felt compelled to harmonize his Celtic diagnosis of the Irish personality with his socio-political diagnosis of the Hebraic English personality. In doing so he provided the Irish revival with one of its most cherished opinions about the utilitarian English spirit's incapacity to deal with the wild freedom of the imaginative Celt. Still, it is necessary to remember at all times what Arnold wrote in "The Future of Liberalism" (1880): "The master-thought by which my politics are governed is rather this—the thought of the bad civilisation of the English middle class" (141).

This fact helps to explain why Arnold's view of Ireland often seems so remote from Irish conditions. Ireland was for him as for John Stuart Mill and even John Morley an exemplary contrast to England. It provided a clue to England's ills but was in itself something of an abstraction, populated by "Celts," "Fenians," "Catholics," and "Northern Protestants," categories that were pliable to a variety of manipulations because they were all essentially foreign to home. As he remarks, ironically, in *Culture and Anarchy*, ". . . we can have no scruple at all about abridging, if necessary, a non-Englishman's assertion of personal liberty. The British Constitution, its checks, and its prime virtues, are for Englishmen" (63). Yet by 1881, in his essay "The Incompatibles," Arnold, under the influence of his recent reading of Burke, feels bound to treat the Irish problem as one of central significance for the resolution of the English problem: "But if we wish cordially to attach Ireland to the English connexion, not only must we offer healing political measures, we must also, and that as speedily as we can, transform our middle class and its social civilisation" (80). That caricature of the Hebraic Englishman, Dickens's Mr. Murdstone, epitomized for Arnold the Irish vision of England and explained the hostility between the two countries. This figure had dominated Ireland and, as a result, Ireland could never be attracted to the English civilization. In the same essay of 1881, he puts the situation like this:

> But the genuine, unmitigated Murdstone is the common middle-class Englishman, who has come forth from Salem House and Mr. Creakle. He is seen in full force, of course, in the Protestant north; but throughout Ireland he is a prominent figure of the English garrison. Him the Irish see, see him only too much and too often . . .
>
> The thing has no power of attraction. The Irish quick-wittedness, sentiment, keen feeling for social life and manners, demand something which this hard and imperfect civilisation cannot give them. Its social form seems to them unpleasant, its energy and industry to lead to no happiness, its religion to be false and repulsive. (68)

The spectacle of Arnold struggling with the Irish University Question, or with the problems of Irish and English secondary schools' syllabus and teaching methods, while advocating sweetness and light, healing measures, mildness of temper, flexibility of intelligence without the slackening of the moral fiber, is more edifying than stimulating. His Hellenized Victorianism seems definitively to miss the quality of the modernist problem and temperament, to offer nothing more than a secularism which would retain the emotion and poetry of religion without being hampered by its beliefs. Yet it is precisely this element in Arnold which is preserved and extended by Yeats and Joyce and which remained for a long time part of the heritage of Irish nationalism. Although it is well-known that Yeats, in his essay of 1902, "The Celtic Element in Literature," acknowledged both Renan and Arnold as sources for his own redaction of the legend of the poetic Celt embroiled with the hard and dull civilization of the English middle classes, it is less widely acknowledged that Yeats, Synge, and Pearse, in taking this over, never quite freed it from the pseudo-chivalric connotations which it had borne in Victorian times.

The Hellenization of England and the Celticization of Ireland (processes despairingly recommended to the middle classes of both countries by Arnold and Yeats respectively) are not just allied movements. They are the same movement. Arnold started more than he knew. In defining the deficiency of the English middle-class civilization, he gave the Irish the cultural distinction which they sought. They took that distinction to its logical terminus—political separation—even though Arnold's aim, in introducing it, had been to use it as an instrument of political and cultural reconciliation between the two, in order to attach Ireland more firmly, because more willingly, to England. In the midst of these ironies, Joyce's role might at first appear to be a characteristically subversive one. Like any good Nietzschean hero or renouncer, he regarded the un-Hellenized and un-Celticized communities as oppressive formations. But once the process of turning Ireland into a Celtic community had been begun by Yeats and his followers, especially through the Abbey Theatre, Joyce's sense of rejection became even more pronounced. English liberalism, in feeding Irish cultural nationalism with the Celtic pap, had exposed its own absurdity. Stephen Dedalus is nicely caught, in *Ulysses,* between the Celtic embodiment of the Sean Bhean Bhoct with the milk and the Hellenic Mulligan with the gift of the gab and a friend from Oxford who, like Arnold, feels that "history is to blame."

If history is to blame, the question then is, What is to be done? Arnold's remedy would seem to be that Catholic Ireland is to be won over to the civilization of Protestant England as Protestant Alsace was won over to Catholic France. The means to be used are Hellenic—sweetness, liberality, attraction. It may be said that Arnold's highly literary conception of the relationship between Celt and Saxon was a sterile illusion that could not survive the demand for any serious constitutional rearrangement of the link between Ireland and England. Two years before he died, he was greatly relieved to see Gladstone's meager Home Rule measure of 1886 defeated, even though that defeat was engineered by Joseph Chamberlain, a Murdstonian Englishman if ever there was one. But the political failure is inevitable when we look again at the racial (even racist) grounds from which it derives. The English, by becoming Hellenized, are going to attract the Irish to English civilization, thereby, at a stroke, canceling the Irish problem by the realization of the perfection of England. The question of Ireland's separateness or separation from England does not even appear on the horizon. The Irish are not conceived of as questioning why any Englishman, dry Nonconformist of the Murdstone type, or sweet Arnoldian liberal, should have the power and authority to conduct this reconciliation. As always, Ireland is really an absence for Arnold. It is merely a term in an argument which has as its goal the ratification of the great project for a perfectly formed and perfectly irresistible English civilization. If it has taken a long time to show itself, especially in Ireland, well, then, "history is to blame."

But this "history" is a protean concept. In Arnold's thought it seems to have two major constituent parts. One is morality, allied always to action, and embodied most powerfully in the Saxon races. The other is poetry, allied always to reflection and culture, and embodied, in a particularly pure manner, in the Celtic races. The conjoining of these two, for which he pleads, would lead to the revival of the full potential of civilization. Arnold wanted to save morality by making his audience nostalgic for it rather than eager practitioners of it. But nostalgia is properly given to something already lost. For him, the Celts were the lost poetry of Saxon morality. The consequence of the fusion of these two races would be an escape from the confusion of history. This can now seem nothing more than an absurdly naive use of racial theory to glamorize (by pretending to solve) the unlovely and brutalized relationship between Ireland and England. Arnold was always better on generalities than on particulars. Celts were more attractive to him than Irish; poetry was always more amenable to his system of hierarchical ranking than were poems. He was an apologist for power. His support for the state (on the Prussian model) and for the categories of race and culture inevitably led to the creation in his work of what Nietzsche, in a different context, called "the pathos of distance." In *The Genealogy of Morals,* Nietzsche writes of the "noble, powerful, high-stationed and high-minded" as the creators of the idea of goodness in order to distinguish themselves from "the low, low-minded, common and plebeian." In addition, "it was out of this *pathos of distance* that they first seized the right to create values and to coin names for values; . . . The pathos of nobility and distance . . . the protracted and domineering sense of the fundamental unity on the part of a higher ruling order in relation to a lower order . . . *that* is the origin of the antithesis of good and bad" (Kaufmann 462). The transposition of Arnoldian hierarchies of values, of the Arnoldian project for a new civilization (Unity of Being), of the racial and cultural implications of this thought, is completed and brought to a new intensity in the writings of the Irish revival and in the writings and actions of Pearsean nationalism. This is one of the sweetest and saddest of all fates. The leading British liberal unwittingly promoted two movements in Ireland, both of which professed contempt for his creed while adapting it to their own purposes.

The "pathos of distance" is especially useful for those who promote racial theories to enhance or support feelings of superiority in the home group and of inferiority in the foreign or Other group. Arnoldian liberalism and Irish cultural nationalism are akin in this respect, one proceeding from the assumptions of the colonizing power, the other from those of the colonized. One of the most effective variations on this concept, rediscovered by those novelists of the last four decades of the nineteenth century who have artists as their favorite protagonists, is that of the heroism of the extraordinary individual who, confronted by the mob, must create a distance from it and, in doing so, develop a kind of chivalry of the intellect. Yeats is the outstanding example of a writer who achieved this in poetry, molding his conception of the heroic artist to his conception of the heroic race and finding the English and the Irish middle classes his figure of the Other, the enemy. Joyce is clearly one of those who finds this an acceptable trope for bringing criticism to bear upon all those institutional forms of authority which he feared or despised, but he differed from Yeats in his readiness to scrutinize the trope itself and in coming to know it as a form of cultural determination from which he needed to find release. His scrutiny began with the assumption that the hero was fated to be homeless, a man permanently disaffected from the surrounding community, a heretic or a criminal who lived in the conviction of his own unimpeachable integrity. This hero-as-renouncer needs the pathos of distance just as much as the racial group or the social class. The scrutiny ended with the destruction of the pathos of distance and all its attendant myths. Within the work itself, the distance between the hero's consciousness and the world against which it is defined becomes increasingly narrow until, in *Finnegans Wake,* it disappears altogether. In addition, the distance between the work and the reader, articulated by the contractual relationship which had supported the realist tradition, was also broken, thereby leaving the possibility of moral decision or of aesthetic satisfaction very remote indeed. With that break, liberalism as a force in the modern novel began to disappear although it did survive the First World War in the work of one great novelist, E. M. Forster. Perhaps it finally disappeared when he confronted the crises of the liberal mind and of liberal discourse in *A Passage to India.* Finding it insurmountable, he lapsed into silence.

Arnold was aware of change; he had the sense of it, but could never define its form. Yet there was plenty of evidence to go on, although it must be conceded that much of it crystallized after Arnold's death in events like the fall of Parnell, the trial of Oscar Wilde, the Boer War. The year of his death saw the publication of the famous and anonymous pornographic work *My Secret Life.* George Moore wondered, in the same year, "why murder is considered less immoral than fornication in literature?" (This was also the year of Jack the Ripper.) The storm over Zola's work, which led to the prosecution of Vizetelly, his English publisher, the obloquy suffered by Hardy for his *Tess of the D'Urbervilles,* and numerous other instances of sexual scandals and censorship all point to the growing unease about the established forms of sexual convention in Victorian England. Yet this is scarcely mentioned anywhere in Arnold's works. Although Arnold was alert to the problems posed by the poverty as well as the numbers of the working classes, he was very far from linking that with changes in the climate of sexual opinion. Oscar Wilde made a characteristically disturbing connection between these facts when he assured an embarrassed friend, just before his trial, that "the working classes are with me—to a boy." Arnold's conception of culture has no element of the erotic. For the erotic was indissolubly associated with the criminal and he was innocent of what the exploration of the possibilities of criminality in relation to art might produce. The world of Wilde, Conrad, Hardy, Henry James, and, of course, Joyce, was beyond his horizon. For him, the problem of contemporary unease could be countered by the revival of a Hellenistic spirit through state intervention in the field of education. He would not have recognized the dramatic interplay between education and love which Hardy described in *Jude the Obscure* as a battle between "nerves" and "primitive feelings." Nor would he have recognized that the Wildean inversions and quips were diagnoses of the moral crisis of the age: "Wickedness is a myth invented by good people to account for the curious attractiveness of others." In the end, we may say that Arnold, and liberalism in general, found that intelligence was inadequate to deal with the problems which its scrutiny had revealed. The belief that there is a crisis is not the same thing as the willingness to let the sense of crisis become an energy in one's thought. This could never be said of Joyce. In 1904, in his sketch "A Portrait of the Artist," he declared ". . . the competitive order is employed against itself, the aristocracies are supplanted; and amid the general paralysis of an insane society, the confederate will issues in action" (*P* 266). These phrases, in which a socialist vision and a medical definition of the terminal stage of severe syphilitic infection are combined, reveal, behind Joyce's radical pose of the young artist, his preoccupation with the linkages between forms of political and forms of sexual convention. These relationships remain unexamined in Arnold. They become central to Joyce. On this issue alone, he transcended the limitations of British liberalism.

Nevertheless, Arnold had offered to Ireland a renovated vision of a new politics based on the idea of racial integrity. Since the early nineteenth century, perhaps even since Burke, this exclusionary notion of the English race had been associated with resistance to revolutionary politics of France and, by a strange extension, to the breakdown of sexual conventions which France seemed to epitomize. The old chivalric movement of the eighteenth century, associated with writers as diverse as Hurd, John "Estimate" Brown, and others, was revived by Burke, Sir Walter Scott, and, most famous of all, by Kenelm Digby in his *The Broad Stone of Honour* (4 volumes, 1828–29; an enlarged edition, in 5 volumes, appeared in 1877). In the meantime, Tennyson's *Idylls of the King* (1855–73), the Christian Socialists, Charlotte Yonge, and even the Pre-Raphaelites all contributed to the idea or ideal of a chivalric society in which the only honor that could be lost was sexual and the only honor worth winning was military. The military element was converted by the Public School system into a sporting element; but that soon reverted to its military origins in times of war—most notably the Crimean and the Boer wars, although World War I provided the long-desired opportunity to transfer chivalry from the playing fields of Eton to the battlefields of Flanders. Mark Girouard has provided the history of this tradition in *The Return to Camelot*. Pertinent here is the transformation of sexual attitudes into military ones and the manner in which male groupings, sports teams, regiments of soldiers, Baden-Powell's boy scouts (born out of the Boer War), came to be regarded as the representatives of all that is noble and chivalric in the race to which they belong. The Irish variation on this theme is Padraig Pearse's educational theories, his school, and the Fianna, all of which are founded on the same conviction that they embody the lost virtues of a noble race which they must revive by their behavior and, finally, by their military action. It takes no great percipience to see that Pearse also transmutes sexual into religious and racial terms. In doing so, he extends the British colonial tradition into an anti-colonial rebellious-ness even while preserving intact the deep, anti-revolutionary conservatism of his forerunners. Sexual purity, gentlemanly conduct, military valor, group loyalty, all contributed to the Irish nationalistic spirit. They were all originally English ideas; or, more precisely, their conflation into a myth of chivalry was originally English. Politics based on the idea of race led to the chivalric apotheosis of violence. This was very far from Arnold's racial conceptions, with their goal of reconciliation. Yet the two are related.

The connection with Joyce can immediately be made if we remember his fury at what he called Sinn Fein's "lying drivel" about the "venereal excess" of the English soldiers in Ireland. His letter of 13 November 1906 to Stanislaus is well-known. But there is a deeper connection. The phalanx of chivalric men represented a bogus form of community, even though it had a powerful appeal. The first great artist to explore this and the political implications of its formation and dispersion was Conrad. The preoccupa-tion with betrayal and the subsequent isolation which dominates his fiction leads to an examination of isolation and criminality as pathological states induced by the failure of communal coherence. Joyce, faced with an Irish version of the same communal vision, also explored the plight of the isolate, the heretic, but he conjoined this with an investigation into the plight of the heroic artist, the Nietzschean renouncer. Then he goes further again and contrasts this with the plight of twentieth-century man, putting such pressure on the form of the novel that he alters it out of all recognition in his attempt to absorb all the traces of a crisis which he inventories and reshapes.

His primary category is history. His aim is to release fiction from its bondage by incorporating it into fiction as one of many possible systems of order. Ireland's long troubles—her relationship with England, her re-bellions, mythologies, her subordination—are included in Joyce's work but do not constitute its subject. The Hellenic and Hebraic distinctions which we meet with in the opening episodes of *Ulysses* are experimental probings, means by which Stephen Dedalus can test the temperature of his contemporary reality. Mr. Deasy's Unionism, Kevin Egan's Fenianism, the most famous heresies of the early church, are comparable tropes. No one of them is finally useful in itself. All are dominated by a consciousness which seeks to know itself through them, not in them. As Stephen says of Shakespeare in "Scylla and Charybdis", "He found in the world without as actual what was in his world within as possible" (*U* 213). But the world without cannot provide a sufficient correlative to the world within. History may be a record of what happened. But there were other possibilities. The deaths of Pyrrhus and Caesar provoke Stephen to ruminate, "They are not to be thought away. Time has branded them and fettered they are lodged in the room of the infinite possibilities they have ousted. But can those have been possible seeing that they never were? Or was that only possible which came to pass?" (*U* 25). The area between the actual and the possible is the area of consciousness. In this, Stephen lives.

Stephen repudiates the solidarity of race, since that leads to falsification and violence. The history of Ireland is a manifestation of that; so too is the history of England. He repudiates the solidarity of the new Hellenism, the aestheticized echo of Arnold's thought, for that leads to the irresponsibility and shallowness of a Buck Mulligan. He also repudiates the solidarity of religion, since that too leads to subordination of the intellect. Thus he is left to cherish isolation, or, more exactly, to create, in his isolation, alternative forms of solidarity—with heretics, artists—which are, nevertheless, unsatisfactory. In this isolation, deprived of communal support and identification, Stephen is stricken by guilt, by the feeling of criminality. His criminality extends from his treatment of his mother to his sexual behavior. He is the artist in the culturally depressed world which Arnold had tried to educate. In such a situation, as R. P. Blackmur says, "To be either a dandy or dirty, and especially where out of keeping, is always a good role; and to be an anchorite or an oracle combines the advantages of both. You are in any case among enemies" (*A Primer of Ignorance 9*). To be among enemies is to find that desire is repressed. History has repressed the possible and substituted in its place the actual. Daily life counters the desire of consciousness, its wish to achieve the potential it feels, by forcing it to conform to the demand of convention: that is, by the rules which make the actual inevitable. Stephen and Bloom are both caught in this silent struggle, dreaming the discourse of freedom, speaking the discourse of repression. As in so many cases in modern literature, the tension between the two is dramatized by Joyce as a sexual tension, a traumatizing of deep energies, a frustration of life itself.

Yet Joyce's work does not rest with frustration. In "The Dead," *Ulysses*, and *Finnegans Wake* he restores to us a sense of community which is too deep-seated to be susceptible to fracture. He changed the terms in which, before him, the dilemma of consciousness and of culture had been understood. Rather than envisaging culture as the goal to be attained, he imagined it as the origin to which we can return. When consciousness is coincident with culture, we are in the world of Molly Bloom, HCE, Anna Livia Plurabelle, Gabriel, Gretta, and Michael Furey. For Arnold, and for liberals in general, the attainment of culture involved the setting-up of a program. It meant the conjoining of separated entities—action with thought, faith with intelligence, purpose with openness. Liberalism, in other words, suffered from the very disease which it sought to cure. It could only conceive of fusion in terms of fission. It begins with the premise of mass culture and sets itself the aim of converting it into authentic culture. Its idea of order had no generosity for the energies of anarchy and thus was bound to be indistinguishable from uniformity. Joyce found the means, formally and substantially, to comprehend what Blackmur has called "the living relation between anarchy and order." He demonstrated that art could indeed achieve what the state had failed to accomplish. In this respect, he goes beyond liberalism, although it is also true that he simultaneously goes beyond socialism and fascism as well. These three modalities of political organization grew out of the conditions which he faced in his art. His success and their failure illuminate one another.

It would be unfair to Arnold to leave the matter at that. There are passages in his work where he anticipates the issues of the future, although he seems to have no premonition of the manner in which art would be forced to deal with them. In *Culture and Anarchy,* he wrote:

> By our every-day selves, however, we are separate, personal, at war; we are only safe from one another's tyranny when no one has any power; and this safety, in its turn, cannot save us from anarchy. And when, therefore, anarchy presents itself as a danger to us, we know not where to turn.
>
> But by our *best self* we are united, impersonal, at harmony. We are in no peril from giving authority to this, because it is the truest friend we all of us can have; and when anarchy is a danger to us, to this authority we may turn with sure trust. Well, and this is the very self which culture, or the study of perfection, seeks to develop in us; at the expense of our old untransformed self, taking pleasure only in doing what it likes or is used to do, and exposing us to the risk of clashing with every one else who is doing the same! So that our poor culture, which is flouted as so unpractical, leads us to the very ideas capable of meeting the great want of our present embarrassed times! (89)

Comparing Arnold's point of view with that of John Stuart Mill, Lionel Trilling found, "if Arnold's position . . . is the more valid, because it forbids the sterile, atomic view of the individual, it nevertheless carried him to a conception of truth which looks to an ultimately mystical sanction" (*Matthew Arnold* 261).

Joyce knew the dangers of "the sterile, atomic view of the individual" and sought to avoid them by locating the individual in the totality of a communal human life which would embrace the past and the present, the accidental and the designed. But he also understood the degree to which the atomization of experience had advanced and how the consequences of this could be discovered in the realms of pathology before they could ever be alleviated in the programs of social and cultural reform. Perhaps the glimpse of Arnold we receive in *Ulysses,* caricatured as it is, has a final, telling accuracy. While Clive Kempthorpe is being debagged in the rooms of a spuriously "Hellenized" Oxford, the gardener cuts the grass, impervious to this undergraduate noise. His solemn and formal gait, his refusal to acknowledge this degraded and degrading romp, is an index of his refusal to accept the anarchy, callow and freakish, bred within the walls of Oxford and culture:

> Shouts from the open window startling evening in the quadrangle. A deaf gardener, aproned, masked with Matthew Arnold's face, pushes his mower on the sombre lawn watching narrowly the dancing motes of grassshalms.
> To ourselves . . . new paganism . . . omphalos. (*U* 7)

Works Cited

Arnold, Matthew. *Culture and Anarchy: An Essay in Political and Social Criticism.* London: Smith, Elder and Co., 1869.

———. "The Future of Liberalism." *Irish Essays, and Others.* London: Smith, Elder and Co., 1882.

———. "The Incompatibles." *Irish Essays, and Others.* London: Smith, Elder and Co., 1882.

Blackmur, Richard P. *A Primer of Ignorance.* Ed. Joseph Frank. New York: Harcourt, Brace & World, 1967.

Girouard, Mark. *The Return to Camelot.* Cambridge, Mass.: Harvard University Press, 1982.

Morris, William. *Hopes and Fears for Art.* Boston: Roberts Brothers, 1882.

Nietzsche, Friedrich. *The Genealogy of Morals.* In *The Basic Writings of Nietzsche.* New York: Modern Library, 1968.

Toynbee, Arnold. *A Study of History.* 12 vols. London: Oxford University Press, 1939. Vol. 4.

Trilling, Lionel. *Matthew Arnold.* New York: W. W. Norton, 1939.

Yeats and Joyce

Ellen Carol Jones

The following is a transcription of the major portions of a panel discussion on "Yeats and Joyce." The moderator was Ellen Carol Jones, Cornell University. Participants were A. Walton Litz, Princeton University; Giorgio Melchiori, University of Rome; and Richard Ellmann, Emory University.

Ellen Carol Jones:

It seems especially appropriate that we discuss the two greatest writers of English prose and poetry of this century in conjunction with each other. There has been relatively little critical work on the topic; although the work that has been done is extremely valuable, significant aspects of the artistic relationship between Yeats and Joyce have not yet been fully explored. It's my hope not only that this panel will discuss more fully those aspects of their relationship which have already been dealt with, but also that it will suggest new areas to investigate.

To provide a context, I'd like to review briefly some of the biographical facts of their relationship.[1] The two writers met in 1902, when Joyce showed Yeats his poems and epiphanies; three years before that meeting Joyce had defended Yeats's work by refusing to sign a petition against the portrayal of the Catholic peasantry in *The Countess Cathleen*. Yet less than one year before their meeting, in "The Day of the Rabblement," Joyce had attacked what he called Yeats's "treacherous instinct of adaptability" to the nationalistic aims of "the most belated race in Europe." The attack continued when the two artists met; according to Yeats in the preface originally intended for *Ideas of Good and Evil*, Joyce questioned: "Why had I concerned myself with politics, with folklore, with the historical setting of events and so on? Above all why had I written about ideas, why had I condescended to make generalizations? These things," Joyce claimed, "were all the sign of the cooling of the iron, of the fading out of inspiration." Joyce's final criticism of the thirty-seven-year-old poet is, of course, famous, ranging from the Dublin street version, "You are too old for me to help you," to the parody in *Finnegans Wake:* "I have met with you, bird, too late, or if not, too worm and early."

However, even if Yeats was too old to be helped by Joyce, he wasn't too old to help *him*—at least materially, if not artistically: he introduced him to editors; encouraged him to offer his poems to magazines; recommended him for grants and publications, acknowledging him to be "a man of genius," and "the most remarkable new talent in Ireland today"; interceded in his behalf—although unsuccessfully—for the publication of *Dubliners;* brought his work to the attention of Ezra Pound, who secured the serial publication of the *Portrait;* defended *Ulysses* before the Senate; and nominated him for membership in the Irish Academy he and Shaw were founding, telling him: "Of course the first name that seemed essential both to Shaw and myself was your own, indeed you might say of yourself as Dante said 'If I stay who goes, if I go who stays?' which means that if you go out of our list it is an empty sack indeed." Promptly, inexplicably, with amicability, gratefully, Joyce declined Yeats's invitation, prefacing his refusal with the acknowledgment: "It is now thirty years since you first held out to me your helping hand."

In art, as in life, both Yeats and Joyce come almost full circle. In a striking renunciation of his elder's vision of art, Joyce has Stephen in his diary differ from Yeats: "Michael Robartes remembers forgotten beauty and, when his arms wrap her round, he presses in his arms the loveliness which has long faded from the world. Not this. Not at all. I desire to press in my arms the loveliness which has not yet come into the world" (*P* 251). Yet Yeats, too, envisions "a loveliness which has not yet come into the world," not only in his art, as in the Byzantium poems, but also in his life, for Ireland in the coming times. And Joyce for his part structures his novel on the ancient legend of Odysseus, of course.

I've given only the briefest outline of moments of intersection and interaction in the lives of these two writers. The questions of artistic influence and interaction that this panel will explore are complex and rewarding ones. Walt Litz will begin our discussion by reviewing past criticism and suggesting ways in which recent ideas about literary influence and literary interaction may reveal new possibilities in exploring the Yeats/Joyce relationship. Giorgio Melchiori and Richard Ellmann will view the broader aesthetic, ideological, and political perspectives of the art of Yeats and of Joyce. Professor Litz.

A. Walton Litz:

Ellen's talk gives you the general outline of the relationship between Joyce and Yeats. I think the contours of their personal relationship will not be changed much by new scholarship. It's possible of course that the complete letters of Yeats being edited now may reveal other details, but it does seem to me that the general outline of the interactions, both personal and artistic, between Yeats and Joyce are now in place. And they're firmly in place in Richard Ellmann's *Eminent Domain* (1967), where the chapter on Joyce and Yeats is an extension, with footnotes and more information, of the Dolmen Press Yeats Centenary pamphlet published in the same year. There's also been, of course, a great deal of scholarship on the topic of Yeats and Joyce, starting from the villanelle of the *Portrait,* as many of you know, and its debt to Yeats, and articles on *Finnegans Wake* and its debt to everything from *The Wanderings of Oisin* to certain diagrams in *A Vision.* One piece of material that I ought to call attention to, since not everyone is aware of it, is in *The Identity of Yeats:* Richard Ellmann prints in full the suppressed or retracted "Preface" to Yeats's *Ideas of Good and Evil* of 1903, a preface written in that year which I think is the most important document about the relationship between Yeats and Joyce, and I'll say a word about it in a moment.

What still remains to be explored and more fully understood are what you might call the more secret relationships, both personal and artistic, between the two writers. Joyce's response to Yeats seems from first to last to have been based primarily on the early works, the works of the 1890s. There's good evidence that Joyce read Yeats throughout his long career, that he knew the poetry, for example, of *The Tower* and even the poetry of the early 1930s. But it seems to me that when Joyce is most closely attuned to Yeats, it is always with the Yeats of the 1890s, the Yeats of the *Rose* poems and *The Wind Among the Reeds.* In 1935, when Joyce was asked in Paris to recite his favorite poems, he recited two hours from memory from the poetry of William Butler Yeats. I'd be willing to bet that all of that poetry, or almost all of it, came from the 1890s: "Who Goes with Fergus?," songs from *The Countess Cathleen,* and so forth. So far as we can see, at his most sentimental and at his most spiritual, which I think is also at his most sincere, Joyce spoke of the poems of the Yeats of the 1890s. Last year when I was reviewing the new collection of all of Yeats's prose fiction of the 1890s for *TLS,* and therefore had occasion to read all of Yeats's prose fiction of the 1890s in the Cornell volume called *The Secret Rose,* I was struck by how much the cadences, the imagery, the language of that prose fiction— not just "The Adoration of the Magi" or "The Tables of the Law," but all of Yeats's fiction of the nineties—how much that is the essential rhythm, the inner life of Stephen Dedalus. In fact at its moments of highest lyrical resolve in the *Portrait,* the Dedalus speech—not just the themes but also the cadences—is that of the Yeats of the 1890s.

Now Yeats's own literary response to Joyce is more difficult and more problematic to understand. I would be willing to suggest—although it would take a good deal of work to give any kind of solid evidence for this—that the Yeats of *Per Amica,* the Yeats of the late teens, who is weltering in esoteric theory, bases at least part of his notion of a creative anti-self upon what Joyce did in *A Portrait* in the creation of Stephen Dedalus. But more work needs to be done on Yeats's literary response to

Joyce than perhaps on Joyce's own uses of the cadences, the rhythms, the essential intellectual rhythms, if you want to put it that way, of the Yeats of the 1890s.

One thing that has struck me when thinking about the topic of Yeats and Joyce is how much certain ideas about literary influence developed over the last decade or more have enabled us to read the relationship in a slightly different way. I'm thinking here of course of Walter Jackson Bate's book on *The Burden of the Past and the English Poet*. I'm thinking even more about the work of Harold Bloom, stretching all the way from *Yeats* and *The Anxiety of Influence* of 1970 to his very strange work published this spring, *Agon*. In spite of the overweening egoism, the resentful language, and the general aberrations of Bloom's writings on literary influence, to me they are the most important objects of literary criticism in a practical way of the last decade. With those notions in mind, I'd like to have a quick look at the suppressed or retracted "Preface" to *Ideas of Good and Evil* of 1903.

It reads in a slightly different way now than it did when I looked at it when *The Identity of Yeats* came out in the 1950s. What one finds here is that Joyce has to assert himself in the face of the greatest writer of his own country and, I think, the greatest writer of any country at the end of the nineteenth century. What Joyce has to seize upon is Yeats's ideas about folk literature and drama as a way, in "The Day of the Rabblement" and what came after that, of putting Yeats at a distance from himself. At the same time Yeats responded to that sense of distance between the young poet and himself by writing those agonizing and in many way anxious pages of the retracted "Preface." The relationship between the two writers is not the classic example of the young apprentice who is somehow in awe of the more powerful and older figure. Because of the accidents of literary history and the personalities of the two writers, Joyce was able to place himself in a position of almost equal power at the same time that their relationship was at its most intense, that is both personally and literarily, in the first years of the twentieth century. There was a very interesting lecture delivered by T. S. Eliot in Dublin in the 1930s at the same time that he was writing the first of the *Four Quartets*. It's a lecture on the English poet and tradition, and it anticipates in every detail the arguments of Walter Jackson Bate and Harold Bloom, except of course that Eliot's final solution is exactly the opposite of Bloom's: it is a solution of humility; it is a solution of compromise and accommodation in relation to the dead master rather than of struggle and anxiety. In that particular lecture, which has never been published and is now at Harvard, Eliot comments on how fortunate he was that at his most formative moments—around 1909— Yeats was in decline in terms of poetic power and, according to Eliot, most local in his interests. Eliot claims that it was his good fortune that he did not have to struggle with Yeats when he was in his formative stage: he could come to Yeats when their styles were already formed; and of course his final accommodation of Yeats—in his encounters with the dead masters in "Little Gidding"—is that of a poet on equal footing. In fact that passage in "Little Gidding" is written on the back of the manuscript of Eliot's magisterial tribute to Yeats delivered here in Dublin in 1940. It would be my argument in conclusion that Joyce was able at least to imagine that he had found Yeats at a moment of weakness, a moment when he was most local, most obsessed with things that Joyce was not interested in, around the year 1903. And that enabled the relationship to be not the classic one of a young poet, overawed and overwhelmed by the imagined shadow of a master, but somehow one of coming to Yeats on equal terms in the first years of the century.

Giorgio Melchiori:

Towers of words. The point I wish to make is simple enough: both Yeats and Joyce felt very strongly the symbolic power of towers, to the point that each of them actually tried to acquire and live in a tower. It goes without saying that the tower is anybody's and everybody's symbol, and we need not bring in Freud or the Bible in order to explain the psychological reasons for the universal appeal of the tower image.

Since I am dealing with two writers deeply conscious of the power and shortcomings of language, I would stress the Biblical implications of the tower of Babel rather than the Freudian, though in both cases the tower is the expression both of the will to conquer and of withdrawal, isolation, the separateness of the ego. For Yeats as for Joyce, their towers are essentially towers of words. The physical objects—the ruined castle at Thoor Ballylee that Yeats bought for thirty-five pounds from the Congested Districts Board in 1916, and the Martello tower at Sandycove for which Joyce (or Gogarty for him) paid an annual rent of eight pounds to the Secretary of State for War—were certainly meant as places to withdraw to, places where the artist could play in seclusion his game with language: ivory towers in fact, according to the aristocratic conception of the function of art promoted by the Decadent movement at the end of the last century.

It is true that Yeats inhabited his tower only occasionally during holidays and never made it his home, while Joyce could not stand the tower at Sandycove for more than a week; but both towers loom so large in their writings as to leave no doubt of the importance they had for the authors.

I'm here merely to suggest some points for discussion: in the first place that there is a basic difference in the approach of the two Irish authors to what they saw symbolized in the tower; and that, by inquiring into their separate attitudes to it, we can realize the deep divergence not only in their aesthetic but also in their political conceptions.

Let us begin with Yeats. His fullest statement about *his* tower came rather late, in a poem first published in 1928, "Blood and the Moon":

I

Blessed be this place,
More blessed still this tower;
A bloody, arrogant power
Rose out of the race
Uttering, mastering it,
Rose like these walls from these
Storm-beated cottages—
In mockery I have set
A powerful emblem up,
And sing it rhyme upon rhyme
In mockery of a time
Half dead at the top.

II

Alexandria's was a beacon tower, and Babylon's
An image of the moving heavens, a log-book of the sun's journey and the
       moon's;
And Shelley had his towers, thought's crowned powers he called them once.

I declare this tower is my symbol; I declare
This winding, gyring, spiring treadmill of a stair is my ancestral stair;
That Goldsmith and the Dean, Berkeley and Burke have travelled there. . . .

. . . . .

IV

Upon the dusty, glittering windows cling,
And seem to cling upon the moonlit skies,
Tortoiseshell butterflies, peacock butterflies,
A couple of night-moths are on the wing.
Is every modern nation like the tower,
Half dead at the top? No matter what I said,
For wisdom is the property of the dead,
A something incompatible with life; and power,
Like everything that has the stain of blood,
A property of the living; but no stain
Can come upon the visage of the moon
When it has looked in glory from a cloud.

At first sight this may sound like a political statement, although couched in a language where each word is a separate autonomous symbol charged with a whole cluster of meanings. I tried many years ago, in *The Whole Mystery of Art* (Routledge, 1960), in the steps of Richard Ellmann, Tom

Henn, Norman Jeffares, and so many other early interpreters of Yeats, to show the peculiar quality of his language and of his symbolism. For Yeats a symbol is:

> . . . not a metaphor for an accepted idea, for a single and definable object, with one specific meaning, but the image which summarizes in itself a number of possible meanings. The overall meaning of a symbol is therefore of itself undefinable: separate facets of it can perhaps be logically explored; but the symbol in its complex unity can be apprehended only through the emotion it communicates, through the feeling it awakens, acting on our senses. It is not so much the sensuous representation of an abstract idea, as the immediate blending of sensuous impression, feeling and thought: it is the intuition of a complex idea through our physical senses. (15)

And again, an "image, for him, was not a static, but a dynamic nucleus, not a stand-in for one particular concept, but a sort of living organism and force-center. It was continually modified, or rather enriched, by his developing thought, and in its turn modified and enriched his thought."

I would still stand by these definitions, but with some reservation about the word "thought." The more one reads Yeats, the more one realizes that thought for him is completely detached from logical reason; it is totally absorbed by physical sensations, visual, tactile, and, more still, phonic— the texture of sounds, the suggestions of lines, shapes, and colors become the only organizing principles of his so-called thought—and this of course accounts for his "system," *A Vision.*

The associations of the tower image in his work are therefore so various and complex that it would take more than one book to trace them all. Among a host of scholars, Jeffares, Henn, and I have tried to show the development and the evolution of the tower image, the accretion of ever new meanings through the years; by the time Yeats wrote "Blood and the Moon" the complexity of the symbol was such that it would be foolhardy to attempt an explanation. Perhaps, however, it is when things are most complex that schematic definitions become acceptable. Such a definition is the one in the last few lines of the poem, where the tower is equated unambiguously with power, violence, and blood in contrast with the moon identified with wisdom; what is more, the poet states bluntly that violence is life and wisdom is death. It is perhaps unfair to reduce to this Yeats's thought, the more so if one takes into account the political implications of such a statement. But how else could one explain that an undoubtedly great poet flirted with the Blue Shirts in Ireland and with the fascist regime in Italy?

The fact is that for all his pronouncements and his apparent involvement, Yeats was to the end of his life that rarest of things, a non-political man; without knowing it himself, he had managed to dissociate completely vision from politics, while believing all the time that he was following closely in the steps of the greatest political visionary in the English tradition, William Blake. For all its complexity, the tower symbol was still linked with the typically decadent impression he had received in April 1907, when he saw a tower rising into the clouds near Urbino, and described it in the essay "A Tower on the Apennines": "I saw suddenly in the mind's eye an old man, erect and a little gaunt, standing in the door of the tower, while about him broke a windy light. He was the poet who had at last, because he had done so much for the word's sake, come to share in the dignity of the saint." Mind you, the word's, not the world's, sake: the two things are completely separate for Yeats. Not so for Joyce. The misspelling in Martha's letter in *Ulysses*, "I called you naughty boy because I do not like that other world," becomes a leading theme in *Finnegans Wake*, which is indeed a world out of the word.

This leads us back to the Martello tower, the *Omphalos* as Gogarty called it, a refuge and a temple from which the two young men, Joyce and Gogarty, were going to preach the gospel of a new paganism. In a fragment probably meant for the rewriting of *Stephen Hero* as the *Portrait of the Artist as a Young Man*, never included in the novel and published by A. Walton Litz in 1961 *(The Art of James Joyce)*, there is a striking anticipation of the opening scene of *Ulysses*. Gogarty is not yet Buck Mulligan, but goes under the name of "Doherty." His mocking tone, however, is unmistakable. He addresses Stephen Dedalus (no longer with the diphthong *ae* as in *Stephen Hero*) with the following words: "The mockery of it! Ireland secretes priests: that's my new phrase. I must go. A woman waits for me. God, the humanity of Whitman! I contain all. I embrace all. Farewell. Did you notice Yeats's new touch with the hand up. It's the Roman salute. *Salve!* Pip, pip! O, a lovely mummer! Dedalus, we must retire to the tower, you and I. Our lives are precious. I'll try to touch the aunt. We are the super-artists. *Dedalus and Doherty have left Ireland for the Omphalos*" (Litz 133). Apart from the curious anticipation of Yeats's peculiar political sympathies (the Roman salute), this passage already explains Joyce's attitude toward the symbol of the tower. "We must retire to the tower. . . . Our lives are precious." The tower represents isolation from the rest of mankind, intellectual snobbery—not the refusal to submit, but the refusal to fight. We all know that *Ulysses* is about leaving the tower, going out into the streets: the young intellectual Stephen Dedalus, who had been tempted by his intellectual pride to isolate himself after his previous failure to escape the paralysis of Dublin, rejects that attitude and finds his spiritual father in the wandering Jew Leopold Bloom. As the Linati schema explains, the "Nostos," the last part of the novel, marks the fusion of Stephen and Bloom, son and father, while Molly completes the human trinity. The tower is the symbol of negation; Stephen's renunciation of the tower is in the first place a political gesture, political in the deepest original sense of the term: it is, like Molly's final "yes," the acceptance of the human condition, of the dimension of history. And *Finnegans Wake*, that formidable structure of words, is not the tower of Babel, but the ultimate attempt to transform the truest means of communication among men, the word, into a world.

Richard Ellmann:

I would emphasize, however, that both Yeats's tower and Joyce's—symbolical as they are—have also a real existence. To be able to live in one's symbol is a special luxury of the literary life since Baudelaire. Material things have a way of doubling their nature. The word *reality* slides between what is beyond appearance and what is within appearance. In Yeats this slide generates poem after poem.

No one doubts that if the metaphysical element which is in almost every poem of Yeats were removed, there would be little left. But we are less prone to acknowledge such an element in Joyce, who like Gautier felt that he was one for whom the visible world existed. But in *Finnegans Wake* (88) he calls it "the audible-visible-gnosible-edible world," and by adding "gnosis" begs the question. He could be contemptuous of occultism, and yet was full of superstitions. Ghosts were not his theme, though he found two in *Hamlet* where most people have seen only one; and he was not as likely as Yeats to practice the evocation of spirits, yet in *Ulysses* Stephen asks rhetorically, "If I call them into life across the waters of Lethe will not the poor ghosts troop to my call?" A reality behind reality seems to be implied also in Joyce's conception of coincidence as an envelope in which the whole world is contained. This idea is as unverifiable as Yeats's of an *anima mundi* in which all the world's images are stored.

Joyce's attention to the grim and grisly may also at first seem different in kind from Yeats's insistent loftiness. But Yeats too holds that the rag-and-bone shop is where we must start, and that even if our goal is "eternal beauty" we must keep hold of "common things that crave." When in "The Tower," he looks out and sees where "tree, like a sooty finger starts from the earth," the tree is bound to treeness and sooty fingers even as it bursts into greater consequence. To pass from one reality to a greater one, as in the poem "Friends," where he "shakes from head to foot," requires anguished love for a known and tangible woman as a starting-point.

In Joyce the word "imagination" is used much more charily than in Yeats. Joyce was inclined to disparage the faculty, and preferred to accept Vico's definition of imagination as memory. A good memory Joyce did not disavow having. In other moods he acknowledged that his imagination was not as creative as Yeats's. But he was needlessly modest. A rhyme quoted in *Ulysses* and attributed to Mother Shipton, "Around the world thought can fly / In the twinkling of an eye," better expresses his view.

Stephen may mock the occultists' notion of the body as a "fleshcase" for the soul, but he ranges as widely beyond his physical confines as they do. Walking past Baird the stonecutter's, he thinks of Ibsen; walking past the North Strand Road provision shops, he thinks of Cavalcanti. He sees not only the ineluctable modality of the visible, as Aristotle prescribed, but also the ineluctable modality of the invisible, as Plato posited it. Dublin has its naturalistic veneer, but this does not prevent it from being also Ulysses' Mediterranean and Hamlet's Elsinore.

In the library episode of *Ulysses,* Joyce sketches his image of the brain as a womb. External things penetrate it, and combine with internal ones; the seen with the unseen. In *Finnegans Wake,* that tower of words described by Professor Melchiori, two levels of reality converge as all the key words (such as *phoenish*) seem to be on the border between the familiar and the strange. Dictionaries quail before the sudden shifts in verbal dimensions, as if from five senses and six. Here, as in *Ulysses,* Joyce voices implicitly a hymn to the imagination, as grand a hymn as Yeats explicitly displays. Joyce, in other words, is metaphysical too.

Note

1. The fullest account of the biographical facts of this relationship is Richard Ellmann, *Eminent Domain: Yeats among Wilde, Joyce, Pound, Eliot, and Auden* (New York: Oxford University Press, 1967), 29–56. Earlier versions of this chapter were published as "Joyce and Yeats," *The Kenyon Review* 12.4 (Autumn 1950): 618–38, the Italian translation in *Inventario* 4 (April 1952): 18–31; and as "Yeats and Joyce," *Yeats Centenary Papers,* 1965, 11 (Dublin: Dolmen Press, 1967): 447–79, included in *The Dolmen Press Yeats Centenary Papers MCMLXV,* ed. Liam Miller (Dublin: Dolmen Press, 1968), 445–79.

See also Richard Ellmann, *Yeats: The Man and the Masks* (1948, rpt. New York: W. W. Norton, 1979); *The Identity of Yeats* (New York: Oxford University Press, 1964); *James Joyce,* New and Revised Edition (New York: Oxford University Press, 1982). Editions of letters are *Letters of James Joyce,* Volume I, ed. Stuart Gilbert (London: Faber and Faber, 1957), Volumes II and III, ed. Richard Ellmann (London: Faber and Faber, 1966); *The Letters of W. B. Yeats,* ed. Allan Wade (New York: Macmillan, 1955).

Works Cited

The Collected Poems of W. B. Yeats. New York: Macmillan, 1956.
Litz, A. Walton. *The Art of James Joyce.* London: Oxford University Press, 1961.
Melchiori, Giorgio. *The Whole Mystery of Art.* London: Routledge, 1960.

Gender and Narrative Voice in *Jacob's Room* and *A Portrait of the Artist as a Young Man*

Karen Lawrence

Both Virginia Woolf's *Jacob's Room* and James Joyce's *A Portrait of the Artist as a Young Man* are *Bildungsromane* that chronicle the development of young male protagonists and the effect of tradition upon them: Jacob Flanders and Stephen Dedalus struggle to find their place amid society's institutions. However, these novels of education reveal something about not only the protagonist's relation to tradition, but the writer's as well, for the genre lends itself to treatment of the general problem of cultural inclusion and exclusion. The narrative strategies of the novels shed light on the writer's position in society and the effect of sex on that position.

In *A Room of One's Own*, Woolf comments on gender, tradition, and writing in a description of a fictitious visit to "Oxbridge" (her hybrid term for the two famous patriarchal academic institutions): "I thought how unpleasant it is to be locked out; and I thought how it is worse perhaps to be locked in; and, thinking of the safety and prosperity of the one sex and of the poverty and insecurity of the other and of the effect of tradition and of the lack of tradition upon the mind of a writer, I thought at last that it was time to roll up the crumpled skin of the day, with its arguments and its impressions and its anger and its laughter, and cast it into the hedge" (24). In *Jacob's Room*, Woolf thematizes the female artist's cultural exclusion by emphasizing the distance between the female narrator and male protagonist. Demonstrating that narrative authority is not a birthright, Woolf raises questions about legitimacy and authority as they pertain to the narrative act.

It should be acknowledged that in many ways both Joyce and Woolf eschew the traditional nineteenth-century form of the *Bildungsroman* in favor of a new kind of novel of education. To borrow Woolf's categories in her celebrated essay "Mr. Bennett and Mrs. Brown," both authors are "Georgian" rather than "Edwardian" writers (*Collected Essays* 1:319–37). They subvert certain thematic and formal conventions of the traditional nineteenth-century *Bildungsroman*. Both *A Portrait* and *Jacob's Room* end on a note of dispossession—the young sons of Ireland and England do not take up the mantles of their fathers. Stephen Dedalus renounces church and country; Jacob Flanders, who has lived in careless rather than rebellious relation to society's institutions, dies meaninglessly in World War I. Both novels, too, eschew the narrative continuity of traditional omniscience or first-person retrospection, providing instead a narrative with lacunae between the various experiences of the characters. Thus neither novel displays the epistemological security of the nineteenth-century form.

But despite the fact that in plot and style Joyce breaks with the traditional novel of education, he nevertheless accepts some of the premises of that form. First, he accepts what Edward Said has called the central element in the classical novel—the development of the "self" of the protagonist (141). Joyce accepts the central notions of identity and vocation in the *Bildungsroman:* Stephen Dedalus has a calling. *A Portrait* moves in the direction of a goal (even if Stephen's aspirations are ironically deflated at times and we may question the greatness of his ultimate destination). Moments of revelation mark the stages of Stephen's journey toward identity, moments when he feels that the prophecy of his name coincides with events in the real world. The basic idea of growth and development, however problematic, is, nevertheless, ultimately accepted.[1]

Secondly, although Stephen rejects his biological father, he accepts the dynastic power of paternity. Stephen disowns Simon Dedalus only to invoke the power of the "old father, old artificer" Daedalus, whose legacy will in turn enable him to become the father of his race and "forge its uncreated conscience." Metaphors of paternity, inheritance, privilege, and authority are at the heart of the novel, charting Stephen's fundamental attempt to understand "himself, his name and where he was" (*P* 15). As Edmund Epstein says in his book *The Ordeal of Stephen Dedalus: The Conflict of Generations in James Joyce's "A Portrait of the Artist as a Young Man,"* the question of symbolic fatherhood is at the center of *A Portrait* and is related precisely to Stephen's destiny as an artist (7). If paternity is a "legal fiction," as Stephen says in *Ulysses* (207), its power as fiction is not fundamentally doubted in *A Portrait*.

Such metaphors of authority and paternity pertain to the narrative as well as to the theme of the novel. As a recent critic has put it, *A Portrait* may be both the author's autobiographical fiction (the portrait of Joyce as a young man) and the autobiography of the fictional character, Stephen Dedalus. Either way, the relationship between narrator and protagonist can be described as paternal: the male narrator/author fathers forth the image of himself as a young man.[2] The close identification of narrator and protagonist is effected largely through the technique of free indirect discourse, which has certain important implications for the notion of narrative authority and privilege. As technically unobtrusive and withdrawn as he may appear, the narrator of *A Portrait* enjoys considerable authority: his voice is authorized to speak about Stephen; he claims, however implicitly, to have access to the thoughts, even the rhythms, of Stephen's mind. ("It was wrong; it was unfair and cruel: and, as he sat in the refectory, he suffered time after time in memory the same humiliation . . ." [53].) What

I speak of has less to do with questions of narrative attitude (e.g., ironic, sympathetic) than it concerns narrative privilege in relation to the main character. Although it may appear paradoxical to call such an unobtrusive narrator authoritative, as recent theorists have shown, narrative authority cannot be related simply to explicit intrusiveness; covert and unobtrusive narrators have their own style of power and authority. Like Stephen's "God of creation" who "remains within or behind or beyond or above his handiwork . . ." (215), the narrator of *A Portrait* exercises power and privilege. He practices what Stephen himself only resolves to practice: "silence, exile, and cunning" (247).[3]

In contrast to Joyce's treatment of the narrator/protagonist relationship, Woolf's narrative strategy and mode of characterization in *Jacob's Room* call into question the concepts of the male ego, patriarchal succession, and narrative power. Unlike Stephen Dedalus, Jacob Flanders is a mystery, in part because Woolf deliberately deprives us of much of his thought. Instead of Joyce's internal focus on the young protagonist, Woolf gives us very little of Jacob's interior life; we see him almost exclusively through the eyes of the narrator and other characters. If Stephen is a complicated and full, experiencing center of consciousness surrounded by "hollowsounding voices," Jacob is himself a blank surrounded by characters and a narrator whose main task is to try to interpret him. To paraphrase Stephen, Jacob himself may very well be the uncreated conscience of his race. Woolf has been criticized for her failure to create real characters in the novel, but the absence of this definitive male ego seems to me intentional. Throughout her works, Woolf subverts the stability of character, that "old stable ego" of which Lawrence, too, complained. As Maria DiBattista says in *Virginia Woolf's Major Novels: The Fables of Anon,* Woolf's work reflects a "critique of [the] presumptuous powers" found in earlier forms of narrative (21). We can see this critique not only as modernist, but as feminist as well, for the world of the self is for Woolf patriarchal, the realm of the male. In part at least, Woolf's decision not to provide a traditional protagonist is a feminist gesture; to quote Jane Marcus, it is evidence of her "feminist attack on the ego as male false consciousness" (9).

Thus, in contrast to Stephen Dedalus, Jacob experiences no epiphanies, no rebellions, no real development in the course of the novel.[4] Unlike Stephen, he doesn't ask himself many questions about the purpose of life: " 'What for? What for?' Jacob never asked himself any such questions, to judge by the way he laced his boots . . ." (161). The narrator's explanation for this lack of curiosity is striking: "He was young—a man" (161). The attributes that for Joyce help to certify Stephen as an interesting center of consciousness seem to disqualify Woolf's protagonist. Jacob is, the narrator tells us, "amiable, authoritative, beautifully healthy" (92), and somehow all this prevents him from being a sensitive interpreter of his surroundings.

Significantly, the main interpreter in this novel of education is a woman, ten years older than Jacob and, by virtue of her sex, excluded, as was Woolf, from the very kind of education he is free to obtain. After describing Jacob's face as he sees his girlfriend walk down the street with another man, the narrator says, "This was in his face. Whether we know what was in his mind is another question. Granted ten years' seniority and a difference of sex, fear of him comes first; this is swallowed up by a desire to help . . ." (94–95). The narrator is not a character in the drama of the plot, but the mixture of sarcasm and awe, resentment and solicitude in her tone, and the presence of rhetorical questions and sudden outbursts of self-reference indeed give her a distinct personality.

Unlike Joyce's cool and unobtrusive narrator who shares Stephen's experiences, Woolf's narrator serves as a kind of voyeur of the male personality. Here is her description of Jacob at Cambridge: "The young men were now back in their rooms. Heaven knows what they were doing. What was it that could *drop* like that?" (42); and, "Was it to receive this gift from the past that the young man came to the window and stood there, looking out across the court? It was Jacob" (45). Nose pressed to the window of that bastion of male privilege, the narrator speculates, chats, comments, all from an excluded position. Jacob's room is precisely the "room of one's own" disallowed to women; "If one is a woman," Woolf writes in *A Room of One's Own,* "one is often surprised by a sudden splitting off of consciousness, say in walking down Whitehall, when from being the natural inheritor of that civilisation, she becomes, on the contrary, outside of it, alien and critical" (101).

The relation between the female narrator and her young male protagonist embodies this splitting off of consciousness, this estrangement and alienation from tradition. Because we are given almost a physical image of the exclusion of the narrator from tradition, "locked out" of the room and, occasionally, the mind of her young male protagonist, technical terms like "narrative distance" and "point of view" take on added meaning. The female narrator's cultural exclusion and aesthetic distance converge, as sexuality creates a gap between character and narrator. "Then consider the effect of sex," the narrator advises us at one point, "how between man and woman it hangs wavy, tremulous, so that here's a valley, there's a peak, when in truth, perhaps, all's as flat as my hand. Even the exact words get the wrong accent on them" (73). Through irony, Joyce's narrator keeps some distance from Stephen who, in turn, exiles himself from his society, but Woolf's female narrator is already estranged from the tradition she describes *and* the young man who should inherit the privileges of that tradition. Indeed, images of exclusion recur in Woolf's writing, whether in the form of Miss Latrobe, the artist in *Between the Acts* who hides behind the bushes while her play is presented, or the speaker in *A Room of One's Own* who is told to keep off the grass, an admonition that reflects larger issues of cultural interdiction, or Lily Briscoe, feeling, as she paints her picture, that she is positioned "on the fringe of the lawn" which is "the world."

Thus, in *Jacob's Room*, Woolf translates female cultural exclusion into a narrative principle. Unlike the restrained but powerful narrator in *A Portrait*, Woolf's narrator overtly abdicates her power. She offers disclaimers, reservations, even retractions. After describing Jacob's appearance, she says "but surely, of all futile occupations this of cataloging features is the worst. One word is sufficient. But if one cannot find it?" (71). And after interpreting Jacob's expression at one point, she retracts her analysis: "But whether this is the right interpretation of Jacob's gloom . . . it is impossible to say; for he never spoke a word" (49). Through her female narrator, Woolf deliberately limits narrative hegemony and the godlike powers of the Joycean narrator.

This reduction of narrative authority is, I think, a strategy to circumvent and expose the pitfalls of the egotism of traditional narration. Instead of the filiality of narrator and protagonist, we find the gap of sexuality, and admittedly fallible observation replaces the knowledge of the protagonist's every thought. In part this may be a bid for a greater realism, a way of writing that acknowledges human fallibility and the enigma of personality. Certainly, Woolf's other novels return to this theme of the mysteriousness of human personality—we can't write about other people definitively because in life we can't really know anyone else. But the self-conscious abdication of authority suggests a further purpose here: an experiment with a feminine alternative to egotistical narration, a transformation of cultural exclusion into an aesthetic boon. The language of gesture Woolf develops in the novel creates a dramatic perspective; exclusion from Jacob's mind forces us to develop our skills of observation and to learn to read a face or gesture, without the privileged access sanctioned by tradition and gender. For Woolf, the other side of female exclusion is the freedom of imagination that comes with being "locked out."

Woolf's deliberate renunciation of power, however, is not, to my mind, her most successful alternative to "egotistical narration." I prefer the wonderfully fluid narration in *Mrs. Dalloway* and *To the Lighthouse*, which does allow privileged entry into the minds of the main characters *and* avoidance of the egotistical narrative self. In her essay "The Narrow Bridge of Art," Woolf alludes to this possibility of access without the arrogance that sometimes accompanies such privilege. She describes the possibilities for prose in the novel of the future, a novel which "will clasp to its breast the precious prerogatives of the democratic art of prose; its freedom, its fearlessness, its flexibility. For prose is so humble that it can go anywhere; no place is too low, too sordid, or too mean for it to enter. It is infinitely patient, too, humbly acquisitive. It can . . . listen silently at doors behind which only a murmur, only a whisper, is to be heard. With all the suppleness of a tool which is in constant use it can follow the windings and record the changes which are typical of the modern mind" (*Granite and Rainbow* 20). In novels like *Mrs. Dalloway* and *To the Lighthouse*, an incarnation occurs in the narrative; consciousness slips in and out of the minds of multiple characters and, thus, inclusion rather than exclusion predominates—our sense of the mystery of personality results from our exposure to the complexity of character rather than our exclusion from interior views. It is the richness, ambiguity, and depth of a Mrs. Ramsay that make her remain a mystery, despite our access to her thoughts.[5]

Nevertheless, the narrative distance between male character and female narrator in *Jacob's Room* provides a fascinating version of the female writer's estrangement from patriarchal tradition. Perhaps the best emblem within the novel for the marginality of female writing, and a good contrast to Stephen's view of the male "God of creation" "within or behind . . . his handiwork," is the letter Jacob's mother writes to her son. It sits unopened on his desk outside the bedroom where he and his girlfriend make love. Although the narrator cites some male writers who have "addressed themselves to the task of reaching, touching, penetrating the individual heart" in letters (93), she identifies these more private, unofficial messages primarily with women. "Poor Betty Flanders' letter" (87), the narrator says, and goes on to describe letters as "the unpublished works of women, written in pale profusion." Within this published novel written by a woman, given over to a female narrator, Woolf reminds us that female writing is often excluded from centers of male power.

Of course, it might be argued that women are not the only ones excluded from power; it is true that Joyce regarded the Irishman as the "servant" of two masters, England and Rome. As he listens to the English dean of studies, Stephen Dedalus thinks, "the language in which we are speaking is his before it is mine" (189). Woolf and Joyce shared a sense of exclusion from the dominant English culture—an Irishman and an Englishwoman are both second-class citizens vis-à-vis British patriarchy. However, in *A Portrait*, Joyce had not yet begun to question certain central patriarchal ideas. It is not until *Ulysses* and *Finnegans Wake* that he mounts a more radical attack on the notions of privilege, authority, and identity, and the whole notion of fathering forth or authoring a text.[6] Also, the types of rebellion against society waged by Joyce and Woolf in *A Portrait* and *Jacob's Room* are very different: Woolf felt oppressed by institutions that tried to lock her out; Joyce (as well as Stephen) felt oppressed by institutions that sought to include him. In fact, Stephen's sense that his artistic consciousness is preempted by the patriarchal institutions seeking to include him sheds some light on Woolf's ability to make the position of marginality a creative source. The different narrative strategies and treatments of patriarchal tradition in *Jacob's Room* and *A Portrait* reflect, in part at least, differences in the writers' perceptions of sexual privileges and burdens.

Notes

1. In their introduction to *The Voyage In: Fictions of Female Development,* ed. Elizabeth Abel et al., the editors observe that although much modernist fiction has tended to call into question the primary assumptions underlying the traditional male *Bildungsroman,* the form is still perceived as viable for contemporary women writing about women (13). As I hope to show, in *Jacob's Room,* Woolf's unusual combination of male protagonist/female narrator radically subverts the underlying assumptions of the traditional form of the *Bildungsroman.*

2. John Paul Riquelme, *Teller and Tale in Joyce's Fiction: Oscillating Perspectives* (51). Advancing the theory that Stephen is the narrator of *A Portrait,* Riquelme says that "Stephen fathers himself in language" (68). Whether one accepts this reading or the more traditional one that posits the work as Joyce's fictional auto-biography, the paternal metaphor still applies.

3. In *The Narrative Act: Point of View in Prose Fiction,* Susan Sniader Lanser presents a "descriptive poetics of point of view," which, although somewhat over-elaborate, does demonstrate that the components of narrative status and stance involve complex questions of power that are unaccounted for in traditional debates about the narrator's attitude. See chapter 4, in particular.

4. For a discussion of Woolf's "playful yet serious rebellion" against the traditional *Bildungsroman,* see Judy Little's very interesting essay *"Jacob's Room* as Comedy: Woolf's Parodic *Bildungsroman"* in *New Feminist Essays on Virginia Woolf* (105). Professor Little is very good on Woolf's ironic treatment of the conventions of the *Bildungsroman,* but I quarrel with her essay on three major points: she fails to distinguish Joyce's *A Portrait* from more traditional *Bildungsromane* and therefore slights Joyce's own brand of "rebellion" against the traditional form; she sees a good deal of identification between narrator and protagonist, whereas to me the gap between them is one of the most significant aspects of the novel; and, finally, I find that the word "comic" does not quite capture the tone of Woolf's attack, which sometimes seems more bitter than the "mild, even cheerful feminism" that Little describes.

5. It is not simply that Woolf gives up representing the inner lives of men. Interestingly, she does portray male consciousness in subsequent novels where the male mind is somehow linked closely to an equally dominant female consciousness. The protagonist in *Orlando,* whose consciousness is recorded by the narrator, metamorphoses from male to female; Septimus Smith in *Mrs. Dalloway* is, as Woolf herself remarked, a "double" for Clarissa; and Bernard, Louis, and Neville in *The Waves* provide the male counterparts to the female chorus of Susan, Jinny, and Rhoda. No longer opaque to narrative scrutiny, the male mind in these novels is presented from the inside as a part of the androgynous consciousness.

6. In a fine essay entitled "Polytropic Man: Paternity, Identity and Naming in *The Odyssey* and *A Portrait of the Artist as a Young Man,*" Maud Ellmann suggests that the ultimate authority of paternity is, in fact, disputed in *A Portrait* and claims that the novel is "omphalocentric." While her individual discussions of certain images are fascinating (for example, her treatment of the word "Foetus" carved in a school desk), nevertheless, the dominant metaphors for artistic creation and for the development of the protagonist seem to me overwhelmingly male-centered (i.e., the "priest of the eternal imagination") and, for the most part, patriarchal.

See *James Joyce: New Perspectives,* ed. Colin MacCabe (73–104). For a discussion of Joyce's subversion of the patriarchal in *Ulysses,* see Karen Lawrence, "Paternity: The Legal Fiction," in Weldon Thornton and Robert Newman, eds., *Joyce's "Ulysses": The Larger Perspective* (University of Delaware Press, 1987).

Works Cited

Abel, Elizabeth, Marianne Hirsch, and Elizabeth Langland, eds. *The Voyage In: Fictions of Female Development.* Hanover, N. H.: University Press of New England, 1983.

DiBattista, Maria. *Virginia Woolf's Major Novels: The Fables of Anon.* New Haven: Yale University Press, 1980.

Ellmann, Maud. "Polytropic Man: Paternity, Identity, and Naming in *The Odyssey* and *A Portrait of the Artist as a Young Man.*" In *James Joyce: New Perspectives,* ed. Colin MacCabe. Bloomington: Indiana University Press, 1982.

Epstein, Edmund. *The Ordeal of Stephen Dedalus: The Conflict of Generations in James Joyce's "A Portrait of the Artist as a Young Man."* Carbondale: Southern Illinois University Press, 1971.

Lanser, Susan Sniader. *The Narrative Act: Point of View in Prose Fiction.* Princeton University Press, 1981.

Little, Judy. "*Jacob's Room* as Comedy: Woolf's Parodic *Bildungsroman.*" In *New Feminist Essays on Virginia Woolf,* ed. Jane Marcus. Lincoln: University of Nebraska Press, 1981.

Marcus, Jane, ed. *New Feminist Essays on Virginia Woolf.* Lincoln: University of Nebraska Press, 1981.

Riquelme, John Paul. *Teller and Tale in Joyce's Fiction: Oscillating Perspectives.* Baltimore: Johns Hopkins University Press, 1981.

Said, Edward. *Beginnings: Intention and Method.* New York: Basic Books, 1975.

Woolf, Virginia. *Collected Essays.* London: Hogarth Press, 1966.

———. *Jacob's Room.* New York: Harcourt Brace Jovanovich, 1922. Rpt. 1978.

———. "The Narrow Bridge of Art." In *Granite and Rainbow.* London: Hogarth Press, 1958.

———. *A Room of One's Own.* New York: Harcourt Brace Jovanovich, 1929.

Virginia Woolf Reads James Joyce:
The *Ulysses* Notebook

Suzette A. Henke

Most of us are familiar with Virginia Woolf's protests against the "enormous indecency" of Joyce's *Ulysses*. An "illiterate, underbred book," she called it, "the book of a self-taught working man, and we all know how distressing they are, how egotistic, insistent, raw, striking, and ultimately nauseating" (*Diary* 54). To Tom Eliot, Woolf described Joyce as "virile—a he-goat." Etched on our minds is her acerbic caricature of the author of *Ulysses* as a "queasy undergraduate scratching his pimples" (57)—a satiric portrait that functions as the verbal equivalent of a David Levine cartoon and evokes images of Joyce, bulbous and bespectacled, staring from a carbuncular physiognomy at a stack of books in the Irish National Library.

After Joyce's death, Woolf reminisced about her first encounter with *Ulysses:* "I bought the blue paper book, and read it here one summer, I think, with spasms of wonder, of discovery, and then again with long lapses of intense boredom. This goes back to a pre-historic world" (*Diary* 334). Woolf, in fact, recorded those initial spasms of wonder and discovery in a small, unpublished notebook on "Modern Novels" presently held in the Berg Collection of the New York Public Library. Far from being antagonistic to Joyce, she appreciated *Ulysses* as a monumental work of fiction and keenly analyzed the novel's avant-garde, experimental techniques.

Reading *Ulysses* for the first time, Woolf admires Joyce's "attempt to get thinking into literature" and appreciates the "undoubted occasional beauty of his phrases." "The thing is that he is attempting to do away with the machinery—to extract the marrow" *(Modern Novels [Joyce])*. Woolf begins to articulate, in nascent form, the ideas that would give birth to her famous essay on "Modern Fiction" and to her insistence that authors should portray what life is "really like" to the subjective consciousness.

Woolf applauds Joyce's "desire to be more psychological" and "get more things into fiction." *Ulysses,* she observes, records the "inner thought" of the individual, "then the little scatter of life on top to keep you in touch with reality." But her reservations about the "damned egotistical self" in *Ulysses* also begin to surface: "Perhaps this method gets less into other people and too much into one" *(Modern Novels)*. Whereas Woolf denounces Joyce's "enormous indecency" in her diary, she expresses greater openness in the notebook: "So much seems to depend on the *emotional* fibre of the mind it may be time that the subconscious mind dwells on indecency" *(Modern Novels)*.

It is somewhat reassuring, as well as enlightening, to watch the initial reaction of a brilliant mind to genius. Woolf tries nobly to get beneath the surface of the text and discover the "stirrings of emotion." But an understanding of Joyce's complex novel was hard-won before the days of Stuart Gilbert and Richard Ellmann—even to a writer as talented and perspicacious as Woolf. First-time readers of *Ulysses* may take heart. Somewhat baffled by Joyce's labyrinthine construct, Woolf wonders if Bloom is the "editor of a paper." She records such banal facts as: "Dignam dies./ Stephen Dedalus—the son of Mr. Dedalus. / Mulligan is his friend." But what, she wonders, can be the "connection between Bloom and Dedalus" *(Modern Novels)*.

We may find Woolf's confusion somewhat amusing, but we have to remember that she was exploring uncharted territory, without the maps, guidebooks, and lexical aids currently available to students weaned on the writings of Tindall, Blamires, and Gifford and Seidman. Slowly and tentatively, Woolf began to piece together the structural innovations of *Ulysses*. Considering her initial amazement, we might assume that the novel made a strong impression on her—and that she gleaned from *Ulysses* the idea of introducing in *Mrs. Dalloway* two separate characters whose paths would symbolically converge at the end of the book.

Surprisingly, Woolf was one of the first critics to recognize the cinematic techniques of *Ulysses*. She observes that the narrative is "possibly like a cinema that shows you very slowly, how a hare does jump; all pictures were a little made up before" *(Modern Novels)*. It is "unfair," she writes in a marginal note, "to approach Joyce by way of his 'method'; and that is on the surface startling." We must in fact, "get out of the way of thinking that the novel is so and so—it is what one chooses to make it." Comparing *Ulysses* to *Tristram Shandy*, Woolf speculates: "For all I know, every great book has been an act of revolution." In modern fiction, "all sorts of new situations become possible. . . . New versions of beauty; demanding, of course, a new form" *(Modern Novels)*.

Woolf would go on to create her own acts of aesthetic revolution by giving us a "new form" in every novel she wrote after *Jacob's Room*. There is no question that her reading of *Dubliners, Portrait,* and *Ulysses* made an indelible impression on her artistic sensibility. Consider, for instance, the similarity between those two romantic martyrs, Michael Furey and Septimus Smith. One dies for love of a woman, the other for a universal, mystical love that cannot survive in a loveless country. Both, like Shelley's Adonais, go out in a blaze of glory and become scapegoats for the spiritual regeneration of those left behind.

Gabriel Conroy thinks of the young man who died for Gretta's sake: "Better pass boldly into that other world, in the full glory of some passion, than fade and wither dismally with age" (*D* 223). Similarly, Clarissa Dalloway evaluates Smith's revolutionary act of suicide: "She had once thrown a shilling into the Serpentine, never anything more. But he had flung it away. They went on living. . . . A thing there was that mattered; a thing, wreathed about with chatter, defaced, obscured in her own life, let drop every day in corruption, lies, chatter. This he had preserved. Death was defiance. Death was an attempt to communicate" (Woolf, *Dalloway* 130). Both heroes have escaped the "contagion of the world's slow stain" (Woolf, *Party* 22).[1]

The two scenes from *Dubliners* and *Mrs. Dalloway* have common roots in Shelley and the romantic tradition. But their resemblance is so striking that it seems more than coincidental. A decade before Woolf's publication of *Mrs. Dalloway,* Joyce provided in "The Dead" a model for a social "party consciousness" invaded by the recognition of death. At the conclusion of his short story collection, he explored the psychic illumination that union with the "living and the dead" can provide. Both works of fiction end on a note of redemptive epiphany.

Was Virginia Woolf contemptuous of Joyce, or did she try to imitate his "stream-of-consciousness" style? Did she feel admiration, rivalry, or artistic comradery with the "working-class" Irishman who was born the same year as she? At the news of Joyce's premature death, Woolf must have felt the same kind of shock experienced by Clarissa Dalloway at Bradshaw's announcement of Septimus Smith's suicide. Woolf wrote in her diary on 15 January 1941: "Then Joyce is dead: Joyce about a fortnight younger than I am" (334). She had always regarded Joyce as a kind of artistic "double," a male ally in the modernist battle for psychological realism. In her own life, Joyce played the role of alter-ego that Septimus Smith had played for Clarissa Dalloway. As if in mirror imitation of her fiction, Woolf, after the sudden and senseless death of Joyce, followed her double to the grave.

Notes

I am indebted to the Henry W. and Albert A. Berg Collection, The New York Public Library, Astor, Lenox and Tilden Foundations for the use of Virginia Woolf's manuscript "Modern Novels."

1. Clarissa Dalloway thinks about this phrase from Shelley's *Adonais* in "Mrs. Dalloway in Bond Street," a short story posthumously published in *Mrs. Dalloway's Party*. Mrs. Dalloway also cites the phrase in Woolf's earlier novel, *The Voyage Out*—perhaps as proof of her "romantic" sensibility.

Works Cited

Woolf, Virginia. *A Writer's Diary*. Ed. Leonard Woolf. 1953. Rpt. New York: New American Library, 1968. Corrected from the manuscript version, Berg Collection, New York Public Library.

———. *Modern Novels (Joyce)*. 2nd of two Holograph Notebooks, unnumbered. New York: Henry W. and Albert A. Berg Collection, Astor, Lenox and Tilden Foundations, New York Public Library.

———. *Mrs. Dalloway*. New York: Harcourt, Brace and World, 1925.

———. *Mrs. Dalloway's Party*. Ed. Stella McNichol. New York: Harcourt Brace Jovanovich, 1973.

What Joyce after Pynchon?

Richard Pearce

My thesis is simply—or not so simply—that we may discover the real James Joyce by reading him not *before* but *after* Thomas Pynchon. Or that we have worked so hard to discover how Joyce put things together, made multiple connections, created an infinitely complex whole, that we have forgotten the shocks of first encounter, the strain of concentration, how unimaginable it was to compare this nondescript Dubliner with Homer's epic hero, how maddeningly the stylistic play obscured key events. Didn't Rebecca West have good cause to describe Joyce as "a great man . . . entirely without taste"? Wasn't Wyndham Lewis right in comparing his mind to a cistern, which collected "the last stagnant pumpings of Victorian Anglo-Irish"? (Givens, ed., xii).

I will press my polemic as far as I can in a short space to see what we can learn about Joyce, about Pynchon, and about the relation between what has been called modernism and postmodernism. And I will focus on *Ulysses* since it was Joyce's ground-breaking novel, where the traditional elements are still strong.

Let me begin by arguing that there is no difference between modernism and postmodernism. It is only that revolutionary writers like Joyce had to be read in a conservative way. And in the process, in a final burst of energy, the old mode gained new life and expanded to its limit—thereby appropriating and domesticating what had actually been made new. At best, then, modernism is the way people learned to read writers like Joyce. It may also be the second-rate writing such reading inspired.

Joyce, after all, chose *not* to title the chapters of *Ulysses*. Or he chose *to* dismantle the Homeric superstructure he needed while writing. As a reader of *Ulysses*, Eliot needed the superstructure. And if Eliot, why not the ordinary reader, who could not approach the imaginative daring of the *Waste Land* poet? Who wouldn't welcome Stuart Gilbert? For fifty years *Ulysses* has been taught (it has been read independently less and less) upon the Homeric superstructure, fortified by new scholarship and new integrating networks. So now we are hardly disturbed by its unbridgable gaps, its intransigent obscurities, its intolerable contradictions, its overwhelming quantity of allusions, its dizzying leaps of perspective.

But after the erratic leaps in *Gravity's Rainbow* from one consciousness to another among hundreds of characters, from London to Holland, over to France, and all through the Zone, before returning to London and then, suddenly, into a California movie house—after accepting, without accommodating to, such jolts and disjunctions—we may rediscover the radical gap between chapters 1 and 2 in *Ulysses*. That is, the leap from the Martello's forty-foot cliff right into "You, Cochrane, what city sent for him?" Where are we? Who says this? Who's Cochrane? Who's the "him" that whatever city it was sent for? We may also wonder how Edmund Wilson could recognize Joyce's kinship with Einstein, but nonetheless legitimize the *Reader's Digest* narrative summary taken up by his successors: "The scene now shifts, as it does in the 'Odyssey,' to the lost Ulysses himself" (195). What a way to describe the leap from fourteen pages of Stephen's erudite musings into "Mr. Leopold Bloom ate with relish the inner organs of beasts and fowls."

And thinking about Leopold Bloom *after* Oedipa Maas may rekindle our amazement, or cause us to wonder how we could have passively accepted the connection between Bloom and Ulysses, even if it is an ironic connection (although Alan Wilde has now helped us understand modernist, as opposed to traditional, irony, which preserves the disjunction after failing to control it). Hearing Buck Mulligan's obscene lyrics as well as the popular songs that punctuate Joyce's epic *after* the corny jingles that interrupt Slothrop's journey may retune our aural imaginations to the jangling clashes of high and pop culture. Working with Joyce *after* Pynchon may reopen the floodgates of information-overload anxiety. It may also help us to recognize the fortuitous joinings, the wild overtones, that arise from Joyce's careful planning. Isn't there something smug about the posture we have taken toward Joyce after years of rereading him and supporting an industry built on the filling in of the holes—or refusing to recognize that *Ulysses* was "ineluctably constructed upon the incertitude of the void"?

Let me begin a thought-experiment focusing on a disjunction in *Ulysses* that has been commonly, and egregiously, bridged: between "Ithaca" and "Penelope." I will come to this disjunction by way of one that has been commonly bridged in the reading of Pynchon's *V.*, the very worst example being my own essay, which has been republished as a key chapter in my book called *The Novel in Motion* (Columbus: Ohio State University Press, 1983). *V.*, I claimed, was designed to generate an experience of senseless motion, unchecked energy, absence of narrative, moral, and political direction. "Where we going?" Benny Profane asks at the end of the first chapter. "The way we're heading," says Pig Bodine, "Move your ass" (8). And we never know where we're heading, as we read along, except that it's the way we're going. Until the end. In the end we know where we are. And we know where we have been. Moreover, we know that the novel has been governed by an omniscient narrator, who has told the story through a series of simple flashbacks, complex rear projections, and the intercutting of one strand of an intricate plot with another. All along he has been holding the pattern in mind, and he ties up the loose ends in the epilogue—where *we* learn what *Stencil* had been searching for and would never know.

Now—having gone through the thought-experiment of reading Joyce after Pynchon, and then coming back to Pynchon's first novel—now I realize that, like the notably few critics who worked with the epilogue, I had read *V.* conservatively. Richard Patterson points out that knowing the answer to Stencil's quest, that his father died in such an "absurdly accidental, ridiculously random way," is to know nothing (30). But even that is conservative. It takes the epilogue as a true epilogue, the purpose of which, according to the Russian formalist Boris Eikhenbaum, is to "set the perspective by a shift in time scale or orientation" (Torgovnick, 11). There has been a shift in the scale and orientation, but what have we gained a perspective upon? Can we take the "Epilogue" seriously? We have learned that Sidney Stencil was ultimately reunited with his old lover, Veronica Manganese, and that they were indeed responsible for the reuniting of Paola's parents. But this double reunion is the most preposterous event in the novel, except for the succeeding account of old Stencil's death; it is a travesty of the marriage ritual that ends traditional comedy, restoring the natural and social orders. Stencil is serving the United States government, which will soon join the Allies in the fight for freedom. V. is serving the Italian Fascists, who are not yet ready to open a second front in the fight for total control. For opposite reasons, therefore, they are both plotting to keep Malta free, and they join forces to compel the double agent Fausto Maijstral to leave their respective services.

And how was Stencil's father killed? Eight lines before the end of the novel, a waterspout appears, which "lasted for fifteen minutes. Long enough to lift the xebec fifty feet, whirling and creaking . . . and slam it down into a piece of the Mediterranean whose subsequent surface phenomena—whitecaps, kelp islands, any of a million flatnesses which should catch thereafter part of the brute sun's spectrum—showed nothing at all of what came to lie beneath, that quiet June day" (463).

This radical parody of an epilogue does not give but denies us a perspective on the events in *V.* It does give us a perspective on the epilogue of *Ulysses.* I, at least, had never thought about "Penelope" as an epilogue, but like most readers had treated it as such. But what are we to make of the perspective established by an epilogue opening with a piece of information—that Bloom asked Molly for breakfast in bed—when this information contradicts what we learned in the last lines of a chapter noted for its fullness, if not overfullness, of objective facts? How reliable is the image of Molly, when we never once saw her in 737 pages of the actual story? Is the evidence about Molly's lovers any more reliable than that given by Bloom and Dublin rumor mongers? What are we to make of Molly's development from stereotype to archetype? How are we to judge Molly's final acceptance of Bloom? And her ultimate "yes"? We may have had differing views on Molly's monologue, but it has been generally accepted as a chapter of equipose, bringing everything together in at least a moment of affirmation. To view it as a parody of an epilogue is to assert the gap between the last two chapters and keep the novel in motion.

"The Incarnate Word," says Baudelaire, "was never known to laugh. For Him who knows all things . . . the comic does not exist." Or, comedy depends upon surprise. We know that Joyce competed with the Creator, that he was a master planner who worked arduously at making connections. But he was, above all, a comic writer and a man who could laugh. Have we overemphasized the way he put things together? Have we taken up too eagerly Joyce's challenge to the detective in us? Or the psychoanalyst? Or have we been misled by the mode of reading that masqueraded as modernist writing, that reached its flower in the new criticism, that we are now recognizing as imperialistic and totalizing? Are we working toward a mastery of the text that would preclude the surprise?

Oedipa Maas, in seeking to understand the Tristero, is driven by the same old humanist impulses. But just before the end of the novel, she begins to wonder whether all the connections she found were the result of paranoia. Or chance. Or a practical joke engendered by someone rich enough to buy a cast of thousands—and capricious enough, and sufficiently imaginative. Doesn't Pynchon give us a new perspective on the real James Joyce?

Works Cited

Givens, Seon, ed. *James Joyce: Two Decades of Criticism*. First Ed. New York: Vanguard Press, 1948.

Patterson, Richard. "What Stencil Knew: Structure and Certitude in Pynchon's *V.*" In *Critical Essays on Thomas Pynchon*, ed. Richard Pearce. Boston: G. K. Hall, 1981.

Pynchon, Thomas. *V.* New York: Bantam Books, 1964.

Torgovnick, Marianna. *Closure in the Novel*. Princeton University Press, 1981.

Wilde, Alan. *Horizons of Assent: Modernism, Postmodernism, and the Ironic Imagination*. Baltimore: Johns Hopkins University Press, 1981.

Wilson, Edmund. *Axel's Castle: A Study of the Imaginative Literature of 1870–1930*. New York: Charles Scribner's Sons, 1936.

Naming in Pynchon and Joyce

David Seed

In experimental fiction there is an inevitable tension between realistic and non-realistic approaches to character, an important factor of which is the author's choice of names. At the realistic end of the spectrum a character receives his name from his family within the narrative; at the opposite extreme the author stands *in loco parentis* in order to give a representative or symbolic label to his characters. Joyce straddles these two broad possibilities by naming his most famous protagonist, Stephen Dedalus, after the builder of the Cretan labyrinth. "Dedalus," from a classical Greek epithet meaning "cunningly wrought," muffles our sense of Stephen's individuality by suggesting a mythical analogue and possible type-quality in his name. But early in *A Portrait of the Artist* Joyce incorporates into the text itself the reader's recognition that Stephen's name is strange. A schoolmate at Clongowes Wood College called "Athy" (after an Irish town) declares that Stephen's name is "like Latin" (25). This recognition disposes of the strangeness and asserts the realism of the name, thereby enabling Joyce at a later stage in the novel to weave it into the text without damaging the name's plausibility. The boys at Belvedere College spin classical variations on his name: "Stephanos Dedalos! Bous Stephanoumenos! Bous Stephaneforos!" (168). Apparently only the ribald games of boys who follow a classical education, these names in fact mock Stephen's secret dream of personal destiny. Joyce draws attention to the etymology of Stephen's forename (*stephanos,* "wreath" or "crown") so that the three names could be rendered as "the cunningly wrought crown," "the crowned ox," or "the crown-wearing ox." Increasingly arrogant behind his mask of detachment, Stephen turns the boys' calls to flattery: "Now, as never before, his strange name seemed to him a prophecy." When at university Stephen's intellectualism has reached disease proportions it is an ironic echo of this earlier scene that Cranly, his friend but also his mocker, should be carrying a book entitled *Diseases of the Ox.* "Dedalus" enables Joyce to conflate different possible fathers, again with ironic effect. Stephen's confident invocation of "old father, old artificer" at the end of *A Portrait* ignores the fact that the mythical Daedalus's son is literally let down by his father's schemes just as Stephen's biological father has let down his family. For Stephen to be named after a mythical figure suggests that Joyce had in mind an archetype, and in *Ulysses* recurrence is developed into a major theme of character. The ironies of *A Portrait* do not destroy Stephen's ambitions because they would be realized after the conclusion of the novel. In *Ulysses,* however, ambition has turned into posture and Stephen imitates the behavior of the biological Dedalus, his hard-drinking father, rather than his mythic archetype.

Throughout *Ulysses* Joyce shows a constant attention to names, partly for political purposes, in "Cyclops" piling them together into Rabelaisian lists to burlesque the chauvinism of the Citizen. R. M. Adams has shown that the list of heroes includes Irish traitors, figures of fantasy, and totally nondescript contemporary figures (152.4).[1] The result is inevitably reductive and deflating. Similarly, the sheer diversity of names makes a cumulative political point about how cosmopolitan Dublin is and raises the question, What is nationality? The two protagonists seem "foreign," as do Artifoni (Italian), Herzog and Dlugacz (East European Jewish, except that Dlugacz is a *pork* butcher), Purefoy (Huguenot), Dandrade (Spanish-American), and Haines (English).[2] The Citizen draws explicit attention to this issue by disgustedly reading out to his cronies the English names from the births and deaths of the supposedly nationalistic *Irish Independent.* The Citizen's point is of course that even these names symptomize the extent of English colonial rule over Ireland, but Joyce ridicules his narrow nationalism by preceding this episode with a ludicrous name-list and by giving the spurious sailor in "Eumaeus" the very name which the Citizen presents as all-Irish, namely Murphy.

As Hugh Kenner has pointed out, it was a fundamental belief of Joyce's "that lives entail roles" (in Hart and Hayman 360). The variability of roles and lack of unity in the self are matched by a corresponding fluidity of names. On the whole the minor characters—the Martin Cunninghams and Paddy Dignams—are relatively stable and form a ground against which Stephen and Bloom manifest themselves. Each of the latter two has a nickname but, instead of implying affection, the nicknames pose a threat. Buck Mulligan calls Stephen "Kinch" (i.e., "knife-blade") presumably in tribute to his scholastic skill, but behind his back mocks him as "wandering Aengus of the rocks," and almost outdoes Stephen's favorite role as intellectual jester.[3] Similarly, Molly calls Bloom "Poldy," but her adultery exerts one of the strongest pressures on his identity in the novel. In *A Portrait* Stephen's surname offered him a possible role which, by the time he reappears in *Ulysses,* he has become acutely conscious of not fulfilling. Hence his intermittent identification with other "pretenders"—among them, Perkin Warbeck and Lambert Simnel—and hence his theatrical mimickry of Hamlet. Bloom similarly emerges as in some sense an imposter. In the past his family name had been changed from Virag (Hungarian for "flower") apparently as part of an effort to cast off Jewish origins.[4] Since Bloom's current name still does not sound Irish he is caught between two identities, and ironically (and unconsciously, since there is no sign that he knows Hungarian) Bloom returns to his earlier name in adopting the pen-name of Henry Flower to carry out a furtive sexual correspondence. Bloom is thus a double imposter, disguising one aspect of himself for his correspondent, and mimicking an earlier and now more or less obsolete racial identity.

During the novel Bloom's name undergoes various kinds of distortion. He appears in the newspaper report of Dignam's funeral as "L. Boom," experiences a musical transformation into "Bloowho" ("Sirens"), has his name declined and made into anagrams. The most bizarre transformations take place in "Circe," where different roles fragment his self into burlesques of his own dreams and fantasies. It is absolutely appropriate to a context of accusation that a member of the watch should challenge Bloom to give his name and address. Bloom forgets in his panic and then takes refuge behind his dentist namesake (who is in fact called *Marcus* Bloom). At this early stage in the mock-trial sequence Bloom's name changes with grotesque rapidity (von Bloom Pasha—Flower—Virag) and his female correspondent appears to try to pin down his forename. Throughout the whole section Bloom's identity is under attack and a crucial feature of this attack is the distortion and obliteration of his name.[5]

In "Eumaeus" the whole question of identity is raised, once again via names.[6] There is some discussion of exactly who the sailor-raconteur is, which gathers together the implications of many earlier transformations and distortions. "Sounds," Stephen declares, "are impostures . . . like names" (622), and the section assembles various examples to confirm his statement. Bloom and Stephen meet a young man facetiously called "Lord John Corley" in mock-recognition of aristocratic descent on his mother's side. The care with which this is explained sets up a context where a passing reference to the case of the Tichborne claimant, a notorious trial revolving around fraudulent identity, and to Parnell's divorce case (where he loses his name in a different sense), become pointedly relevant. Bloom introduces Stephen to his wife obliquely through a photograph identifying her by her stage name of Madam Marion Tweedy. And so the examples proliferate. Names slide off their owners and generalize the process that has been happening in "Circe" to Bloom in particular. The culmination of the process, at least as far as Stephen is concerned, is reached in "Ithaca," where the scholastic prose extends outward to the broadest abstractions. Bloom is now, as it were, generalized out of existence as "Everyman and Noman."

Joyce uses a variety of means to alert the reader to names in *Ulysses*. A bizarre example of accident takes place when the mysterious mourner at Dignam's funeral is christened McIntosh by the reporter. The sandwich-boards advertising H.E.L.Y.S. give an early example of fragmentation. Bloom/Virag/Flower is woven into a series of metaphors of fertility and growth. To compound the reader's confusion Joyce duplicates names (two Simon Dedaluses, two Blooms, etc.) and mingles fiction with historical names in an idiosyncratic and often private biographical way (Adams 222–23, 237–42).

Thomas Pynchon takes Joyce's skepticism about the authenticity of names a considerable step further. His first novel has as its title *V. A Novel,* an initial which teasingly suggests a name behind it. As many critics have noted, however, the various meanings of the title multiply, partly through names. V. goes through a series of transformations from historical allusion (Victoria Wren), through displacement onto an animal (a rat called Veronica), duplication in two simultaneous female characters (Vera Moroving and Hedwig Vogelsang) to displacement onto a setting (a priest in Valletta). Pynchon undoubtedly took his title from the obsessive seeker in Nabokov's novel *The Real Life of Sebastian Knight* (1941), where the narrator (V.) sets out to write a biography of his cousin and assimilates his subject into narcissistic self-description.[7] The fact that Pynchon gives *his* seeker the name of Stencil suggests that his character *is* his search for V., and, like Nabokov's protagonist, he begins to impersonate his own subject. For that reason he is described at one point as a quick-change artist. The patent subjectivity of Stencil's quest and the multiplicity of personifications of V. ("v" is also the logical symbol for "or") tempt the reader to engage in a similar decoding of the text and at the same time discourage him. Pynchon even breaks down the distinction between personal names and things as V-shapes proliferate endlessly (a V-8 engine, a jazz club called the "V-Note," and so on).

The permutations of V. are far more extreme than anything Joyce attempts in *Ulysses* and reflect a general absurdist treatment of names on Pynchon's part. A small number are straightforward, realistic ones, usually with some implication of a fuller personality (for example, Fina Mendoza, a Puerto Rican girl; or Paola Maijstral from Malta, named after the northerly wind which sweeps her island). Otherwise most names fall into four broad categories: they personify functions (Stencil; Shale Schoenmaker, a cosmetic surgeon); transform their owners into synthetic materials or consumer objects (Morris Teflon, "Bloody" Chiclitz); parody English colonial types (Bongo-Shaftesbury, Rowley-Bugge); or they are simply facetious (Harvey Fazzo, Hanky and Panky).[8] Like his friend from Cornell, Richard Fariña, Pynchon takes delight in inventing names which jump from mathematics and literary allusion to pop culture and obscenity.[9] What virtually all of these names have in common is a comic inventiveness which makes it well-nigh impossible for the reader to credit the characters with any identity. They constantly remind us of the virtuosity of the writer and live up to the absurdity of their names. Unbeknown to themselves, they are participating in a general process of decline, a steady atrophy of humanity which culminates in ridiculous figures like Slab. Appropriately named after an inert object, he forms part of Pynchon's attack on fashionable New York artist-intellectuals. Like the other members of the Whole Sick Crew he acts out his inertia, painting endless variations of cheese Danishes.

The problem in the names of Pynchon's first novel is that he can't do very much with them. Given the absurdity of their initial bestowal, they can do little more than demonstrate the overlap of people into things. There is some use of distortion ("Godolphin" into "Gadrulfi"), impersonation (Paola pretends to be a negress called "Ruby"), and repetition ("Porpentine" reappears as "Porcépic"), but Pynchon's rhetorical exploitation of the names loses its point because we do not believe that identities are at stake. This is not the case with Oedipa Maas in *The Crying of Lot 49,* who is a more substantial character than either Stencil or Benny Profane, *V.*'s second protagonist. Her name combines a suggestion of role (Oedipus confronting the Sphinx) with a plausible Dutch-American surname, whereas "Benny Profane" is part label and part synecdoche, being named after the benzedrine pills of the profane culture which he inhabits. Instead of demonstrating a diffuse absurdity, the characters relate closely to Oedipa's predicament. She gets information from a theater producer called "Randolph Driblette," the mannered style of whose name obscures its purely functional significance—"driblet" meaning a small piece. Similarly she gets different information from one Mike Fallopian, whose name is mock-Armenian and also fits the character into a series of metaphors of impregnation and gestation which articulate the growth of Oedipa's theories. A pop group called "The Paranoids" and an actor/lawyer called "Manny di Presso" offer deceptively comic comments on the paranoid possibilities in Oedipa's experience which pose a stronger and stronger threat to her. As in *Ulysses,* one sign of this threat is that Oedipa's name becomes vulnerable. She finds herself in a homosexual bar with a badge identifying her as "Arnold Snarb," and at another point becomes "Edna Mosh" when her husband broadcasts her name over the radio. In *Lot 49* names have a comic or absurd surface but they also become a means of interpreting or commenting on the narrative. Thus Richard Poirier has indicated the philatelic significance of "Pierce Inverarity" without explaining the more immediate relevance of the name (in Levine and Leverenz 22). The tycoon whose will Oedipa has to execute *pierces* her in a whole variety of ways, revealing and exploiting her vulnerability.

Gravity's Rainbow presents a protagonist whose identity goes through even more bizarre transformations. Tyrone Slothrop's name hints at an allegorical type-quality (sloth), but more importantly Pynchon repeatedly draws attention to his family ancestry. Instead of filling out Slothrop as a character, his family background rather suggests that he has inherited a set of Puritan attitudes and reflexes, and thereby decreases his identity, especially when Slothrop discovers he has been sold to a big business combine as a child. The structural linkages between him and the Nazi V-rockets transform Slothrop into an apparently valuable prize for the competing intelligence agencies, and it seems at first that the variety of disguises he undergoes would protect him and allow him to maneuver around the Zone

(Germany between Nazi collapse and Allied partition) with comparative freedom. Rather than preserving Slothrop's national identity, however, these disguises gradually fragment him as a character in a process very similar, if more extreme, to that Bloom undergoes. The disguises are forced on Slothrop by circumstances. He becomes variously "Ian Scuffling," an English war-correspondent, a temporary personification of a local pig-deity ("Plechazunga") and a comic-book figure ("Rocketman"). Pynchon complicates the already intricate sense of masquerade by multiplying resemblances. Thus, as Scuffling, Slothrop compares himself to Hemingway and to Ralph Ellison's zoot-suited Rinehart. At another point under the alias of Max Schlepzig he meets an actress called Greta Erdmann who was lover to the "real" Schlepzig. After forcing Slothrop to go through a ritual flagellation she then tells him that "Schlepzig" anyway wasn't her lover's real name. Names, in short, recede into multiple layers of impersonations. This is one reason why a fictional actress (Greta, described as the "anti-Dietrich") and a historical film-actor (Rudolf Klein-Rogge) should be such important secondary characters.

In *Gravity's Rainbow* we find the same kind of names as in Pynchon's earlier fiction. Some (particularly the English ones) have a comically "period" ring to them ("Webley Silvernail," "Maurice ['Sax'] Reed") or draw attention to their nationality (like Slothrop's one English friend—"Tantivy Mucker-Maffick").[10] Another mainly German group repeat from *V.* the transformation of people into things, specifically minerals or chemicals: "Smaragd" (emerald), "Feldspath" (felspar), "Säure" (acid). But these names work on the surface of the text. *Gravity's Rainbow* weaves more important names into the narrative with astonishing intricacy, setting up many more connections than any individual character could recognize, and constantly enriching the novel's thematic issues. In a novel so extensively preoccupied with espionage we might anyway expect an element of disguise; we have already seen another element of theater in naming. But neither factor gives us an adequate explanation. Greta Erdmann tells Slothrop that she adopted a more *völkisch* name because such names formed a kind of code, reinforcing racial and political solidarity. Decoding some of the German names thus becomes important for the reader to gain access to the collective mentality lying behind them. The most important single example of a name rich with meaning is Captain Weissmann (i.e., "White man") who first appeared in the South-West Africa section of *V.* On joining the SS he takes as his new name "Blicero" after an Old German nickname for death, *Blicker*. It is uncertain whether Weissmann completely understands his new name—he is merely "enchanted" by it. It is a highly strategic change for Pynchon's purposes because it enables him to establish various verbal linkages which develop the symbolism of whiteness in the novel. If Death is the bleacher to the early Germans, "Bleicher" comes from *bleichen* (to shine) which is cognate with *blicken* and with the noun *Blitz* (lightning). The pronunciation of "Blicero" would link it with the latter term, particularly with the Nazi coinage *Blitzkrieg* (literally, a lightning war). Blicero is after all participating in a belated blitz by sending the V-rockets to Britain. Meanings proliferate outwards away from the captain to include the place where the rockets were made, Nordhausen/*Bleiche*röde—the latter emerging as a place of death within the meanings of the novel's symbolism. Unknowingly, Slothrop is even participating in these connections when he dresses as a pig-deity called "Plechazunga," since the pig's name means "lightning" in Old High German. Pynchon draws attention particularly to the theme of whiteness in these meanings, but the second area of meaning—shining/lightning/radiance—would relate to Nazi mysticism.[11] The interconnections between these names and the fact that they play on etymological origins deeply embedded in the German language imply that for instance Weissmann is acting on some kind of race-memory in changing his name. The change becomes alarming and exciting to him (he describes it as "this sinister cryptography of naming") because he only dimly understands its meaning and rationalizes his limited understanding by reference to an ultimate goal or destiny.

Apart from being an exercise in self-mystification, naming in *Gravity's Rainbow* can also be an act of power. When in South-West Africa, Weissmann appropriates a young Herero boy as a catamite and names him "Enzian," after the mountain gentian in Rilke's ninth "Duino Elegy." The name, or more correctly the metonym, represents an individual act of colonization since Weissmann forces Enzian to conform to his own fantasies. "Enzian" was also the name given to an anti-aircraft rocket Messerschmidt was testing in 1944, which broadens Weissmann's individual appropriation and, as it were, involves Enzian in the Nazi military enterprise. Enzian's white *Doppelgänger* Gottfried (which Pynchon translates ironically as "God's peace") has to conform even more to Weissmann's dreams.[12] At first being only sexually exploited, he is later shot to death in a rocket. Bernard Duyfhuizen has commented interestingly on a taboo against naming in this novel which harks back to the primitive belief that a name was an integral part of the self (31).[13] He sees Slothrop's reluctance to name names as a defensive strategy in order to protect himself. It is of course an effort which fails since Slothrop discovers in some records that he has been given the cryptonym "Schwarzknabe" (black boy) which signals his conversion into raw experimental material and which links him with Nazi hardware like the Schwarzgerat. Spiritual names usually appear in this novel emptied of their spiritual content or distorted, just as the names of God and Christ appear in "Cyclops" primarily as profane exclamations. Enzian uses the Herero name of God when he makes love to Weissmann, and a brigadier racked with guilt from World War I performs a ritual of submission to the accompaniment of voices from the Kabbala ("Meta-tron"), pornography ("Savarin" from "Severin" in *Venus in Furs*) and Black Magic.[14] Mythical analogues, spiritual names, etymological word-play, and aliases give some examples of the extraordinary breadth of expression Pynchon gives to names in *Gravity's Rainbow*. They form a rich seam of meaning in the text, despite the difficulty at times of decoding them, and help to locate characters within a network of thematic and symbolic correspondences.[15]

Notes

1. Adams makes invaluable comments on, among other things, Joyce's inter-mingling of fictitious and actual names.

2. The Jewishness of Dlugacz is in fact ambiguous. Bloom sees polonies (Polish sausages) in his window and sure enough *w dlugacz* is Polish for "in debt." Bloom picks up a page from a pile of "cut sheets" and reads about the settlements in Palestine, but the pages are obviously used for wrapping and could have come from anywhere. Adams (215) derives the name from a Polish historian (Jan Dlu-gosz), but the Random House edition of *Ulysses* spells the butcher's name "Dlugacz" (58). It is an indication of Joyce's detailed attention to names that, for instance, Paddy Dignam's son should go to a butcher's called "Mangan's, late Fehrenbach's"; that is, that a Jewish name should get historical precedence over the name of one of the most famous Irish poets.

3. See J. H. Maddox on Mulligan's threat to Stephen in *Joyce's "Ulysses" and the Assault upon Character* (23).

4. Joseph Prescott has shown that during revision Joyce increased the Jewish content of Bloom's thoughts but also made them realistically vague (3–4).

5. A more recent American novel which is heavily indebted to Joyce, Edward Wallant's *The Tenants of Moonbloom* (1963), has as protagonist Norman Moon-bloom, a rent-collector. As he feels his tenants making more and more demands on him, the last letter of his name painted on his office window is scratched off by an anonymous joker.

6. I am particularly indebted to Gerald L. Bruns's discussion of this section in Hart and Hayman, *James Joyce's "Ulysses": Critical Essays (363–83)*.

7. The similarities between the two writers are examined by David R. Mesher in his "Pynchon and Nabokov's *V*." (43–46).

8. The names in this novel have been surveyed but not analyzed by Kelsie B. Harder in her "Names in Thomas Pynchon's *V*." Terry P. Caesar's "A Note on Pynchon's Naming" is also useful.

9. Fariña's only novel, *Been Down So Long It Looks Like Up To Me* (1966), has characters named either for ironic/absurdist purposes or to shed light on its pro-tagonist, Gnossos Pappadopoulis. The novel's comic use of Homeric allusion is one of the many signs of its indebtedness to Joyce.

10. "Tantivy Mucker-Maffick," grotesque as the name sounds, is in fact made up from three common nouns: "tantivy" is a hunting-cry; "mucker" has various

meanings, the most relevant one being "mate" in British army slang; and "maffick" means the noisy, exuberant behavior of a crowd when celebrating good news (like the relief of Mafeking).

11. The key section of *Gravity's Rainbow* in this context reads: "And Enzian's found the name Bleicheröde close enough to 'Blicker,' the nickname the early Germans gave to Death. They saw him white: bleaching and blankness," (Viking/Picador editions 322). *Bleichen* means "to shine or bleach," but "Blicker" is rather from *blicken,* meaning "to shine or look." "Blankness' has as German cognate the Old Germanic name "Blanka" (Slothrop later meets a young German girl called "Bianca"). "Plechazunga" (or "blekezunga" alternatively) is cognate with the verb *blicken* and noun *Blitz.* Steven Weisenburger has pointed out that Pynchon takes many of his details about Germanic names from Jakob Grimm's *Teutonic Mythology* (3–15).

12. Wagnerian names form an obviously important theme in *Gravity's Rainbow* and always in a context of masquerade. Slothrop acts out the role of Tannhäuser briefly; Gottfried is compared with Siegfried; Greta has a guardian called Sigmund; and so on.

13. One of the key statements on primitive names appears in J. G. Frazer's *The Golden Bough* (321–22).

14. The common source in Sacher-Masoch is only one of the many connections between this section and "Circe."

15. A small part of the Pynchon section of this paper appeared in a preliminary form in *Pynchon Notes* 6 (June 1981).

Works Cited

Adams, R. M. *Surface and Symbol*. New York: Galaxy Books, 1967.

Bruns, Gerald L. "Eumaeus." In *James Joyce's "Ulysses": Critical Essays*, ed. Clive Hart and David Hayman. Berkeley and Los Angeles: University of California Press, 1974.

Caesar, Terry P. "A Note on Pynchon's Naming." *Pynchon Notes* 5 (Feb. 1981): 5–10.

Duyfhuizen, Bernard. "Starry-Eyed Semiotics: Learning to Read Slothrop's Map and *Gravity's Rainbow*." *Pynchon Notes* 6 (June 1981): 5–33.

Frazer, James George. *The Golden Bough*. London: Macmillan, 1963.

Harder, Kelsie B. "Names in Thomas Pynchon's *V*." *Literary Onomastics Studies* 5 (Feb. 1981): 5–10.

Kenner, Hugh. "Circe." In *James Joyce's "Ulysses": Critical Essays*, ed. Clive Hart and David Hayman. Berkeley and Los Angeles: University of California Press, 1974.

Maddox, J. H. *Joyce's "Ulysses" and the Assault Upon Character*. New Brunswick, N.J.: Rutgers University Press; Hassocks, England: Harvester Press, 1978.

Mesher, David R. "Pynchon and Nabokov's *V*." *Pynchon Notes* 8 (Feb. 1982): 43–46.

Poirier, Richard. "The Importance of Thomas Pynchon." In *Mindful Pleasures:*

Essays on Thomas Pynchon, ed. George Levine and David Leverenz. Boston: Little, Brown, 1976.

Prescott, Joseph. "The Characterization of Bloom." *Literature and Psychology* 9 (1959): 3–4.

Weisenburger, Steven. "Notes for *Gravity's Rainbow.*" *Pynchon Notes* 12 (June 1983): 3–15.

2. Sirens Without Music

Joyce's Lipspeech: Syntax and the Subject in "Sirens"

Derek Attridge

The English language allows very little independence to the organs of the body: most verbs of conscious behavior require a grammatical subject implying an undivided, masterful, efficient self of which the organ is mere slave or satellite. In *James wears a ring* or *He turns the page* it is only from the verb and its object that we deduce the role of finger or hand, since they make no appearance in the sentence; and if it becomes necessary to stipulate the organs involved, we do so by suggesting that they are places where, or accessories by means of which, the controlling individual performs the activities in question: *James wears a ring through his nose; He turns the page with his toes.* We seldom stop to question that easy transition from subject to verb, to consider what a totalizing and naturalizing gesture it is to constitute in language a complete, homogeneous, individual subject ("James," "he"), a single, coherent, separable activity ("wears," "turns"), and a relation between them of pure transitivity. If, however, the verb is given a subject that is only a part of the whole individual, the sentence immediately registers as anomalous: *James's finger wears a ring; His hand turns the page.* It is not just the feeling of tautology that produces the oddness here; we are even more unsettled by sentences in which the subject is *not* implied by the rest of the sentence—*James's nose wears a ring* or *Joyce's toes turn the page.* What is worrying is that the grammatical subject is no longer a human subject: syntax and our sense of the world have ceased to coincide. Even when the activity is fully localizable in the conscious mind, we prefer to specify the individual as a mental and physical unity: *She thought hard,* not *Her mind thought hard.* The totalizing pronoun "she" satisfies us by providing a fully constituted human subject, answerable to the rules and norms of the society which confers identity upon all subjects; "her mind" disturbs us as an isolated and ungovernable potency.[1]

Ulysses, however, fails to conform to these syntactic expectations. Take for example, the following statement: "His hand accepted the moist tender gland and slid it into a side pocket" (60). Such a sentence, in which the transaction between Bloom and Dlugacz becomes a transaction between two organs, hand and kidney, challenges momentarily our untroubled belief in the human subject as unitary, unconstrained, and capable of originating action from a single center of consciousness; the sharp focus which is the goal of traditional realistic narrative has been narrowed to a point at which it threatens the subjective unity it usually serves to sustain. Only when the unity of mind and body is actually broken does it seem legitimate—though still troubling—for the organ to command its own intentional verb, as in young Dignam's memory of his father's death: "I couldn't hear the other things he said but I saw his tongue and his teeth trying to say it better" (251). Even the body acting as a whole must be behaving abnormally if it is to be permitted the privilege of functioning as the subject of a verb of this kind: "once, sleeping, his body had risen, crouched and crawled in the direction of a heatless fire and, having attained its destination, there, curled, unheated, in night attire had lain, sleeping" (692).[2] The verbs we are accustomed to finding with organs of the body as subjects usually involve completely involuntary and localized muscular behavior (or behavior which is perceived in this way by a particular character or narrational point of view): thus in "Aeolus," "His mouth continued to twitch unspeaking in nervous curls of disdain" (138)—and even here "disdain" seems to reintroduce the intentionality expelled by "twitch."

Not surprisingly, among the organs whose independent initiative is stringently circumscribed by these linguistic norms is the voice itself: we guard the right of the "speaking subject" to be master of the speech apparatus, to speak through it, not to let *it* speak. However, ten lines into the main body of "Sirens," the chapter most closely concerned with voices, we come across this: "—In the second carriage, Miss Douce's wet lips said, laughing in the sun" (257). Here is a sentence which refuses the usual automatic move from vocal activity to a free, originating subject; we stop at the lips, which have somehow managed to displace Miss Douce as the author of the statement. An indication of the barmaid's mindlessness as she produces mechanical chatter—or, rather, lets her speech organs produce it for her? Perhaps, but the device occurs too often in the "Sirens" chapter, and in relation to too many characters, to be seen only as the reflex of a particular state of mind. Lips act again and again beyond the reach of a mastering self:

> Her wet lips tittered:
> —He's killed looking back. (257)

> Lenehan's lips over the counter lisped a low whistle of decoy. (264)

> Lenehan still drank and grinned at his tilted ale and at Miss Douce's lips that all but hummed, not shut, the oceansong her lips had trilled. (265)

> Down she sat. All ousted looked. Lips laughing. (275)

> Sour pipe removed he held a shield of hand beside his lips that cooed a moonlight nightcall, clear from anear, a call from afar, replying. (279)

> See. Play on her. Lip blow. (285)

Miss Mina Kennedy brought near her lips to ear of tankard one.
—Mr Dollard, they murmured low. (287)

Yes, her lips said more loudly, Mr Dollard. (288)

Here are six pairs of lips all engaged in activities we normally regard as the proper province of the whole individual acting under the command of a central will: they say, titter, lisp, hum, trill, laugh, coo, blow, murmur, and say loudly. We might add to this list of independent speech organs the "boot-snout" that sniffs a rude reply to Miss Douce (258), Bob Cowley's Adam's apple that "hoarsed softly" (271), and Richie Goulding's breath and teeth that "fluted with plaintive woe" (272), as well as the reversal in "Speech paused on Richie's lips" (272). Although examples cluster most thickly in the "Sirens" chapter, they occur in many other places too, with no shortage in the earlier, stylistically more "normal," episodes— we might note that Mulligan's voice speaks in the opening pages (4, 5—where it is a "wellfed voice," 10), that the milkwoman "bows her old head to a voice that speaks to her loudly" (14), that Mr. Deasy's voice speaks to Stephen (33), and that Bloom hears his own voice say something (56).[3] (In "Circe" the attribution of intentions and speech to organs and subjects is of course concretely dramatized.) There is clearly too much vocal and emotional energy of different kinds being expended here to allow "mechanical behavior" to stand as a satisfactory explanation.

Another way of attempting to account for the independence of these speech organs would be to appeal to the figure of *synecdoche*. We find a familiar textbook example, somewhat fragmented, among Bloom's meditations in this chapter: "Beerpull. Her hand that rocks the cradle rules the. Ben Howth. That rules the world" (288), and in "Circe" Stephen recites the customary description of this trope in connection with another example: "Doctor Swift says one man in armour will beat ten men in their shirts. Shirt is synecdoche. Part for the whole" (588). This definition in terms of a straightforward substitution implies a reassuringly reversible movement which allows the momentarily challenged unity to be retrieved, so that we are not shaken in our assurance that it is mothers who rock cradles (and rule the world), not hands. It would also be possible, however, to regard the naming of the whole individual when only a part of the body is active as itself a figure of speech, albeit one which we use all the time and therefore take for granted; in fact, the substitution of whole for part is included in the classical definition of synecdoche. The variously busy lips of "Sirens" can therefore be seen as a more *literal* rendering of human vocal activity than is normally permitted by linguistic conventions. Joyce's transgression of the selectional restrictions of English syntax can be regarded as a stratagem which liberates the body from a dictatorial and englobing will, and allows its organs their own energies and proclivities.

A further effect of this organic liberation is erotic power: sexuality thrives on the separation of the body into independent parts, while a sexually repressive morality insists on the wholeness and singleness of body and mind (or soul). One of the most striking whole-for-part synecdoches is the substitution of the entire individual for the genital organs in euphemistic references to sexual activity: "You can . . . play with yourself while I just go through her a few times," says Boylan to Bloom in "Circe" (566). The business that all these lips are about in "Sirens" is in one way or another sexual: Lenehan's flirting, Molly's first appearance to Bloom, Simon Dedalus's memory of moonlight barcaroles, Bloom's fantasies of oral sex, and of course the titillating ministrations of the Sirens themselves. Miss Douce and Miss Kennedy, like their Homeric counterparts, know the power of a sexuality radiated from a single organ: the Sirens heard by Odysseus sing both of and in a "honey-sweet voice that issues from our lips" (*The Odyssey of Homer* 12:187–88),[4] and the Ormond Hotel barmaids offer not only erotically independent lips and voices, but a rising and falling bosom, a smackable thigh, and a masturbatory finger and thumb.

The "Sirens" chapter teems, in fact, with the names of organs (as so often, Joyce's schema, which singles out the ear, gives a misleading emphasis); and once the parts of the body are separated in this manner, the possibility arises of replacing one by another. When lips are said to hum, coo, and murmur, they are doing duty for other parts of the vocal apparatus. In this chapter, a bust hums (266), eyes ask (279), lips and eyes listen (262). Bloom even tries, in a fantasy of remote-controlled seduction, to commandeer another organ to serve in place of both voice and lips: "Ventriloquise. My lips closed. Think in my stom" (285). (His most notable utterance in the chapter does indeed proceed from the lower rather than the higher organs.) We hardly need Freud to persuade us that sexual development and variety depend on this substitutability of organs. Lips may be a synecdochic substitute for the whole individual of which they are a part, but they may also be a metaphoric substitute for another organ which they resemble.[5] Miss Douce's lips are twice given the adjective "wet," and she complains after her laughing spree, with undecidable reference, "I feel all wet" (260). (Compare this with Molly's "I'm drenched," which Bloom remembers her screaming as she laughed in the wake of Dollard's tight-trousered departure [270].)

This traffic between vocal and sexual organs occurs throughout the chapter, the word "organ" itself providing one of the bridges:

> —Sure, you'd burst the tympanum of her ear, man, Mr Dedalus said through smoke aroma, with an organ like yours.
> In bearded abundant laughter Dollard shook upon the keyboard. He would.
> —Not to mention another membrane, Father Cowley added. (270)

(In the background here is the displacement from vagina to ear in one account of the Virgin's conception in Christian mythology; it becomes more explicit in "Circe" when Virag produces the anti-Christian alternative: "Panther, the Roman centurion, polluted her with his genitories . . . Messiah! He burst her tympanum" [521].) Words occur which suit both voice and genitals, whether male: "Tenderness it welled: slow, swelling. Full it throbbed" (274), or female: "Gap in their voices too. Fill me, I'm warm, dark, open" (282). In Bloom's musings on Ben Dollard, voice and testicles are associated through the obvious physiological connection: "With all his belongings on show. . . . Well, of course, that's what gives him the base barreltone. For instance eunuchs" (270); or "Good voice he has still. No eunuch yet with all his belongings" (283). And in Tom Kernan's highly condensed anecdote, the context of adulterous sex encourages a double reading of the word "throat": "Authentic fact. How Walter Bapty lost his voice. Well, sir, the husband took him by the throat. *Scoundrel,* said he. *You'll sing no more lovesongs*" (281).

Molly, also, is to be seen with her "belongings on show" (284), and the parallel with Dollard extends to the association, thanks to the double applicability of the word "full," between them and the voice: "Full voice of perfume of what perfume does your lilactrees. Bosom I saw, both full, throat warbling" (275). The vocal and the vaginal became indistinguishable; Simon Dedalus, agreeing that Molly has a fine voice, adds, "The lower register, for choice" (289). (Once again, "Circe" is outrageously explicit: Bella's "sowcunt barks" [554].) And returning to the wetness with which we began, we can trace a pattern whereby the flow of the singing voice flows into the flow of genital arousal, a language of flow that, like the language of flowers, is the language of Henry Flower's synecdochic love:

> Flower to console me and a pin cuts lo. Means something, language of flow. Was it a daisy? Innocence that is. (263)

> Tenors get women by the score. Increase their flow. Throw flower at his feet when will we meet? (274)

> Flood of warm jimjam lickitup secretness flowed to flow in music out, in desire, dark to lick flow, invading. Tipping her tepping her tapping her topping her. Tup. Pores to dilate dilating. Tup. The joy the feel the warm the. Tup. To pour o'er sluices pouring gushes. Flood, gush, flow joygush, tupthrop. Now! Language of love. (274)

One could almost conceive of the chapter as a version of Diderot's *Les Bijoux indiscrets:* a conclave of talkative (not to say musical) genitalia.

Nor is it the vocal organs alone that prove sexually substitutable: ears, hair, skin, hands, fingers, nose, and eyes all function as genital surrogates during the course of the chapter.[6] Bloom's allusion to the synecdochic hand that rocks the cradle also involves sexual substitution, the barmaid's hand on the beerpull recalling the stimulating activity of Molly's hand on Ben Howth (which in another passage is displaced onto a harpist's touch on the strings of her instrument: "The harp that once or twice. Cool hands. Ben Howth, the rhododendrons. We are their harps" [271]). It is not, after all, maternal but sexual instincts that rule the world, and they exercise their power through specific organs. (We might recall that during the "Sirens" episode Boylan and Molly are brought together for their adulterous act by a duet in which genital union is euphemized as a union of hands: Mozart and Da Ponte's *Là ci darem la mano.*) And the sexual innuendos by means of which the two barmaids urge one another into orgasmic laughter (259–60) are all achieved by displacement: "And your other eye!", "With his bit of beard!", "Married to the greasy nose!" (Lenehan uses the same technique in his advances to Miss Kennedy: "Will you put your bill down inn my troath and pull upp ah bone?" [262].)

In all these processes of displacement, decentering, and exchange can be seen one aspect of the interpenetration of the categories of "form" and "content" that characterizes *Ulysses,* going well beyond (and indeed undermining) any notion of mimesis or iconicity. The liberation of the part from the whole, and the possibility of condensation and substitution, come about only because the meaning of an organ is not exhausted by its place and function in the economy of the unified individual, as determined by the cultural and ideological context; it has its own physical properties and patterns of behavior which displace and subvert the central, commanding, conscious will, and open up the possibility of continual reinterpretation. In just the same way, every item of speech or writing has its own sound and shape, independent of its authorized function in the language system, and this material specificity and independence prohibit transparency, fixity, and singleness of meaning; words, even letters, have lives of their own in *Ulysses* (and even more so, of course, in *Finnegans Wake*). In "Sirens," these two processes come together: bodily displacements and substitutions are enacted in the displacements and substitutions of language. It is the regular patterning of syntax that makes it possible for one item in the chain to be paradigmatically replaced by another in defiance of semantic restrictions ("her lips" for "she"), and it is the arbitrariness of the material signifier that makes it possible for one word to point in several directions ("swelling," "throbbed," "warm," "flow/er"). (Bloom himself reflects on this potential in language—and achieves another vocal/genital transfer—in bringing to mind Molly's urination: "Chamber music. Could make a kind of a pun on that" [282].) The "Sirens" episode insists that neither language (in its materiality) nor the body (in its physicality) can be seen as merely secondary and subservient to a nonmaterial, transcendent, controlling principle, whether that principle is called "meaning" or "the self"; more importantly, it demonstrates some of the pleasures, sexual and textual, that we owe to this fact.

Notes

1. We do, however, say "My head hurts" where French, for example, has *J'ai mal à la tête:* an even more stringent insistence on a dominating central subjectivity. In other languages, the fusion of individual and action extends to a verbal system that can do without personal pronouns (*cogito*—"I think").

2. Roy K. Gottfried comments briefly on the occurrence of such sentences in the novel, finding in them a "drift into apparently mere patterning and mechanics" which leaves Bloom "almost a passive object" (70); he views them, that is, as having a traditional expressive function, representing human behavior as mechanical.

3. The attribution of volition to the voice in these examples should be distinguished from the use in narration of phrases like "A voice spoke" to signify a point of view from which no other information is available. This is done by Joyce—with slightly parodic scrupulousness—in introducing Haines: "A tall figure rose . . .— Have you the key? a voice asked" (11).

4. Tr. Richmond Lattimore (New York: Harper & Row, 1967).

5. In his survey of studies concerned with the equivalence between the mouth and the vagina, Ivan Fónagy notes that in several languages the word for "lips" metaphorically designates both the vocal cords and the lips of the vulva as well (85).

6. The term "fetishization" offers itself here, but because it implies a long-term transference of libido I would resist it. What is at stake is a matter more of erotic (and verbal) play than neurotic fixation.

Works Cited

Fónagy, Ivan. *La Vive voix: Essais de psycho-phonétique.* Paris: Payot, 1983.
Gottfried, Roy K. *The Art of Joyce's Syntax in "Ulysses."* Athens: University of Georgia Press; London: Macmillan, 1980.

To Sing or to Sign

Maud Ellmann

"Par it's Greek: parallel, parallax," muses Bloom in "Lestrygonians." "Sirens" parallels "Proteus," and provides it with a kind of parallaxative. Like "Proteus," "Sirens" sets the audible against the visible, time against space, voice against writing: but Bloom's fart escapes both of the modalities which these two chapters pose as ineluctable.

As magicians of the voice, the Sirens stand for the enchantments of the audible. To resist them, Bloom must discover a new lure, and open an alternative modality. While the ear surrenders to the blandishments of voice, the roving Odyssean eye pursues the letter, and it is through writing that Bloom begins to make his getaway. What the ear hears, the eye reads; and in particular, the eye reads names and signatures. "Signatures of all things I am here to read" (*U* 37), thinks Stephen, while in "Sirens," "Bloowhose dark eye read Aaron Figatner's name" (259). As well as reading signatures, Bloom's task in "Sirens" is to write his name to Martha Clifford. Here he must summon all his polytropic cunning. For while he signs the letter, he must still preserve the incognito he imposes on himself, the law that Nosey Flynn nosed out in "Lestrygonians":

> O, Bloom has his good points. But there's one thing he'll never do.
> His hand scrawled a dry pen signature beside his grog.
> —I know, Davy Byrne said.
> —Nothing in black and white, Nosey Flynn said. (178)

So Bloom must find a pseudo-signature: and more than that, a countersign (for Molly's countersign, see R. Ellmann, *Ulysses on the Liffey* 162). This mark enables him to face the music without unstopped ears, but it also gives him the guts to shun its charms. Because it sneaks *between* modalities, this autograph will open forth a heresy. The Greek root of "heresy" implies a middle voice, a middle way. "Heresy" resembles "odyssey," for both pursue a middle course of action or of thought, between antitheses or rocks and whirlpools. By eluding binarism, both condemn themselves to endless errancy.

"Proteus" and "Sirens" meditate the heresies couched in "contransmagnificandjewbangstantiality." In "Sirens," song and signature compete for the annunciation of the Virgin. Ben Dollard would take her with his voice: "Sure, you'd burst the tympanum of her ear, man, Mr Dedalus said through smoke aroma, with an organ like yours" (270). Bloom foregoes the penetrations of the voice, but he would ravish with his writing. "Blank face," he thinks. "Virgin should say: or fingered only. Write something on it: page" (285). This image harks back to "Proteus," where Stephen envisions Eve's unnaveled flesh as a "buckler of taut vellum," an unwritten page (38). The writing that blemishes this vellum is the navel, which undersigns the strandentwining cable of maternity. Because he would deny maternity, and beget a father for his name, Stephen must erase the navel from the page. But his own logic means that he can never write. If writing is the scar upon the belly where the mother's namelessness engraves itself upon the flesh in mockery of Stephen's name and patrimony, to write is to unname and to unman. This is why Bloom can only write his name in womantalk, the language of flowers, the language "they" like because "no-one can hear" (78). He foregoes his father's name to write "an anenome's letter," and to disseminate maternal countersigns (*FW* 563).

How is Bloom to write umbiliform? An answer may be found in Plutarch's essay "On the E at Delphi," for the letter *E* was carved into the navel of the world, the stone of the Delphic oracle *(Plutarch's Morals* 173–96). When he countersigns his pseudo-signature with two "Greek ees," Bloom commemorates this ancient graffito, and hollows out an omphalos within his name. The difference between a Greek *E* and a Roman *E* cannot be enunciated; nor can it pierce the tympan of the ear. Only the eye can see the *E*. Through this navel strategy, our latter-day Odysseus eludes the Sirens and the perilous pleasures of the voice, as Homer's Noman once escaped the eyeless Cyclops.

So far, so good. Bloom supplants the phallus with the omphalos. He escapes the myth of vocal penetration by writing Greek *E*'s on the virgin page. The voice does not deflower Henry Flower, for his silent *E* subverts its whole modality. If, as Bloom says, "time makes the tune" (*U* 278), it would seem that space and writing had outdone the Siren time, the Siren music. But the etymology of heresy involves the notion of a middle course, and Odysseus is one who steers *between* antitheses. Besides, Stephen indicates that the father governs *both* modalities. "The man with my voice and my eyes," he says (38), the man who orders all the audible and visible. Bloom, the new womanly man, must uncover a new language which eludes both voice and eyes, both music and writing: a language which evades antithesis itself, as Penelope will add a dangerous supplement to the binary order of paternity.

The Greek *E* belongs to this new discourse, for it does not confine itself to one modality. Indeed, it crosses both and double-crosses their duality. Bloom's "kakography" is such a consummate escape that it escapes the text itself, and we only read the *E* in its transliterated form: "ee" (*U* 279; also see *FW* 180). Besides, Bloom listens for the *E* as well as reading it and writing it. "There's music everywhere," he thinks. "Ruttledge's door: ee creaking" *(U* 282). He hears ees creaking, he sees ees Greeking: and while the *E* enjoys the charms of both modalities, it also opens a defect in both, an unvoiced, unseen residue. Is it possible that we have missed a *third* modality? Bloom seems to think so when he muses, "Words? Music? No, it's what's behind" (274). What's behind is Bloom's behind, and it is Bloom's behind that enunciates the missing ee. "Pwee! A wee little wind piped eeee. In Bloom's little wee" (288). This is an *E* that Bloom neither sings nor signs. He farts it. This ee outdoes Odysseus himself, the very principle of slippage and escape, for the fart escapes its own escaper. A new voice, its eeee belongs to music, but it also seeps into the written word, to vex the opposite modality. The fart explodes in the very letters of the word "written" which constitutes Bloom's epitaph: "My eppripfftaph. Be pfrwritt" (257). As writing, the fart cajoles the eye: as voice, it saturates the ear. But there is a third organ which can detect the fart when it is neither audible nor visible.

This organ may be found at the end of "Sirens" and of "Proteus," for these two endings mirror one another. In "Sirens," Bloom makes sure there is "No-one behind" (291), before he lets his behind utter its last word. Stephen mimes this gesture in "Proteus," turning his eyes "over a shoulder, rere regardant" (51), before he dares to pick his nose. Later, Bloom appropriates his words in "Circe," when he stammers "rerererepugnant," guiltily (538). If this is a coincidence, Bloom twice indicates in "Sirens" that coincidence is the order of the day (263, 275). How do Bloom's and Stephen's stealthy gestures coincide? Is there some link between the nose and rear, between the nose and what's behind?

If Bloom's fart escapes the father's ear, the father's eye, it leaves its "eppripfftaph" for the nose alone. It is in the nose that heresy has found its middle course, for the art of the fart could find no greater connoisseur. Similarly, when Stephen deposits his dry snot in "Proteus," he countersigns his carefully constructed patriarchal universe. Snot has become a matriarchal signifier, since the "grey sweet mother" is the "snot-green sea." For Bloom, the nose outdoes the phallus, and in the end defeats the suitors in "Penelope." While Molly broods of Boylan and "that tremendous big red brute of a thing," she wonders that "his nose is not so big" (742). "Married to the greasy nose" (260), she, too, has left the ear and eye behind in a voyage towards a new olfactory modality.

Why should the nose be greasy? It would be far-fetched to turn to Freud, and to the famous fetish of the shine on the nose that marked and masked the loss of the maternal phallus ("Fetishism," *Complete Works* 147–57). (Freud also argued that civilization with all its discontents came into being when the eye took over from the nose [*Civilization* 99n, 106n].) It is perhaps more pertinent that "grease" is slang for "unction," or that it eases entries and odyssean exits. Moreover, the Greek *E* whispers in greasy (Greece-ee), so that Bloom's nose may glisten with his secret signature. In "Sirens," nose becomes "knows" (*U* 260), and since the word "knows" derives from "gnosis," it is as if knowledge itself were rooted in the wayward odysseys of heresy. By writing Greek "ees" where Roman "ees" should be, Bloom supplants the Roman Church with a nosey gnostic jewgreek heresy. What the ear hears, and the eye sees, give way to what the nose knows.

Works Cited

Ellmann, Richard. *Ulysses on the Liffey*. New York: Oxford University Press, 1982.

Freud, Sigmund. *Civilization and its Discontents*. Standard Ed. 21. London: Hogarth Press, 1953–54.

———. "Fetishism." In *The Complete Psychological Works*. Standard Ed. Tr. James Strachey. 21. London: Hogarth Press, 1953–54.

Plutarch's Morals: Theosophical Essays. Tr. Charles William King. London: George Bell, 1882.

Echo or Narcissus?

Daniel Ferrer

What song the syrens sang may not be *beyond all conjecture,* but perhaps there are more important problems to be solved now: I am not satisfied with a purely musical analysis of the "Sirens." The general analogy between the technique of this chapter and a *fuga per canonem* seems particularly unilluminating for a real understanding of the nature of Joyce's stylistic achievement. Of course, with some distortion of both terms of the comparison, one can demonstrate a certain similarity between this chapter and a fugue (although it is obviously much closer to a bel canto opera). Of course, the *fuga per canonem* theory is authenticated by Stuart Gilbert's *authorized* commentary. But this is precisely the point. It is high time it was said that the denominations of the various techniques in the Joyce/S. Gilbert chart are so vague, so impressionistic, that they mean very little and hide, rather than reveal, the individuality of the different chapters. This can be demonstrated indirectly, but I think convincingly, if we show that any one, or at least several, of the techniques assigned by Joyce/S. Gilbert to the other episodes could be used to describe the "Sirens" as well as, if not better than, the original.

The chapter "Lestrygonians," being centered around food, is supposed to have a *peristaltic* technique. Couldn't we perhaps use this term more appropriately for the "Sirens"? At the beginning of the episode, a mass of material ("the overture") is fed into the text like data into a computer, or like highly concentrated nutriments into a digestive system. Then, through a long and thorough process of transformation, this inert matter is assimilated, transmuted into the living substance of the fiction. At the other end of the *tract,* expulsion takes place: the chapter actually finishes with an anal evacuation, Bloom's fart. Moreover, a general identification between music and excretion is suggested (from Molly's chamber pot [*U* 283] to the echoes reverberating along the bowels of the earth [*U* 283]) which will be taken up, reworked, and amply developed in *Finnegans Wake.* (See the whole passage about "shamebred music" in *FW* 164.15–165.7, with a suggestion that even the "Bronze by Gold" motif may have an excremental connotation.)

The numerous mirror effects, the importance of the process of identification with gratifying images (Bloom seeing himself as Henry-Lionel, Miss Kennedy fancying herself as the perfect lady), could suggest that we call this technique *narcissism* (originally assigned to the "Lotus-Eaters"), for the identifications are not only imagined by the characters, they are wrought into the texture of the chapter through free indirect style, or what Hugh Kenner has called the "Uncle Charles principle" ("Ladylike in exquisite contrast" [*U* 258]; "haughty Henry Lionel Leopold dear Henry Flower earnestly Mr Leopold Bloom envisaged candlestick . . ." [*U* 290]). But we shall come back in a moment to the problem of narcissism, which is central in this text and closely related to all the themes of our discussion.

The stylistic features that we have just mentioned could also be interpreted as a ghostly intrusion of the character's voice upon the narrator's discourse. In some cases this results in a gross violation of its integrity, engendering grammatical monsters, such as "That must have been highly diverting, said he. I see. / He see" (*U* 263), which is very free indirect style, indeed. There are also passages in which the "Uncle Charles principle," so useful to explain the early Joyce and a good part of *Ulysses,* proves to be totally inadequate to account for what is happening. The two barmaids are not thinking about Bloom; they probably do not even know him and yet, by a curious process of contamination, they find themselves "married to Bloom, to greaseaseabloom" (*U* 260). (It is significant that a literalist like H. Blamires is completely taken by surprise here and misreads this passage.) In the same way, Bloom is unaware of the existence of "Greasy eyes," but he is nevertheless haunted by his presence, so that nightmarish hybrids are born of their unnatural copulation: "greaseaseabloom," "Greaseabloom." This uncanny process, very characteristic of the "Sirens," perfectly deserves the name of *incubism* (normally reserved for the technique of "Hades").

Let us add that these stylistic encroachments usually produce a comical effect, but they still assume this ghostly character because they are connected with a general, if unobstrusive, encroachment of death upon life. Music being the center of this episode, we discover death hidden at the core of music: "upholding the lid he (who?) gazed in the coffin (coffin?) at the oblique triple (piano!) wires" (*U* 263); "Numbers it is. All music when you come to think . . . symmetry under a cemetery wall" (*U* 278); "Sings too: *Down among the dead men*" (*U* 272). From this core death radiates through the text in all directions. Its presence is particularly conspicuous in the closing words of the chapter, which are precisely supposed to be the *last words* of Robert Emmet. These last words are automatically compared by Bloom to Christ's last words, which were, if we believe St. John, "Everything is finished" (according to St. Luke, these were only the penultimate words), although they actually announce anything but an ending, a quiet resting in the grave. In the case of Robert Emmet, things are still more intricate. His very last words are: "I have done," but this is not a simple descriptive statement. It is subordinated to an imperative: "When my country takes her place among the nations of the earth, then and not till then, let my epitaph be written: I have done." Since the past perfect is suspended by a hypothetical condition, it is prospective rather than accomplished. The actual *writing* of the epitaph, although its grammatical form is the first person singular, is postponed beyond the death of the subject. These "last words" are the ultimate spoken words, but they will not be the last written in the name of this "I." Long after speech is consummated, writing is to begin. The enunciation is torn apart by death. Language is confronted with its unutterable limit.

Since these words coincide with the last words of the chapter, the whole text is affected by their ambiguous status. The highly unstable nature of this ending is made even more precarious by the fact that, in the "overture," this epitome of the episode, *done* is not the last, but the penultimate word (cf. Christ), and it is followed by *Begin!,* the only word of the overture that is missing in its place in the chapter. Thus, after the end, after the last words, after death, a suppressed beginning lies in wait.

The shadow of death does not spare the addressee of the text anymore than it does the subject of the enunciation. When Bloom is writing his letter to Martha (the girl who wanted so much to know about the "other world"), he is forced to split his personality between his respectable self and his secret *persona,* Henry Flower: "Bloom mur: best references. But Henry wrote: it will excite me." When the time comes for writing the address, Bloom:

> murmured: Messrs Callan, Coleman and Co, limited. Henry wrote:
> Miss Martha Clifford
> c/o P.O.
> Dolphin's barn lane
> Dublin. (*U* 280)

The "innocuous" names that come to Bloom's lips as a decoy are taken directly from the obituary page of the newspaper which he has just been reading (*U* 279). Through a kind of symmetry ("symmetry under a cemetery wall"), the epitaph that cannot be written at the end of the chapter reappears here, in the form of this obituary, replacing the addressee of the letter by a pair of freshly buried corpses. The official words that are supposed to lay the dead to rest, to insure the insertion of the Unnameable in the Symbolic Order, are indeed out of joint in the "Sirens." And let us not forget that we, the readers, are the ultimate addressee of this letter and of this mortifying chapter.

It would be possible to try other techiques assigned to other chapters, and see if they work here. One could show that other chapters work like a *fuga per canonem,* and "Wandering Rocks" seems to be a promising subject for experiment along those lines; any episode would do since polyphony is the most striking characteristic of *Ulysses* as a whole. But the point has already been made clearly enough. What we have been doing seems to prove the inadequacy of Joyce's stylistic denominations. If they are not simply hoaxes (we never can be sure), they betray a rather naive ideology of the correspondence between form and content. They probably were important to Joyce, but so was the fact that *Ulysses* was published on his birthday and that Bloomsday coincided with the day on which he first went out with Nora Barnacle. We should take these things into account, but not let them obstruct our way. These denominations are metaphors, and we should not refuse them as such. But it is well to remember that other metaphors may be quite as valid and fruitful.

The little experiment which we have attempted perhaps has the merit of pointing to some new correspondences between the episodes. It may also suggest the importance of some neglected elements in the make-up of the "Sirens": the digestive and excretive process, death and its encroachment upon life, narcissism.

I would like now to consider this last aspect: narcissism and the imaginary register in general. The musical analysis of the "Sirens" is often disappointing because it usually remains purely formal. It is based on a conception of music which is very close to that of Bloom: "Numbers it is. All music when you come to think Two multiplied by two divided by half is twice one. Vibrations: chords those are. One plus two plus six is seven. . . . Musemathematics. And you think you're listening to the ethereal. But suppose you said it like: Martha, seven times nine minus x is thirtyfive thousand. Fall quite flat" (*U* 278). Obviously, the formal element is capital in this chapter, the work on the signifier is extraordinarily intense. But upon this symbolic framework, a huge imaginary construction rises ("Pour qu'il y ait du fantasme, il faut du prêt à le porter" [Jacques Lacan]), and we must not fail to take this into account. The prevalence of this imaginary element is what distinguishes the "Sirens" from "Circe," in which the theatrical technique ultimately by-passes the imaginary, so that the symbolical and the real come into direct contact and create hallucination.

We have already mentioned the importance of the mirror reflections (only writing has no mirror image in this chapter because it is cancelled by superposition: when he writes his secret letter, Bloom makes sure to "blot over the other so he can't read") and of the narcissistic identifications throughout the "Sirens." Everywhere, the imaginary is at work, trying to heal wounded egos (while simultaneously, under the surface, the polyphonic nature of the enunciation destroys the illusion of the unity of the subject). Surprisingly in a chapter which is supposed to be devoted to the world of sounds, but quite logically (Lacan speaks of the "visual pregnancy that this Imaginary shape [the ego] retains from its origins [i.e. the mirror stage]"), we find that the visual element plays a very important part. It would take several pages to make a list of all the occurrences of *look* ("peep, peer . . ."), *see* and *eye,* and this list would be comparable in length to an enumeration of all the forms of *listen, hear,* and *ear.* The words connected with vision are made all the more conspicuous by the fact that they are often found in duplicate forms, indicating variations of the typical imaginary situation ("He's looking. Mind till I see" [*U* 257]; "See, not be seen" [*U* 265]; "Molly great dab at seeing anyone looking" [*U* 284]; "See real beauty of the eye" [*U* 286]; etc.), or even in multiplied forms ("Look: look, look, look, look, look: you look at us" [*U* 282]; "she knows his eyes, my eyes, her eyes" [*U* 286]). It might be possible to consider that, between the singers and their audience, a kind of auditive voyeurism-exhibitionism takes place—but the situation remains fundamentally incomplete without the relay of vision. A can see B seeing him, but A can't hear B hearing him, and in this respect, the ear is ultimately subordinated to the eye.

However, the infinite multiplication of this specular process proves that it is powerless to heal the narcissistic wounds. The image remains incomplete (because the restoration of the ego is perpetually undermined by the flight—*fugue*—of the signifier) and a whole economy of substitution is at work to try to compensate for what is missing. This is another difference between this chapter and music conceived as purely formal play of sounds: in music, a note stands for nothing other than itself, while here everything *represents* something else. What represents what, and for whom? Basically, the events in the Ormond and what is sung there represent for Bloom what is happening simultaneously at home between Molly and Boylan, and this in turn is a re-presentation of the primal scene. But the limits that are normally constitutive of representation (the limit between the stage and the audience; the limit between the theater and the "real" outside world; and the limit between the stage and the invisible space at the back of the stage where the scenographer stands) are constantly transgressed. Beyond the reciprocal voyeuristic relationship (A sees B seeing A), a transitive relation is always present in the "Sirens" (A sees B seeing C seeing D). Bloom, in the dining room, sees the barmaids behind their counter, who see the clients in the bar, who see the singers in the saloon. Let us not forget, moreover, that Bloom can hear the singers directly, and that all these relationships are reversed at one point or another (the singers eventually hear Bloom going out). It soon becomes impossible to situate the first limit, and even to say which is the stage and which is the audience.

The second limit is also extremely unstable. An outdoor spectacle (the viceregal cavalcade) passes outside the theater (the Ormond): from within, the barmaids watch the show, but they become themselves a spectacle for a member of the viceregal party. As could be expected, the inside world constantly reflects events happening outside, but we see also that events in the outside world are affected by what happens inside. For instance, Boylan's desire is certainly aroused by Miss Douce's *sonnez la cloche* trick, and who knows if he will not take Molly as a mere substitute. As for the third limit, it is quite as unsettled as the others. Bloom, the arch-spectator, is at the same time the scenographer of what is happening at 7 Eccles Street. He does not exactly arrange the event, but he could stop it at any moment by simply coming home. Moreover, it is absolutely impossible for us to decide that one passage is Bloom's fantasy of the scene ("Jing. Stop. Knock. Last look at mirror always before she answers door. The hall. There? How do you? I do well. There? What? Or? Phila of cachous, kissing comfits, in her satchel. Yes? Hands felt for the opulent" [*U* 274]), and that another is the author's description of what is actually happening ("One rapped on a door, one tapped with a knock, did he knock Paul de Kock, with a loud proud knocker, with a cock carracarracarra cock. Cockcock" [*U* 282]). There is nothing to tell us that the second passage should have more authority. Our overhearing of the mysterious conductor, ordering the representation to *Begin!* at the end of the overture, is another transgression of this limit. More generally, we could say that for the first time in *Ulysses* the scenographer/narrator comes to the front of the stage to perform his antics and becomes openly part of the show. Representation, then, is everywhere, but it is also nowhere; it is impossible to situate it within its usual bounds.

The perversion of representation rather than the apotheosis of music, the importance of vision rather than the supremacy of audition, narcissism rather than object relation, orality and anality rather than genitality, death rather than sex—it is this constellation of related themes which should now be explored for a renewal of our perspective on this most elusive chapter.

"Sirens": The Emblematic Vibration

André Topia

Particularly striking in the "Sirens" chapter is the process of dislocation and fragmentation of the figures, and more precisely the dissemination of the bodies into isolated, autonomous parts. Partial fragments and specific attributes attached to particular characters take on so much importance that they substitute themselves for the whole and stand for it. Hence the abundance of metonymic and synecdochic devices. The characters never appear as homogeneous units but as fragmented parts which have been dissociated from the wholes to which they belonged. We have the feeling that all the intensity of meaning has concentrated on a part which stands for the whole, so that whenever the character appears, it is enough to call up the part which represents him. Hence also the emblematic dimension of the chapter.

A good example of this synecdochic dislocation is the recurrence of references to lips throughout the chapter. When a character speaks or laughs or sings, the lips are often the grammatical subject of the sentence, so that we have the impression that the activity of speaking or laughing or singing does not originate in the person as a whole, but is limited, in a nearly fetishistic way, to the precise part of the body from which the sounds are seen to issue. And the lips seem to become the only source of these sounds: "Miss Douce's wet lips said" (*U* 257); "Her wet lips tittered" (257); "Lenehan's lips over the counter lisped a low whistle of decoy" (264); "Lips laughing" (275); "he held a shield of hand beside his lips that cooed" (279); "Yes, her lips said more loudly" (288). The characters seem to be emblematically reduced to that part of themselves which utters the sounds. The body seems to take over the whole activity and to have a speech of its own.

The lips are not only the subject of sentences but also often the complement of a verb, so that the action is directed not at a person but at his or her lips specifically. Thus Miss Douce with Boylan: "dealing from her jar thick syrupy liquor for his lips" (265). Or Lenehan smiling to Miss Douce: "grinned at his tilted ale and at Miss Douce's lips that all but hummed" (265). Or Simon Dedalus and Miss Douce: "He smiled at bronze's tea-bathed lips, at listening lips and eyes" (262).

By creating this intimate link between the voice and the physical organ from which it is issued Joyce makes the voice indissociable from a physical pantomime, so that its poetic, rhythmical, auditory aspect is constantly counterbalanced and, as it were, deflated by the physical *compositio loci* which accompanies its utterance. Indeed, it is quite significant that in a chapter which is under the sign of the voice, the lips should be so omnipresent. They have a double value: they are the place of both sound utterance and erotic flirtatiousness. They are at the same time the privileged place of romantic, ethereal, idealized figures such as they appear in love songs or heroic ballads—and a part of the body associated with erotic caresses, drinking, eating, sensuality in general. Through the presence of the lips, the body is never forgotten even in the most idealized moments. They are a basically ambivalent orifice, disembodied *spiritus* and carnal lure.

We would find the same kind of subtle metonymic displacement with the transfer of the activity of singing towards a part of the body which is associated with it, but which is not its origin. Thus with Father Cowley singing: "Hoarsely the apple of his throat hoarsed softly" (271). His Adam's apple seems to become the very center and origin of the emission of the song, and the song becomes physical, nearly muscular. In the same way, Bloom will remember Molly singing, "throat warbling" (275).

This simultaneous process of pulverization and reorganization into new units can be paralleled with the relationship between the phonic network and the syntactic framework of the sentence. Indeed, in a first phase, the syntactic framework (the internal order and hierarchy within the sentence) is systematically broken by Joyce, who substitutes a mere horizontal juxtaposition of isolated units to the vertical hierarchic integration which characterizes a syntactic pattern. As a result, the reader is confronted with a succession of punctual, mobile, fluid, interchangeable units which can move in all directions along the chain of the sentence. But in a second phase, once the internal limits are broken and replaced by this fluid exchange, Joyce reorganizes his material by coagulating it into new units, this time according to phonic patterns (variation/permutation/echo/symmetry) which, as it were, interfere with, subvert, and often replace the syntactic framework of the sentence.

Take for example the following paragraph: "Miss Kennedy sauntered sadly from bright light, twining a loose hair behind an ear. Sauntering sadly, gold no more, she twisted twined a hair. Sadly she twined in sauntering gold hair behind a curving ear" (258). We can first notice the aleatory dimension of the passage, which is made of permutations and variations. We have the impression that this limited linguistic material could be rearranged indefinitely. The linear progress of the sentence is arrested by phonic structures based on recurrence, echo, symmetries, permutations. Four words ("sauntered," "sadly," "twining," and "hair") appear in all three sentences and seem to be likely to be recombined again and again. We have the feeling that there is no stable syntactic framework able to maintain the words in specific positions. The sentence becomes a kind of dance, or is like a pattern in a tapestry. It ceases to unfold in time but becomes, as it were, projected into space. From linear it becomes tabular.

One of the consequences of this is the immobilization of all movement, the transformation of all the dynamic pulse of the sentence into a static, emblematic tableau. Particularly significant is the use of the present participle, here the change from "sauntered" to "sauntering." A subtle counterpoint seems to take place between the main action and the accompanying action, which become interchangeable and whose hierarchy is neutralized. First we find "sauntered . . . twining," then "sauntering . . . she . . . twined," then "she twined in sauntering." The finite form becomes present participle and the present participle becomes finite form. The chronological relationship supposedly linking the two actions is disrupted and becomes totally ambiguous. What was originally a punctual action suddenly freezes, seems to be unable to come to an end, and lingers indefinitely.

We find further evidence of this blurring process with the various places of the word "sadly," first in fourth position, then in second position, then in first position. The linguistic chain becomes totally fluid. The words are used like counters whose spatial position indicates subtle shifts of meaning. The same kind of undecidable ambiguity is to be found with "twisted twined," which should be read not as succession but as juxtaposition. The two actions must be coagulated into one global entity, a kind of imagistic tableau including successive actions in its simultaneous stasis.

We must also notice, at the end of each of the three sentences, the presence of successively "ear," then "hair," then again "ear." Because of the phonic proximity of these two words a kind of hesitation occurs: the two phonic patterns seem to overlap somehow, which corresponds to a kind of blurring of the differences between the various parts of the bodies. The fluidity of the sentence connotes the same fluidity in the bodies. All the parts of the characters' bodies keep vibrating and migrating. The physical proximity of ear and hair becomes in the sentence much more than mere spatial contiguity: the two elements of the body seem to become part of an intricate game, of a kind of dance in which their places can vary though their relation remains the same. A kind of inner tension, of paradoxically static movement, seems to animate the bodies.

A consequence of this proximity is that the specific functions of the bodies are often blurred and neutralized and some parts of the bodies usurp each other's function. We have the feeling of a continual fluid circulation. Words which normally apply to certain specific zones migrate towards other zones, introducing in the text a kind of general vibration. (This blurring and dissolving function of the music can already be found in the *Portrait,* when Stephen listens to a group of young men singing: "The music passed in an instant, as the first bars of sudden music always did, over the fantastic fabrics of his mind, dissolving them painlessly and noiselessly as a sudden wave dissolves the sandbuilt turrets of children" [*P* 160]).

Thus lips and eyes listen: "He smiled at bronze's teabathed lips, at listening lips and eyes" (262). Or: "A liquid of womb of woman eyeball gazed under a fence of lashes, calmly, hearing" (286). The fluid circulation of the musical substance seems to break all barriers and to include all senses in the activity of listening. The auditory function takes on such importance that it penetrates the bodies through all their openings.

Eyes eat: Lenehan eyes Miss Douce's breasts greedily, "small eyes ahunger" (266). Eyes can also talk: "—Answering an ad? keen Richie's eyes asked Bloom" (279). Functions are transferred not only from one organ to another but also to bodily parts, to partial zones. Nostrils shout: Miss Douce's nostrils "quivered imperthnthn like a shout in quest" (259). The nose sings: "Simon trumping compassion from foghorn nose" (287). Breasts sing too: Miss Douce appears to Lenehan "bust ahumming" (266). In the same way as, from a linguistic point of view, the phonic patterns emancipate themselves within the sentence structure and give birth to autonomous processes, here the bodily parts become, as it were, micro-systems which are more active than the groups to which they belong.

In the case of the deaf waiter, Bald Pat, the mouth becomes an equivalent for the ear: Simon Dedalus's voice "also sang to Pat open mouth ear waiting to wait" (275). The mouth seems here to receive the song just as legitimately as the ear. All the orifices are open to the musical penetration.

Sometimes these migrations and permutations result in the junction of bodily parts which belong to highly differentiated symbolic poles: thus in Bloom's reverie triggered off by the sight of Miss Douce listening in the shell. Through a series of gradual metaphorical shifts we come to an identification of ear, mouth, and sex (281).

Other symbolic conjunctions of the same type occur in the chapter. Thus the membrane of the eardrum becomes for Father Cowley the hymen (285). And when Bloom's belly begins to rumble Joyce uses the word "ventrilo-quise" (285), thus preparing the final telescoping of mouth and anus with Bloom's fart, which is his final answer to the emphatic rhetoric of the singers.

One of the barmaids' eyes appear as "A liquid of womb of woman eyeball" (286), thus telescoping eye and sex. The word "liquid" is here important: it is the omnipresent fluidifying power of the music which dissolves the symbolic limits and barriers within the bodies. Just as it is a musical analogy (blowing into an instrument) which will connect and unify the various orifices in a woman's body in Bloom's monologue at the end of the chapter: "Blow gentle. Loud. Three holes all women" (285).

Another recurrent stylistic trait of the "Sirens" chapter is the absence of an article where an article would be expected. For instance in the passage already quoted: "from bright light," "she twined in sauntering gold hair." This absence creates the impression that we have to do not so much with specific objects in a specific place and time as with a vague, all-pervasive, fluid, little differentiated substance which can vary infinitely in aspect and form: hence, the slightly hazy and hesitant outline of figures and objects—their emblematic, a-temporal quality. In Joyce the words and the real never fold over each other exactly. There is always an interstice where the vibration can be felt.

Joyce's very characteristic use of the present participles further contributes to this vibration: "Again Kennygiggles, stooping her fair pinnacles of hair, stooping, her tortoise napecomb showed, spluttered out of her mouth her tea, choking in tea and laughter, coughing with choking, crying:" (260). What is striking in the internal organization of this sentence is that the only two finite verbs are islanded at the center of the sentence, but totally immobilized and paralyzed by the participial clauses which seem to encroach upon them. Between the subject ("Kennygiggles") and the first finite verb ("showed") the two participial clauses seem to stretch the sentence infinitely and to prevent the action from even beginning, so that this action finds itself arrested. In the second part of the sentence the second finite verb ("spluttered") is accompanied by four present participles as by appendices, by a series of echoes, so that the sentence seems to vibrate infinitely without really coming to an end. The paradoxical result of this proliferation of present participles is that the action in this sentence first cannot begin and then cannot end. It acquires an eternal, permanent, emblematic quality. It is arrested in mid-air between tableau and narrative, neither of which manages to take control of the text.

The same unresolved tension between tableau and narrative can be found in another sentence: "The boots to them, them in the bar, them barmaids came" (258). Because of the repetition of "them" with each time a more specific determination, the sentence advances in a succession of touches which have to be read as simultaneous. The combination of growing precision in the details and of indecision in the structure gives the impression that the scene is constantly being at the same time built and dissolved in front of our eyes.

Sometimes the tension between differentiated syntactic functions and fluid, undifferentiated phonic patterns gives birth to such ambiguities that they prevent any visualization of a "scene" in progress and contribute to the dream-like aspect of the whole action. "—Imperthnthn thnthnthn, bootsnout sniffed rudely, as he retreated as she threatened as he had come" (258). The three repetitions of "as" have each a different grammatical function (simultaneity, causality, comparison), but these differentiated functions are blurred and subverted by the repetition which produces analogy and equivalence instead of difference.

Another example of this deliberate dissolution of the usual syntactic sentence patterns and their replacement by subtle rhythmical variations is the sentence "Douce gave full vent to a splendid yell, a full yell of full woman, delight, joy, indignation" (260). We can feel there two distinct movements: First, a kind of infinite stretching of the first half of the sentence due to the expansion of "yell" by a juxtaposed clause and to the repetition of the word "full" which gradually passes from abstract meaning to concrete image; it is the very body of Miss Douce which seems to be yelling. Thus the phonic repetitive patterns reorganize the text gradually and imperceptibly. Then, in the second part of the sentence, we find a sudden, rapid juxtaposition of the three words "delight, joy, indignation." Consequently, we find initially a minimum of information stretched and expanded (and giving the impression that it could be still more expanded), then a maximum of information condensed in as little space as possible. In the first part of the sentence the words seem to proliferate by repetitive analogy, then, on the contrary, the substantives are given without determinents, in a bare, nearly programmatic abstraction. This alternation of repetitive expansion and programmatic condensation is one of the recurrent traits of the chapter. In their tension, in this static movement, neither tableau nor narrative, lies the emblematic vibration.

The Silence of the Sirens

Jean-Michel Rabaté

> That's joyful I can feel. Never have written it. Why? My joy is other joy. But both are joys. Yes, joy it must be. Mere fact of music shows you are. *(U 282)*

I have shared with some friends a growing dissatisfaction with the classical and current types of analysis of the "Sirens" chapter in *Ulysses:* it is generally taken to represent one of Joyce's most daring experiments with the musicalization of language. More than this thesis, which can be elaborated and qualified, since no one will agree on the term "musicalization," it is the demonstration which appears to be debatable. The musical terms, those used by Stuart Gilbert for instance, are all metaphorical and arbitrary. A combination of simple rhetorical tropes such as those used for the analysis of "Eolus" seems apter for describing the technique of this "musical" episode. This wish to tidy up our critical vocabulary does not by any means imply that one could evolve an entirely non-metaphorical language. On the contrary, I shall not attempt to resist the drift of metaphors, but shall underline their possibly neutralized coloration, their silent working. Any critical language may gain by becoming aware of its own metaphorical nature, and start by describing an explicit tropology as part of its interpretive strategies, thereby opening the possibility of a more adequate approach to the text taken as point of departure.

I shall take one simple example of "musical trope" as supposedly exhibited by Joyce's text, the famous "hollow fifth" which Stuart Gilbert—no doubt helped by Joyce—identifies in "Are you off? Yrfmstbyes. Blmstup. O'er ryehigh blue. Bloom stood up" *(U 286)*. Here is the commentary: "Examples of the 'hollow fifth' *(quinto vuoco)* are such words as 'Blmstup,' where the 'thirds,' the letters *oo* and *ood* (Bloom stood up) are omitted . . ." (Gilbert 223). To take the third letter or group of letters as the equivalent of a chord, or "third," is more a way of expanding the punning process already at work in the text. The term indeed belongs to the text, since it gives a musical key to Stephen's theory of paternity in "Circe" (Stephen plays a series of "empty fifths" before explaining his view on the "fundamental" and the "dominant" [504]). In this sense, the commentary, especially if it may appear "authorized," is part of the text, and I would not disagree. But it may beg important questions of procedures, and presuppose that we know what a "musical metaphor" is before we go on talking about "musicalization."

My contention is that classical rhetorics can describe all these musical figures as well, if not better than, the vocabulary of musicology. Thus, the "hollow fifth" is just a kind of syncope (loss of sounds in the interior of a word) and could introduce us to a list of suppressions shown by the text. I give just a few examples:

apheresis (loss of a syllable or letter at the beginning of a word): "Idolores, a queen, Dolores" (269);

apocope (same device at the end of a word): "language of flow" (263); "How will you pun" (280); "Bloom ate liv" (271); "Best value in Dub" (271);

ellipsis: "Bloo smi qui go. Ternoon." (264); "That is to say she" (265);

telescoping of words: "Siopold" (Simon + Leopold [276]); "Maas was the boy. Massboy" (272).

From the suppressions, one can shift to the additions, among which I will rapidly list:

anadiplosis (repetition of words in echo): "Heartbeats her breath: breath that is life" (286);

prosthesis (addition of sound or syllable to a word): "endlessnessnessness" (276) and all the drawing out effects;

epenthesis (intercalation of a consonant in a word): "*I care not foror the morrow*" (270);

diaeresis: "waaaaaaalk" (286);

tmesis: "Miss voice of Kennedy answered . . ." (262); "a flush struggling in his pale, told Mr Bloom, face of the night . . ." (277);

gemination: "Big Benaben . . . , Big Benben. Big Benben" (287);

augmentation in echo: "Luring. Ah, alluring" (275); "inexquisite contrast, contrast inexquisite non exquisite" (268);

anaphoric extension: "The boots to them, them in the bar, them barmaids came" (258);

interpolation: "he (who?) gazed in the coffin (coffin?) . . ." (263).

This easy selection of available rhetorical terms must be related to broader syntactical devices and expanded to include larger rhythmical units. I shall again give selected examples:

chiasmus: "Like lady, ladylike" (264);

apposition: ". . . Bloom, I feel so lonely Bloom" (287);

asyndeton: "Will? You? I. Want. You. To." (285); ". . . said he. I see. He see. He drank." (263)

coluthon: with increasing or decreasing rhythm: "Tank one believed: Miss Kenn when she: that doll he was: she doll: the tank" (287);

oxymoron: "Aimless he chose with agitated aim" (266).

The sound effects and the rhythms are of course dominant throughout all these examples, but this does not absolutely require a musical vocabulary to be accounted for. One can use terms such as:

onomatopoeia: "Jiggedy jingle jaunty jaunty" (271);
assonance: "muffled hammerfall in action" (263);
imitative harmony: "lovesoft oftloved word" (274);
mimology or *contamination:* "Essex bridge. Yes . . . Yessex" (261–62);
echolalia: "Imperthnthn thnthnthn" (258);
simple echo: "Bloom mashed mashed potatoes" (270).

The widest category of all is then that of the pun, or *paranomasia* (for instance the numerous puns on "rose": "rose of Castille . . . she rose . . . rose of Castille" [264]; "her rose that sank and rose" [266]). It is no accident that one is able to witness the shift of apocope to punning in the question "How will you pun?" (280). Other terms would have to be combined so as to describe all the complicated rhythms, with their varied admixture of puns. In *"Cloche. Sonnez la Cloche. Sonnez la"* (276), the displacement of the punctuation cuts the sentence in a different way, enhancing the repetitive and circular nature of the echo, and of male desire, while adding a French pun on "donner la la," "to give the A."

All this leads one to describe the style of this episode as a highly *mataplastic* idiom, exploiting the flexibility of signifiers for their evocative power. Echolalia and mimology are dominant, coupled with the structural use of leitmotives which dynamically structure the text. Music appears then both as a *pretext* for the radicalization of such a process—which will not be forgotten in "Circe"—which implies that the only purely musical passage is the overture, precisely because it is devoid of syntactical articulation, and a *theme:* not the organization of the signifiers in their interplay, but the signified of such an interplay.

Thus the puns tend to become literal adaptations of stocks of musical phrases, such as "transposed . . . low" (258), "conduct himself" (258), "chimed in" (259) for laughter; "ringing in changes" (260), "a great tonic in the air" (261) for mountains, "he yet made overtures" (262) for Lenehan's insistent banter. There are so many musical proverbs and terms concealed throughout the episode, that such a lexical saturation should not invade our language, and we face a process which is very similar to that of "Lestrygonians" for food. Nevertheless, the puns and tropes all tend to assert the imitative quality of language—but not in the sense that they attempt to imitate formal music; indeed, while playing on music as a theme, the different voices—not so easily identifiable with characters—constantly imitate each other: "Luring. Ah, alluring" (275). The language of this episode opens up a system of echoes, which is the direct introduction to the "echoland" of *Finnegans Wake*. One paragraph provides the best summary of such a process:

> A low incipient note sweet banshee murmured all. A thursh. A throstle. His breath, birdsweet, . . . fluted with plaintive woe. Is lost. Rich sound. Two notes in one there. Blackbird I heard in the hawthorn valley. Taking my motives he twined and turned them. All most too new call is lost in all. Echo. (272)

Richie Goulding explains the beauty of the song Simon Dedalus is going to sing in the other room. He tries to impress Bloom by the fact he has heard Maas sing it, and Bloom is convinced it is a lie, or self-deception. But such a "rich sound" becomes a reminiscence of the songs of birds, then of one bird, he had heard before. It shows the "call" as containing the "all" in a system of natural echoes. The bird was stealing Bloom's motives, and "twining," and "turning" them. This is close to the old sense of *trope*—to turn—since tropes proliferate, redouble, and invert a motive which does not belong to Bloom any more, while not having an origin in the bird. Such a twining is also a "binding," similar to Bloom's apotropaic gesture of twining the elastic band when hearing the songs ("Bloom . . . wound it round his troubled double, fourfold, in octave, gyved them fast . . ." [274]).

This strange song deprived of an origin may throw some light on the nature of the Sirens' song. Indeed, the Sirens rarely sing in the episode, while they constantly insist on having other people hear. They conform to their literal function of *binders* and of *birds*.

Victor Bérard explains that *sir-hen* is a compound of two semitic roots (*sir*, "song," *hen*, "grace") which can be paralleled with "H.n.n.," a semitic root meaning "to bind, to attach" (akin to fascia/fascination). They sing a "song of grace" which binds, enthralls, just as Ulysses obeys this pattern by asking to be bound to the mast. But according to the most ancient Greek tradition of etymology, the Sirens are primarily winged beings, like sea-birds, and they belong to the long series of bird-like women met and loved by Ulysses: Circe, a hawk-owl; Calypso, a nocturnal bird of prey; Penelope, a teal, daughter of Ikarios, the partridge; and the Sirens, possibly cormorants. The link between the Sirens and Molly-Penelope is stressed by the text, when it puts their remarks about laughing and sexuality in parallel ("I feel all wet" [260]; "O saints above, I'm drenched!" [270]). All these birds bind and inhabit an "echoland" in which mirrors are the visual equivalent of whatever enchantment they achieve. The mirror-effect of the Sirens can be shown by a simple consideration of their activities at the beginning of the chapter. After the overture, which somehow exhausts in advance all the elements functioning as leitmotives, the Sirens tend to anticipate Bloom's strategies when he has to escape from their charms. This was apparent with Simon Dedalus as well, since he enters the bar and conforms to the logic of the echoes: "And what did the doctor order today? . . . Whatever you say yourself" (261). The Sirens literally "twine" and "turn" Bloom's motives, for Miss Kennedy plugs "both two ears with little fingers" (259); in a gesture reminiscent of the Homeric sailors, she unplugs them to hear and speak. She then concentrates on her paper, which she reads absorbedly in order to ward off Lenehan's importunate "overtures," just as Bloom writes to Martha in order to avoid the lure of the air from Martha which is sung, and hides his letter-writing under the pretence of answering an ad for the newspaper.

The Sirens possess one major emblem, that of the huge mirror behind the bar. This mirror revealingly enough bears gilded letters, and reflects the scene in the central room: "to see her skin askance in the barmirror gildedlettered where hock and claret glasses shimmered and in their midst a shell" (259; see also 261, 275, 284), and "He spellbound eyes went after her gliding head as it went down the bar by mirrors, gilded arch for ginger ale, hock and claret glasses shimmering, a spikey shell, where it concerted, mirrored, bronze with sunnier bronze" (267). This shell in the mirror is later relayed by a real shell which metaphorizes the enchantment exerted by the Sirens on Lidwell. Bloom watches one of them working her spell: "Bloom through the bardoor *saw* a shell held at their ears. He *heard* more faintly that that they heard, each for herself alone, then each for other, hearing the plash of waves, loudly, a silent roar" (281; italics mine). The ear becomes a shell which conjures up an imaginary sound, a sound which exists without actual presence. Seeing turns into hearing just because of that imaginary nature. It is there that the function of the echo-chamber is revealed. This proves that the real song of the Sirens is a song of silence. The healing "grace," and the tempting enthrallment are bound together not as by the complicity of the Virgin and the prostitute, but by the oxymoron of "silent roar." All this is part of a general spatial mechanism which can only be sketched here, and which presupposes the disjunction of the three main actions of singing, hearing, and seeing, a disjunction central to the ruse of the Homeric hero who hears but whose voice remains without effect on his men:

saloon	*bar*	*dining-room*
Simon, Ben, Cowley . . .	Sirens + Customers	Bloom, Richie, and Pat
SONG	TALK	LOOK
mouth: production		eye: production of images
eye: passive function	EAR	mouth: ingestion

The role of the echo is to redouble both song and look. The space of the shell is necessary for the reciprocal transformation of song into image (an imaginary song) and of vision into music (a hallucination). Such a trope, which looks very much like a chiasmus—optical or auditory—corresponds to the movement of the text, in which music and language fight against each other, striving for total mastery, but in fact destroying each other.

Boylan seems almost fascinated at one point by the "Sonnez la cloche" of the Sirens in a sentence which enhances the repetition at work: "Boylan, eyed, eyed" (267). The two striking commas emphasize the element of duplication. Bloom, on the other hand, cannot flee back to another bird, to Molly. He endures because he thinks he can see without being caught, hear without being seen, see without being noticed (Simon and his friends only realize he was there after he has left). He thinks "See, not be seen" (265) as he chooses to have lunch in the dining-room, thus offering his version of the Homeric myth: the main thing is not to hear without risking destruction, but to see from a chosen vantage-point (this is why he asks Pat to leave the door of the bar ajar, although he will not see the singers, but only the barmaids who hear the same song).

It is as if he had to see their ear in order to hear the song: "Still hear it better here than in the bar though farther" (275). A key to this audio and visual disposition is given by Bloom when he is about to decide to write to Martha: "Wish I could see his face, though. Explain better. Why the barber in Drago's always looked my face when I spoke his face in the glass" (275). The barber looks at his customer's lips while the customer only sees his reflection in a mirror; otherwise he would turn and present his face to the razor. This structural difference or inequality of status is to be found in the scene of the "Sirens," with a mirror-shell which reflects only emptiness, and emptiness which nevertheless allows for the exchange of imaginary products. The scene differentiates between "voice production" and a "retrospective kind of arrangement," to use the two "critical" concepts yielded by the dialogues of the passage:

organistic phallic tenors	bosom	incestuous fathers
	Virgin/prostitute	
singers	Sirens	Bloom/Goulding
"voice production"	echoes	"retrospective arrangement"

What Bloom can "see" is not simply a "phantasmal sea-surge" (Pound) roaring in a paradoxical silence. It is the very function of alterity in the binding, blending mixture of opposites, an alterity which is disclosed to him, and to him only, as soon as he understands that the song of the Sirens is both a natural noise, be it inhuman or purely material, and utter silence. He thus meets Kafka's remarkable insight, that the power of the song of the Sirens lies in its silence: "But the Sirens have a more terrible weapon than their song: it is their silence" ("The Silence of the Sirens," *Hochzeit-vorbereitungen auf dem Lande* [58–59]). Bloom merely reflects: "It's in the silence you feel you hear. Vibrations. Now silent air" (277). The *air* is not simply the invisible modality of the audible, but the *bar* of music which bars itself, constituting the silent song of songs which allows all other songs to reverberate, diffract, disseminate themselves. The pure modality of looking would afford no solution: "She listens. . . . Time to be shoving. Looked enough" (285). The solution can only be reached with a non-musical resolution of the antagonism: a fart.

The fart is not a compromise, but a parodic dissolution of the violent antagonism opposing words spoken to words printed, history as learned by heart and history as recorded in documents, patriotism as the main theme of Irish songs and the raceless and nationless language of the body. As emanation of air and food, it participates in the combined logics of "Eolus" and "Lestrygonians." Bloom is not "giving the A" to the text; he opposes the "naturalness" of the Croppy Boy who was so easily deceived by the disguised Captain, as well as the angelism of the blind tuner. (They are united by the curious leitmotiv of "God's curse on bitch's bastard" [263], first thought by Simon Dedalus [?], then in the mouth of the yeoman Captain, with the following "Tap" belonging to the tuner [285].) Being at the same time *pianissimo* and *fortissimo,* Bloom reaches the truth of his own position; he "views" the text of the last words of Robert Emmet, is seen by no one, heard by no one except the reader. Facing which, we can only say, like the Sirens: "Ask no questions and you'll hear no lies" (264).

Or to quote from Blanchot's post-Kafkaian meditation on the other navigation of the narrative which is opened by the Song of the Sirens:

> The whole ambiguity comes from the time which is here implied, which enables one to say and feel that the fascinating image of experience is, at a given moment, present, while this presence itself belongs to no present, and even destroys the present into which it introduces itself. True enough, Ulysses was really sailing and one day, at a certain date, he met the enigmatic song. He then can say: now, this happens now. But what happened now? The presence of a song only still to come. And what did he touch in the present? Not the event of a presence becoming present, but the opening of this infinite movement which is the meeting itself, and which is always at a distance from the place and time where it is affirmed, for it is this very distance, *this imaginary distance through which absence is actualized and at the end of which the event only starts happening:* a point in which the truth of the meeting is accomplished, and from which, in any case, the speech which utters it wishes to be generated. (16–17)

Works Cited

Blanchot, Maurice. *Le Livre à Venir*. Paris: Gallimard, 1959.
Gilbert, Stuart. *James Joyce's "Ulysses."* London: Faber & Faber, 1932.
Kafka, Franz. *Hochzeitvorbereitungen auf dem Lande*. New York: Schocken Books, 1953.

The Language of Flow

Robert Young

> —Grandest number in the whole opera, Goulding said.
> —It is, Bloom said.
> Numbers it is. All music when you come to think. Two multiplied by two
> divided by half is twice one. Vibrations: chords those are. One plus two plus six
> is seven. Do anything you like with figures juggling. Always find out this equal
> to that, symmetry under a cemetery wall. . . . Musemathematics. And you think
> you're listening to the ethereal. But suppose you said it like: Martha, seven times
> nine minus x is thirtyfive thousand. Fall quite flat. It's on account of the sounds
> it is. (*U* 278)

If anything could evade the Sirens it would be the reduction of music to
Bloom's erroneous mathematics. But even in math, numbers flow: technically, to flow means to increase or diminish continuously by infinitesimal
quantities. And the numbers that swirl so thickly past the Sirens do not
evade their allure:

> —Two pence, sir, the shopgirl dared to say.
> —Aha . . . I was forgetting . . . Excuse . . .
> And four.
> At four she. (264)

Everything is absorbed by the Sirens and turned into the capturing sounds
of their insistent song.

"When love absorbs my ardent soul": love, its old sweet song, its old
sweet sin, devours and secretes; it lures and accretes, glances and sweats.
Bloo Bloom is so lonely blooming, transmigrating into the flowers, the
tropes, the deceits and wiles that allure him with their decoys of desire,
their round o's, enticing embellishments of love and war. His transmigra-
tions are always paralyzing—into Pat's brother, Pat's deafness, the strip
ling's blindness, the old Fogey's goggle eye, "croppy bootsboy Bloom."
Blue Bloom is absorbed in the Sirens like the blotting paper which sips the
last wetness of his letter to Martha; he is constantly written over again like
the address which he blots over the traces of his letter in order to conceal
its vestigial remains. Bloowho is covered and uncovered by the secrets
which he conceals about his person; he gets written by them: "Up the quay
went Lionelleopole, naughty Henry with letter for Mady, with sweets of
sin with frillies for Raoul with met him pike hoses went Poldy on" (288).

Like sex, writing in the "Sirens" is a furtive act of veiled secretions.

Letters, of words, of music, become the flow of letch-water. Bloom, sea-bloom, greaseabloom, secretes his letter to Martha not only behind the covers of the *Freeman,* but also beneath the folds of his repeated "Bloo mur" or bloomers. And like the "not yet" of desire, writing is an activity that merely fingers the hymen, delays and defers: "Nothing doing I expect," Bloom remarks of the advertisement to which he pretends to reply, and also, ironically, of the fetishized letters of his romance with Martha. Nothing will come of it. Like Robert Emmet in his last words, Bloom puts off writing: "Please write me a long letter and tell me more," Martha had written. "Remember if you do not I will punish you. So now you know what I will do to you, you naughty boy, if you do not write." Bloom in replying is so seduced by the Siren music, so captured by and in its letters, that he finds it impossible to write that day: "It is utterl imposs. Underline *imposs.*" Transbloomed by the music, his letter becomes nothing more than a mere note, interspersed with notes, "notes chirruping answer," and the long letter dwindles to the "sad tail" of its P.S.'s: "P. P. S. La la la ree. I feel so sad today. La ree. So lonely. Dee" (280). Bloom obeys Martha's injunction with his long p.s.'s, his long letters, la la la ree, but at the same time disobeys her demand for a long letter and relishes her threatened punishments. Excitedly, he blots the secreted ink.

Music and writing, far from being set in antithesis, join in "the thrill they itch for," the secretions of pen and ink and of the bodily organs. "Soap feeling rather sticky behind. Must have sweated: music." When the two belles peal with laughter at the idea of being married to the old Fogey at Boyd's—goggle eyes, greasy eyes, greasy nose, Greasy I knows—Miss Douce's "other eye," her "eye hole," her "cave of the dark middle earth," becomes "all wet," just as Molly is "all drenched" when she sees Ben Dollard in his tight dress suit "with all his belongings on show." Music and eyes, like writing, produce surreptitious secretions to be savored. By Boylan, for instance, as he drinks the sweets of Miss Douce's sinful smack: "Boylan, eyed, eyed. Tossed so fat lips his chalice, drankoff his tiny chalice, sucking the last fat violet syrupy drops" (267). Bloom, who relishes the tinkling drops of Molly's "chamber music," and even the idea of the "foghorn" nose-blow ("That's music too. Not as bad as it sounds"), similarly laps up the sticky traces oozing from Martha's song:

> Words? Music? No: it's what's behind. . . .
> Bloom. Flood of warm jimjam lickitup secretness flowed to flow in music out, in desire, dark to lick flow, invading. (274)

The "language of flow" is not restricted to the gushes that throb through the sluices of the mouth, the sexual organs, and their "wet lips." It flows too through Pat Bloom's "blind eye" or arse. Before his grand finale, his epifart, Bloom contents himself with a "blind—fart"—defined in the dictionary as a "noiseless but particularly noisome breaking of wind." Just as Simon Dedalus had "puffed a pungent plumy [?bloomy] blast," so "Bloom sang dumb," "then all of a soft sudden wee little wee little pippy wind. Pwee! A wee little wind piped eeee." Bloom observes profoundly, "It's in the silence you feel you hear. Vibrations. Now silent sir."

Sex, excreting, farting, and writing are the concealed, illicit activities, the "seen unseen," like Bloom's idea for an advertisement for Hely's stationery: "I suggested to him about a transparent show cart with two smart girls sitting inside writing letters, copybooks, envelopes, blotting paper. I bet that would have caught on. Smart girls writing something catch the eye at once. Everyone dying to know what she's writing" (154). As Bloom's trick here suggests, sex and writing are also the acts of duplicity, a duplicity projected in Bloom's fantasy of painting the back of bald Pat's head so that he becomes a Janus: "Paint face behind on him," thinks Bloom, "then he'd be two." The specific deception of the Sirens involves, of course, Molly's rendezvous with Boylan; while Boylan advances on his journey towards Molly the intervals of music attempt to arrest his flow, to arrest emission by omission: "He stopped. . . . stopped. . . . stopped again." But the flow can't be stopped: "Jingle jaunty. Too late. She longed to go. That's why. Woman. As easy stop the sea. Yes: all is lost" (273). It can't be stopped because the insistent refrain of the silence in the music, the stop, only exacerbates the very condition that it is meant to forestall. For at the same time as topping arrests, it also stops up, like Bloom fingering the three holes of Lydia Douce's body, "a flute alive," or Molly's "They can't manage men's intervals. Gap in their voices too. Fill me. I'm warm, dark, open." And as well as stopping up, the stop stops, or punctuates, like the refrain of the blind boy's "tap tap tap," or Miss Kennedy minding her stops, or, crucially, Boylan: "Jing. Stop. Knock."

Stopping succumbs to the "lett and flow" of music and loses its "crooked ess" to become topping, just as when Bloom crosses the Essex Bridge it acquires a *y*, to become the Yessex—or "Yes Sex"—Bridge. To succumb to the jingle of music, the repetition of the same or similar sounds, is to be led to music's lickerish secretions and its secret betrayals, its toppings and tuppings: "in desire, dark to lick flow, invading. Tipping her tepping her tapping her topping her. Tup. Pores to dilate dilating. Tup. The joy the feel the warm the. Tup. To pour o'er sluices pouring gushes. Flood, gush, flow, joygush, tupthrop. Now! Language of love" (274). While Bloom stops at the fetishized veil and contents himself with "tambourining" gently with his fingers on Pat's pad, with writing on the blank page of Miss Douce's hymen, "fingered only," Boylan's rap, tap, knock of Paul de Cock returns insistently with the tapping of the blind boy, the cry of "tiptop," Molly's "last tip to titivate," as well as in the letters of "lickitup" and "Blmstup." As Boylan knocks with a loud proud knocker, with a cock, to tup Molly, "Full tup. Full throb," Bloom at the same moment compulsively tips tipped Pat tuppence. And when Molly is at last topped, so is Bloom, appearing in the sandwichbell as a topped sardine:

> —Very, Mr Dedalus said, staring hard at a headless sardine.
> Under the sandwichbell lay on a bier of bread one last, one lonely, last sardine of summer. Bloom alone. (289)

While Molly and Boylan play at tops and tails, Bloom, headless and castrated, topped and tailed, returns to his voyage, his journey, on a Germanic pun. From his one remaining organ, he delivers his own unwritten epitaph, one last, one lonely, last raspberry of summer.

3.   Aspects of *Finnegans Wake*

Beyond Explication: The Twice-Told Tales in *Finnegans Wake*

Bernard Benstock

For decades we have concerned ourselves with the near-impossibility of explicating *Finnegans Wake,* laboring under the misapprehension that knowing the meaning of words results in the total comprehension of a work of literature, that the phoneme is the basic unit of Joyce's *collideoscape.* Yet it should be apparent by now that *collision* and *evasion* are far more important in Joyce's schematics than any tangible element that can be isolated and trapped: the essence of a kaleidoscope is not the unit of color but the architectonics of change. *Finnegans Wake* is indeed overly jammed with words, some of them quite likely Albanian or Armenian, but they are little more than mechanical counters compared to the tonal structure that activates the aesthetic entity. Perhaps it is time to leave the exegesis of words to verbal entomologists and concentrate on the dynamics of the text.

No narrative line lasts for very long on its own in the *Wake:* it is swiftly overtaken, bypassed, short-circuited, bifurcated, trivialized, even quadri-vialized. The local train that starts out so well is quickly drowned out by the roar of the express train that leaves it temporarily at a standstill; the terrestrial advance is undercut by underground and elevated lines of nar-rative flow. The quantum energy of such narrative depends on multiple directions of near-simultaneity, far beyond what *Ulysses* had dared prepare us for, where questions-and-answers replaced declarative direction, where internalization displaced external discourse, and a busybody of a narrator usurped the narrative prerogative for an entire chapter. No "rivverun" in the *Wake* lingers for very long at Eve and Adam's, but modulates by swerves and bends, and if it recirculates occasionally to Howth Castle and Environs, underground streams bob up elsewhere as often—in Laurens County's gorgios, for example. The tracking of narrative flux in *Finnegans Wake* demands more than just a "hand" that "from the cloud emerges, holding a chart expanded." A discussion of narrative dysplasia might best be served by an examination of the various self-contained narratives within the Wak-ean structure, those "fables" or "set-pieces" that intrude as narrational units in the text and operate by their own laws of self-generation.

Even as a distinct sub-genre these inserted pieces are not easily classifi-able, no two of them much resembling each other except as set off in some way from what appears to be the mainstream of the text. One can dispute what is actually the first such intrusion in *Finnegans Wake:* the Museyroom segment (a single paragraph less than a page in length), or the Mutt-Jute confrontation (which derives so much more naturally from the preceding text and flows so comfortably into the next portion), or the Tale of Jarl van Hoother and the Prankquean. The last certainly qualifies: it extrapolates cleanly from the context, is presented in a consistent voice, and is bracketed at beginning and end with formulaic storytelling opening and closing. "It was of a night, late, lang time agone, in an auldstane eld" *(FW* 21.5) satisfies Joyce's demand for traditional folk tale openings, and "Thus the hearsomeness of the burgher felicitates the whole of the polis" *(FW* 23.14–15) sounds the concluding moral in succinct aphoristic tone and structure. Yet here are deceptive shadows marring the clean lines of this simple monolith: a firm narrative closure ("And they all drank free" [23.7–8]) has been allowed to foreshadow the end of the tale, an especially conclusive unit since it echoes the phrase that Joyce himself cited as the basic close of the folk tale in our culture, "Polly put the kettle on, and they all drank tea." It is immediately followed by a basic declarative statement that smacks of the moralistic aphorism: "For one man in his armour was a fat match always for any girls under shurts" (23.8–9). The active narration had terminated with the sound of the fall, but a series of eight sentences follow that event, an embarrassment of narrative closures that call into question the efficacy of the tight storytelling pattern.

Nor was the crisp, succinct opening of the tale without its own encumbrances. Only a few lines prior, a blurred version of "It was of a night" breaks through, as if a tentative narrator is attempting to begin the van Hoother tale, trips over the simple words of introduction, pleads for the attention of an audience, is interrupted by that audience assuring the teller of its attentiveness, but interrupting nonetheless. The cumulative effect is of a bumbled attempt at storytelling from a hesitant narrator, clearing his throat in anticipation before actually finding his voice: "Het wis if ee newt. Lissom! lissom! I am doing it. Hark, the corne entreats! And the larpnotes prittle. It was of a night . . ." *(FW* 21.2–5).

These deviations in what on the surface appears to be a direct and uncomplicated tale testify to the inherent complications of any story: the tale has a life of its own independent of any determined storyteller, a racial memory of analogues and variants, while the teller competes with colleagues and rivals invested with stories of their own, and an audience that "contributes" by its attentiveness as well as interference. Telling a story is not leading a tame horse down a straight road, but riding a self-willed maverick on a crooked path. The Tale of Jarl van Hoother and the Prankquean remains one of the simpler set pieces of *Finnegans Wake,* and its vagaries can be applied to one of the most complex "tales"—The Mookse and the Gripes.

The fable of the Mookse and the Gripes, self-contained between an announced title ("The Mookse and The Gripes" [152.15]) and a direct withdrawal from tale-telling ("No applause, please!" [159.19]), is a rather long and somewhat rambling narrative, yet it is folded into multiple layers of packaging. At its outer limits it exists within the eleventh question of the riddles chapter—actually within its response, which runs for nineteen pages (149.11–168.12). The Shem question receives its Shaun answer, a very blunt and immediate "No," which then expands into multiple explanations and justifications, all ancillary to that conclusive negative, and eventually self-defeating. A pedantically professorial voice elaborates a complex scientific-metaphysical theory, apparently for highly sophisticated auditors, only to evolve into a lower-level teacher spinning an exemplary tale for a roomful of pupils (The Mookse and the Gripes), after which he takes on still another voice and format to narrate the tale of Burrus and Caseous. In an important sense everything after the opening *No* is digression, tale-spinning for its own purpose, and consequently along the lines that the tale dictates rather than in support of the motives of the tale-teller. The question itself requires no answer, since its cute, wheedling, lilting, self-effacing and self-deprecating song-and-dance contains the impossibility of a positive reply ("we don't think, Jones, we'd care to, would you?" [149.11]).

Once the questioner christens his adversary "Jones," the personality of the Shaun figure is presumably fixed for the duration of his performance: he has had the negative prerogative handed to him and quickly assumes it, his four immediate "questions" ("So you think I have impulsivism?" etc. [149.11–14]) revealing his personal defensiveness in direct colloquy with his interrogator; Jones is a typical bourgeois rationalizing his stinginess. Thereafter he adopts the tone of a lecturer, and christens Shem "Schott," as if in direct debate with him, but with a condescending note of familiarity. Shem's plea having been summarily set aside, Jones settles down to a one-sided theoretical debate, setting up examples for refutation and puffing himself up with self-congratulations.

There is still nothing in this one-character monologue, executed in a modulating but individual voice, to prepare us for the presentation of the fable. Jones fabricates a professorial adversary to refute and demolish ("Professor Loewy-Brueller"/"Professor Levi-Brullo"/"Professor Llewellys ap Bryllars" [150.15/151.11/151.32–33]), but the learned debate becomes at times a political pose, that of a hectoring legislator, as well as that of a pub blatherer cadging drinks with non-stop anecdotes and arguments. With a sudden shift, however, he lowers the pedantic tone, totally condescending: "As my explanations here are probably above your understanding, lattlebrattons . . . I shall revert to a more expletive method which I frequently use when I have to sermo with muddlecrass pupils" (152.4–8). The major transformation now is not in the speaker but in the audience which he has utterly transformed ("Imagine for my purpose that you are a squad of urchins" [152.8–9])—the nature of the story, as much as the motives of the storyteller, creates its analogue in its listeners. And the story that he tells is his own "easyfree translation of the old fabulist's parable" (152.12–13). The auditors have been transformed by a standard convention ("Imagine for my purpose"); the story has been transformed from a pre-existing text that we will never see ("my easyfree translation"); all that remains is for the teller himself to undergo a transformation.

In invoking the fabulist Jones becomes the fabulist: he assumes a total disregard for any existing auditors, and the fable begins with epic depiction, grandiose and inflated, although with the folk tale opening: "Eins within a space and a wearywide space it wast" (152.18–19). As long as he concerns himself with his Mookse alterego he can maintain the elevated tone, the Mookse in effect engendering his own discourse: "our once in only Bragspear, he clanked, to my clinking, from veetoes to threetop, every inch of an immortal" (152.33–34). The narrator makes little secret of his direct association with the Mookse (and the Mookse's way of thinking), so that a mutual disdain can be expressed for both the "boggylooking stream" (the mother) and the pathetic figure overhanging the stream, the Gripes (the brother). The auspicious tone has been replaced by the supercilious, stream and Gripes affecting the method of narration, but both are easily expected from Mookse-directed narrative. Yet in the paragraph describing the Gripes the narrative voice dissolves into a chatty, folksy, snide, lilting tone, as befits the lower-level Gripes rather than the loftier Mookse, paralleling the tone of Shem's begging question that incurred Shaun's wrath and this lengthy apologia. To portray the Gripes as "cheek by jowel with his frisherman's blague, *Bellua Triumphanes,* his everyway addedto wallat's collectium, for yea longer he lieved yea broader he betaught of it, the fetter, the summe and the haul it cost, he looked the first and last micahlike laicness of Quartus the Fifth and Quintus the Sixth and Sixtus the Seventh giving allnight sitting to Lio the Faultyfindth" (153.28–34) may not be as demotically pedestrian as what the fabulist describes as the Gripe's "wherry whiggy maudelenian woice" (153.36), but it is a far cry from the tone that proclaimed the Mookse "every inch an immortal."

The situation has come full circle, an uncomfortable (for Shaun) parallel to the question asked by the "poor acheseyeld from Ailing" that engendered the enraged "No, blank ye!" (148.33, 149.11). The Gripes also asks the begging question ("Will you not perhopes tell me everything if you are pleased, sanity? All about aulne and lithial and allsall allinall about awn and liseias? Ney?" [154.3–5]), which also contains its own hopeless negative. The Mookse responds true to form. His "Blast yourself and your anathomy infairioriboos! No, hang you for an animale rurale!" (154.10–11) is dangerously close to the original. In constructing his fable Jones has abandoned his monologue debate with an adversary unable to reply, and saddled himself with a narrative form in which Shem-Gripes has an active voice.

Narrators maintain their advantage over the discourse of their tales as long as they can control the monologue. Once they permit colloquy among their characters, the distinct possibility of an opposing voice presents itself, and although readers suspect that functioning narrators have their own means of "recycling" the speech of their characters for their own purposes, the Gripesean "woice" breaks through the Mooksean control. And most of the confrontation between them exists primarily in dialogue, with Jones allowing himself the prerogative of editorial comment after each of the Gripes's statements: "Think of it! O miserendissimest retempter! A Gripes!" (154.6). No pretense to objective narrative now exists: Jones is the Mookse, and the enemy is the Gripes. The narrative is consumed within the Mookse's perspective, yet the Gripes is eloquent in his self-deprecatory thrusts: "My tumble, loudy bullocker, is my own. My velicity is too fit in one stockend. And my spetial inexshellsis the belowing things above" (154.33–35).

When the tale returns to a "narrative norm," the Mookse having had the last word in the exchange, Jones regains his control through the usual means: matter-of-fact setting of scene, cataloguing, name-dropping in pompously pedantic fashion. The Mookse, assumed by the narrator to be in ascendency, reopens the dialogue this time, but even with Jones's continued support, he cannot conceal that he is going deaf, as the Gripes is going blind. And these separate and distinct personalities, the teller's hero and his *bête noire,* become inseparable and indistinct, merge into undifferentiated antagonists in the growing darkness:

> And they viterberated each other, *canis et coluber* with the wildest ever wielded since Tarriestinus lashed Pissasphaltium.
> —Unuchorn!
> —Ungulant!
> —Uvuloid!
> —Uskybeak!
> And bullfolly answered volleyball. (157.1–7)

The Nuvoletta portion of the fable that follows totally disarms the putative narrator. As a character in *his* tale she completely takes possession of the mode of narration. No longer are we privy to the Jonesian pontifications ("While that Mooksius with preprocession and with proprecession, duplicitly and diplussedly, was promulgating" [156.8–9]) or Mooksean disdain ("It looked little and it smelt of brown and it thought in narrows and it talked showshallow—" 153.5–6) or masculine straight-from-the-shoulder talk ("The Pills, the Nasal Wash (Yardley's), the Army Man Cut, as british as bondstrict and as straightcut as when that brokenarched traveller from Nuzuland . . ." [156.28–30]). The entire Nuvoletta section, which dominates the final third of the fable, is recounted in a feminine, young, wistful, serene, romantic tone, befitting the nature of the character but inappropriate for the character of the narrator. This concluding capsule of the tale of the Mookse and the Gripes, a moralistic fable of didactic intent, removes the thrust of narration from the teller and reconstitutes it in the domain of Nuvoletta herself, with no more bias for the Mookse and what he represents than with the Gripes. The powerful force of the character eliminates the narrator, and the tale finally tells itself.

The Nuvoletta portion of the tale is entirely subsumed by the Nuvoletta voice, from the opening sentence ("Nuvoletta in her lightdress, spunn of sisteen shimmers, was looking down on them, leaning over the bannistars and listening all she childishly could" [157.8–9]) to the closing sentence ("But the river tripped on her by and by, lapping as though her heart was brook: *Why, why, why! Weh, O weh! I'se so silly to be flowing but I no canna stay!*" [159.16–18]). The style is reminiscent of that of the first half of the "Nausikaa" chapter of *Ulysses,* where any pretense of objective narration is foregone and a narrative mode that is romantically young and feminine is in full swing. Compare the opening of "Nausikaa": "The summer evening had begun to fold the world in its mysterious embrace. Far away in the west the sun was setting and the last glow of all too fleeting day lingered lovingly on sea and strand" (*U* 346). There are, of course, modulations within this mode, as there are in the comparable section of "Nausikaa," dictated by the narrative changes internally. But essentially a vocal approximation of Nuvoletta's attitudes and interests dominates the portion of the tale in which she is central, even past her actual departure ("She was gone. And into the river that had been a stream . . ." [*FW* 159.10–18]), as her influence is still felt. When Jones "returns," the Tale is ended and the classroom scene re-emerges as a frame ("No applause, please! Bast!" [159.19]): the magician reappears and takes credit for his magic; the puppeteer assumes that the puppets acted according to *his* volition. In reality the sorcerer's apprentice has unleashed powers beyond his meager control.

It is Nuvoletta who is mainly responsible for the equalization of the Mookse-Gripes situation, despite the didactic intentions of the presumed "narrator," Shaun-Jones, and his boast (after the tale), "As I have now successfully explained to you my own naturalborn rations" (159.24–25), is comically absurd. Nuvoletta may be making important distinctions between the Mookse and the Gripes when she sees the former as "Shouldrups in his glaubering hochskied his welkinstuck" and the latter as "Kneesknobs on his swivvel was makeacting such a paulse of himshelp" (157.10–13), but she maintains equal interest in the two prospective lovers—the romantic daydreaming of a Gerty MacDowell over Leopold Bloom. When each proves equally inaccessible she despairs of either, and is then quite clinical in her evaluations of their failings, dubbing the Mookse "a dogmad Accanite" and the Gripes "a dubliboused Catalick" (158.3–4). And finally she groups them under a single plural heading, "menner" (158.5), where Jones had been so persistent in distinguishing between the advantages of one and the disadvantages of the other.

Nuvoletta's actual voice is only rarely heard, most specifically in that verdict ("—I see, she sighed. There are menner" [158.5]), and in her cry before departing (*"Nuée! Nuée!"* [159.9]). Two other cries in this section are logically comparative in tone: at dusk "the tired ones" are heard crying *"O! O! O! Par la pluie!"* (158.21–23), for which some sort of collective attribution is made—"as we weep now with them." And the river closes the tale with her own *"Why, why, why! Weh, O weh!"* chorus, which also sounds very much within the Nuvoletta sound pattern. More unusual than the intrusive *we* is the casual introduction of a first person singular in the scene in which both the Mookse and the Gripes are mysteriously carried off: "Then there came down to the thither bank a woman of no appearance (I believe she was a Black with chills at her feet) and she gathered up his hoariness the Mookse" (158.25–27). Not since early in the tale has the narrative "voice" sounded in its own rights ("And, I declare, what was there on the yonder bank" [153.9]), and its return here seems to indicate a desperateness to take back the narrative from the Nuvoletta locus, and swing the balance for the Mookse after all: "So you see the Mookse he had reason as I knew and you knew and he knew all along" (158.30–31). The auditors are made fellow conspirators in the exoneration, identifying narrator and audience with the chosen subject. And although there is a note of sympathy for the Gripes, howbeit condescending, his demise is reported without editorializations: "And so the poor Gripes got wrong; for that is always how a Gripes is, always was and always will be" (159.1–2). A tension has arisen between the narrator's projected bias and Nuvoletta's disappointed sympathy, but her disappointment plays into the hands of the Mookse's proponent.

Whatever margin of success Jones has snatched from the brink of defeat is not enough to allow him to vacate the stage: The Tale of The Mookse and The Gripes is not the parable that will prove the Shaunian case in reply to the begging question, and the "answer" goes on into still another phase, and eventually another tale. Burrus and Caseous replace the Mookse and the Gripes as exemplary characters, but the tale (if there is a tale) is difficult to extrapolate from the Jones tendency to be discursive and digressive: where does it begin and where does it end? No title as such is advanced and emblazoned, set off in the text as definitively as "The Mookse and The Gripes." Instead, the last sentence of a digressive paragraph mentions that "I cannot now have or nothave a piece of cheeps in your pocket at the same time and with the same manners as you can now nothalf or half the cheek apiece I've in mind unless Burrus and Caseous have not or not have seemaultaneously systentangled themselves, selldear to soldthere, once in the dairy days of buy and buy" (161.9–14). That last echo of the opening lines of "Love's Old Sweet Song" is the closest that Jones comes to an introductory catchphrase for the new fable, although much later on, as if to remind us that the tale has never been properly introduced, *"ill tempor"* (164.34–35) recalls the beginning of a gospel reading, *in illo tempore*. Once the tale has got under way ("Burrus, let us like to imagine, is a genuine prime" [161.15] is a narrative commencement not unlike "Eins within a space and a wearywide space it wast ere wohned a Mookse" [152.18–19] despite the absence of a clearcut "Once upon a time"), a disquieting note is soon sounded with "Duddy shut the shopper op" (161.23–24): "Polly put the kettle on and they all had tea" is a narrative closure arriving much too early. The Shaun-Jones narrator, despite his tenacity, is a pathetic bumbler at his task.

He has emerged from his Mookse-Gripes effort as a praiser of his own performance, and immediately appears from behind his storyteller's mask, not even Professor Jones as such but obviously and basically Shaun: "I feel in symbathos for my ever devoted friend and halfaloafonwashed, Gnaccus Gnoccovitch. Darling gem!" (159.26–28); and in exiling his brother to a treeless Tristan da Cunha, he loses himself in the forest of his own words and digresses endlessly on forestry. The pedagogic Jones has once again gained the upper hand ("If I weren't a jones in myself I'd elect myself to be his dolphin" [160.18–19]), until he has to admit openly that he has been rambling: "But I further, feeling a bit husky in my truths" (160.23–24). Although no actual dichotomy exists between Shaun and Jones, they are at odds with each other over tale-telling methods: Shaun would prefer to use direct discourse to overwhelm his adversary; Jones is incapable of any discourse which is not circumloquacious and tangential. In opting for direct address ("Will you please come over and let us mooremoore murgessly to each's other down below our vice" [160.25–26]), Shaun suspends any pretense of storytelling, although admitting to deafness ("I am underheerd" [160.26]) identifies him with Jones's Mookse. The serial reversal to a bela-boring of a space-time theory returns the podium to Jones and his new effort, with Burrus and Caseous as his protagonists.

The new narrational technique is to be simple and low-keyed in expo-sition, even somewhat surreptitious ("Burrus . . . is a genuine prime, the real choice, full of natural greace . . . whereat Caseous is obversely the revise of him and in fact not an ideal choose by any meals" [161.15–19]), since highflown rhetoric in the previous fable proved to be Jones's undoing. The colloquial discourse, however, opens the gates for Shaun's direct thrusts ("The seemsame home and histry seeks and hidepence which we used to be reading for our prepurgatory, hot, Schott?" [161.22–23]), so that although the opening sentence deals with Burrus and Caseous, the rest of the paragraph dissolves into childhood recollections of foodstuffs, as Shaun reverts to lording it over Shem: "snob screwing that cork, Schott!" (161.32–33). Once again, as if in desperation, the taleteller resorts to talking down to "muddlecrass pupils": "to understand this as well as you can, feeling how backward you are in your down-to-the-ground benches, I have completed the following arrangement for the coarse use of stools and if I don't make away with you I'm beyond Caesar outnullused" (161.33–36).

Two competing voices simultaneously embark on the Burrus-Caseous narrative, one, that of a reasonably chatty, somewhat comic, even playful storyteller, the other a moralistic historian with an axe to grind and a tendency to openly attack. For a while they compete, with the teller carrying the narration and the moralist interrupting parenthetically, so that if the reader were to separate the texts from each other and place them in parallel juxtapositions, these two sets of texts would co-exist on the printed page:

The old sisars . . . become unbeurrable from age, . . . having been sort-of-nine-knived and chewly removed . . . the twinfreer types are billed to make their reupprearance as the knew kneck and knife knickknots on the deserted *champ de bouteilles.* . . . *Ostiak della Vogul Marina!* But that I dannoy the fact of wanton to weste point I could paint you to that butter . . . if you had some wash. Mordvealive! Oh me none onsens!	(Tyrants, regicide is too good for you!) (the compositor of the farce of dustiny however makes a thunpledrum mistake by letting off this pienofarte effect as his furst act as that is where the juke comes in) (this soldier - author - batman for all his commontoryism is just another of those souftsiezed bubbles who never quite got the sandhurst out of his eyes so that the champaign he draws for us is as flop as plankrieg) (A most cursery reading into the Persic-Uraliens hostery shows us how Fonnumagula picked up that propper numen out of a colluction of prifixes though to the permienting cannasure the Coucousien oafsprung of this sun of a kuk is as sattin as there's a tub in Tobolosk) (cheese it!) (162.1–19)

Although the parenthetical voice is dominant in this opening series of exchanges, it soon loses ground and almost disappears. The colloquial narrator takes control and holds his advantage through to the conclusion of the long paragraph, at the end of which two succinct summations are offered to differentiate Burrus from Caseous: the historian resorts to Latin and employs a Vulgate Psalm, stepping out of parentheses in the process (*"Butyrum et mel comedet ut sciat reprobare malum et eligere bonum"* [163.3–4]), while the storyteller slogs along with vulgar German and gets the last word: *"Der Haensli ist ein Butterbrot, mein Butterbrot! Und Koebi iss ein Schtinkenkot! Ja! Ja! Ja!"* (163.5–7).

Text and countertext interact throughout the segment dealing with Burrus and Caseous, and as a result no story line manages to develop. The dominance of the colloquial voice is resounded in a short passage of triumph, almost a proclamation of triumph, as if the battle over Caseous has been won: "This in fact, just to show you, is Caseous, the brutherscutch or puir tyron: a hole or two, the highstinks aforefelt and anygo prigging wurms" (163.8–10). Yet the following paragraph undercuts the victory: the pedant is back in harness, balancing the parts as if in scientific objectivity, and it weaves itself into still another philosophic involvement—in lieu of storytelling: "Thus we cannot escape our likes and mislikes, exiles or ambushers, beggar and neighbour and—this is where the dimeshow advertisers advance the temporal relief plea—let us be tolerant of antipathies" (163.12–15). It is difficult not to be suspicious of this voice of reason, although it is almost exclusively concerned with the superiority of space over time (as if the Burrus-Caseous personifications hardly existed), so that while the calm conclusion that "the Bure will be dear on the Brie" (163.27–28) sounds like a dispassionate equation of two French cities, it is nonetheless clear that the butter is in ascendancy over the cheese. Where the extreme voice exults over the trouncing of Caseous by Burrus, the moderate one gives Burrus the narrow edge—victory nonetheless.

This scientifically balanced tone persists even longer, and it is soon apparent that such careful moderation is in practice: just as Nuvoletta intruded herself upon the Mookse-Gripes situation, so a female presence comes to the fore in this case, and the present narrator is gingerly working toward incorporating her into the narrative, unwilling to take the chance which allowed her predecessor to usurp his narrational directions:

> Positing, as above, too males pooles, the one the pictor of the other and the omber the *Skotia* of the one, and looking wantingly around our umdistributed middle between males we feel we must waistfully woent a female to focus and on this stage there pleasantly appears the cowrymaid M. whom we shall often meet below who introduces herself upon us at some precise hour which we shall again agree to call absolute zero or the babbling pumpt of platinism. And so like the former son of a kish who went up and out to found his farmer's ashes we come down home gently on our own turnedabout asses to meet Margareen. (164.4–14)

There seems little doubt that the august arranger of the scenario has no choice but to allow Margareen her entrance, and he does his best to put a good face on it. Already his tone has descended from the lofty philosophical: the last sentence smacks of the colloquial, as the first sentence of the next paragraph comes dangerously close to positively lilting: "We now romp through a period of pure lyricism of shamebred music . . . evidenced by such words of distress as *I cream for thee, Sweet Margareen,* and the more hopeful *O Margareena! O Margareena! Still in the bowl is left a lump of gold!"* (164.15–20). The latter is designated as more hopeful since it is Burrus's, while the former song title is Caseous's, but there is really little to choose between: both are smitten with her and she is the active subject of the tale.

The ploys undertaken now by the functioning narrator are numerous, each intended in some way to "objectify"—and therefore dispel—the strong feminine influence. By posing behind numerous journalistic styles and guises he seeks to prevent her female voice from usurping the directional tone; consequently, we hear from a food specialist: "(Correspondents, by the way, will keep on asking me what is the correct garnish to serve drisheens with)" (164.21–22); the cosmetics adviser: "Criniculture can tell us very precisely indeed how and why this particular streak of yellow silver first appeared" (164.25–26); and the music critic: "I would advise any unborn singer who may still be among my heeders to forget her temporal diaphragm" (164.35–36). Nonetheless, he sways under her spell (music was his mistake) and succumbs: "O! to cluse her eyes and aiopen her oath and see what spice I may send her" (165.4–5).

Pulling himself together he tries once again, using the same ploys for narrative disinterest, adopting various guises for the presentation of Margareen, the first as music manager ("the acoustic and orchidectual management of the tonehall" [165.8–9]); but orchidectomies are hardly suitable under the circumstances, and mathematical instruction may be safer ("to pursue Burrus and Caseous for a rung or two up their isocelating biangle" [165.12–13]). As a self-advertising portrait painter he can distance himself from the alluring female form ("Every admirer has seen my goulache of Marge" [165.13–14]), and as an advertiser can describe the packaging rather than the contents ("The boxes, if I may break the subject gently, are worth about fourpence pourbox" [165.30–31]). But every attempt now leads him further into double-entendres. Nonetheless, he plunges ahead as a gossip-and-fashion columnist, distancing Margareen as an isolated object to be observed and commented upon: "Now there can be no question about it either that I having done as much, have quite got the size of that demilitery young female (we will continue to call her Marge) whose types may be met with in any public garden, wearing a very 'dressy' affair" (166.3–6). From which point on through the rest of the paragraph a distinct voice carries on rather stridently, familiar to us as that of Percy Wyndham Lewis, pronouncing his published prejudices, and especially apparent in the numerous single words set out in the text by quotation marks (nine of them in the single-sentence paragraph). It is quite an unpleasant and arch voice, anti-feminine in his derision of Margareen. And even when the narrator recaptures the narrational prerogative, he is supercilious in his insistence on dealing harshly with the young woman: "My solutions . . . must stand over from the moment till I tackle this tickler hussy for occupying my uttentions" (166.27–29).

The *tickler hussy*, of course, has a strong mind and personality of her own, and as soon as it becomes necessary to relate her part of the tale, the tone generated moves especially close to hers ("Margareena she's very fond of Burrus but, alick and alack! she velly fond of chee" [166.30–31]). (Compare this, for example, with the cloying cute voice of the tale of Peaches and Daddy Browning: "he is downright fond of his number one but O he's fair mashed on peaches number two" [65.24–26]). The subject is Margareena, and consequently the narrational indicators are Margareena's, while the anti-feminine, pro-Burrus source that we know as Shaun-Jones strives to undermine her possession of the tale, using the parenthetical intrusion as his vehicle: "(The important influence exercised on everything by this eastasian import has not been till now fully flavoured though we can taste it in this case. I shall come back for a little more say farther one)" (166.30–34).

What Margareen has to announce, and what the text has been preventing by the irrelevancies and evasions, is that not only does she view Burrus and Caseous as relatively interchangeable (an idea that is anathema to the Jonesian controlling voice), but she has bypassed them both for a more suitable male: "A cleopatrician in her own right she at once complicates the position while Burrus and Caseous are contending for her misstery by implicating herself with an elusive Antonious" (166.34–167.1). Margareena has learned from Nuvoletta's experience not to accept limited options, and aware that there are many other men *(menner)*, she has moved out of the narrative restrictions imposed by Professor Jones in his role as dominating fabulist, and not only imposed her own tone on the story but her own plot directions. Jones has little option now but to salvage as much of his position as he can, by the now-familiar techniques of lecturing on *talis* and *qualis* once again, reducing life to mathematical equations. He had attempted to glide by the unpleasant subject of Margareen's choice of Antonious by a pseudo-objective tone, merely presenting the Argument of the piece quite matter-of-factly (*A cleopatrician in her own right she . . .*), but once the cat is out of the bag, no amount of "*talis* on *talis*" (167.5) can conceal his annoyance, and he goes off in a tirade against "a boosted blasted bleating blatant bloaten blasphorus blesphorous idiot who kennot tail a bomb from a painapple" (167.13–15).

It is now apparent that there is to be no Tale of Burrus and Caseous, that Jones has been even less successful with this venture than with that of the Mookse and the Gripes, and intends cutting his losses as soon as he can. His "solution" is to climb as high on his horse as possible and pontificate in olympian fashion, in effect abandoning narration for an argumentative and moralistic laying down of the law. A resounding negative introduces the last paragraph of the Shaunian response to Shem's begging question ("No! Topsman to your Tarpeia! This thing, Mister Abby, is nefand" [167.18–19]), both denying Shem and terminating the tale-telling process. Even without sufficient evidence he dictates his terms, pronouncing the victory of Burrus over Caseous ("Merus Genius to Careous Caseous!" [167.23–24]), and proceeds to add moral tags to close the proceedings, including the marriage vows:

> My unchanging Word is sacred. The word is my Wife, to expouse and expound, to vend and to velnerate, and may the curlews crown our nuptias! Till Breath us depart! Wamen. Beware would you change with my years. Be as young as your grandmother! The ring man in the rong shop but the rite words by the rote order! *Ubi lingua nuncupassit, ibi fas! Adversus hostem semper sac!* (167.28–34)

These declamations even when not isolated as individual imprecations, recall the closing moments of the Tale of Jarl van Hoother and the Prankquean, the morals tagged on to the end:

> For one man in his armour was a fat match always for any girls under shurts. And that was the first peace of illiterative porthery in all the flamend floody flatuous world. How kirssy the tiler made a sweet unclose to the Narwhealian captol. Saw fore shalt thou sea. Betoun ye and be. The prankquean was to hold her dummyship and the jimminies was to keep the peacewave and van Hoother was to git the wind up. Thus the hearsomeness of the burger felicitates the whole of the polis. (23.8–15)

The addition of a *sweet unclose* which encapsulates a moral is traditional for such cautionary tales, but somewhat excessive when, with the aborted narrative of Burrus and Caseous, the conclusions greatly outweigh the evidence. Quotations and mottoes continue on toward the end of the Shaun reply, full of sound and fury and high seriousness, and at one particular instance revealing the "relayed" tone of an underlying voice, that of a sermonizing preacher. "She that will not feel my fulmoon let her peel to thee as the hoyden and the impudent!" (167.34–35) has surely been heard before (although apparently not by any of the explicators of *Finnegans Wake*): it is the "rector's pedantic bass" none-too-infrequently heard by the muddlecrass pupils of Belvedere College, and we best remember it (not having heard the rector himself) as transmitted second-voice by Vincent Heron in *A Portrait of the Artist as a Young Man*. Heron's attempt at vocal imitation is admittedly not successful; the true mimic is Stephen Dedalus, and it is *his* rendition that Heron is attempting to duplicate: *"He that will not hear the churcha let him be to theea as the heathena and the publicana"* (P 76). As a coda-statement to the fable of Burrus and Caseous it is replicated at third or fourth remove, an echo of an echo, a voice adopted for the purpose.

For all of his half-successful and unsuccessful attempts at telling a tale, and despite his deployment of a narrator accustomed to public speaking, Shaun can only really resort to the bald *No*—in thunder. In his overlong discourse elaborating that expletive, he weaves himself in and out of story, fable, myth, and multiple performance, yet at the end it is Shem's lilting voice that dominates even Shaun's reply, a return to the rhythmical patterns of the eleventh question itself: "if he came to my preach, a proud purse-broken ranger, when the heavens were welling the spite of their spout, to beg for a bite in our bark *Noisdanger,* would meself and MacJeffet, four-in-hand, foot him out?—ay!" (168.3–6). Shem frames the question in his own mockpoetic voice, and in its negative, self-defeating formation determines the foregone answer; and Shaun eventually fails to find the proper narrative mode of discourse to deal directly with the shaming situation, returning the query at the end to Shem's area of discourse.

Finnegans Wake as a History of the Book

Carol Shloss

"I was in a printing house in Hell," William Blake tells us in *The Marriage of Heaven and Hell,* "& saw the method in which Knowledge is transmitted from generation to generation. In the first chamber was a Dragon-Man, clearing away the rubbish from the cave's mouth; within, a number of Dragons were hollowing the cave." As he expands this great, apocalyptic vision, Blake embellishes his description of the printing press, making it into a purifying agent, the tool of regeneration, a door to infinity. "I shall . . . print," he says "in the infernal method, by corrosives" (154). Viper, eagle, and lion, Blake's stable of symbolic animals, contribute to this process, eating away the restrictive texts of the past, building palaces to replace narrow caverns of knowledge, molding new books that will enable men to understand their own bondage and to escape into plenitude. The printing press, in its infernal guise, obliterates all that is small and mean about the past and replaces it with infinity—Blake's designation for all that is great and joyful and repressed in our world. As Harold Bloom has commented, it becomes "the voice of desire and rebellion crying [out] against restraint" (76).

When we think of James Joyce and the book, we are not likely to imagine him as the creator of another grandiose scheme for the press, but to remember instead the thousand, wearing details that dogged him on his way into print. Where Blake became a printer and incorporated the language and the techniques of impression-making into a system of human liberation,[1] Joyce seemed worn down by the whole process, more at the mercy of printers than their master. In 1912 he villainized John Falconer, the printer who burned the Maunsel edition of *Dubliners,* in a wretchedly scatological broadside; and though he never went to such extremes of vengeance again, his sentiments about printing seem to have remained consistently negative. In 1921, he was still complaining about it with regard to the proofs for *Ulysses:* "I am extremely irritated by all those printer's errors," he lamented to Harriet Shaw Weaver. "Working as I do amid piles of notes at a table in a hotel I cannot possibly do this mechanical part with my wretched eye and a half. Are these to be perpetuated in future editions? I hope not" (*Letters* I.176). Even Harriet Weaver, who had engineered *Ulysses'* publication by locating Maurice Darantière, a Dijon printer who would ignore threats of libel, found it necessary to apologize for a faulty first edition (1922): "The publisher asks the reader's indulgence for typographical errors unavoidable in the exceptional circumstances."

Like most of Joyce's experiences, these annoying incidents were transformed into literature. In *Ulysses* the evening edition of the newspaper makes Leopold Bloom into "L. Boom," and later, in the *Wake,* Joyce personifies typographic error as "misses in prints." You will "finally (though not yet endlike) meet with the acquaintance of Mister Typus, Mistress Tope and all the little typtopies" (20.11–14). If Blake had visualized the printing press as a vehicle of regeneration, Joyce considered it a means of miscegenation. Error always engendered its own vile offspring.

These attitudes are of particular interest to us now since it is our generation of scholars which is attempting to recover authentic texts of Joyce's work out of the "midden heap" of erring transcriptions of faulty copies of ill-typed drafts. We would like to know Joyce without thousands of typographic errors intervening. Hugh Kenner's essay about "The Computerized *Ulysses*" firmly establishes what we have all known distantly—that a core of dedicated Joyceans has spent years tracing the corruptions which occurred as texts were reset for successive editions. He has shown, too, the international cooperation and technology that are required to arrive at a base text that Joyce himself never left to us.

But Joyce's annoyance and his beleaguered efforts to transfer manuscripts to printed pages are more than incidental biographical details that require our own efforts to correct. Experience is powerful, and for Joyce, his own experience was always paradigmatic: one found the fate of the collective in individual lives. One finds, consequently, the analogue of all cultural transmission in Joyce's own fate in print. We should not underestimate the imaginative claim of Joyce's struggle with the machinery that allowed his work to be read in book form. T. S. Eliot has written about the "shadow" that falls between the intention and the act; but for a writer like Joyce who habitually composed on successive stages of proof, the printing press was more than an intervening shadow. It was, along with the typography which preceded it, a series of minute, human interventions that carried knowledge, more or less accurately, from one human being to another and from generation to generation. It was also the meeting point of art and commerce, the means by which a book is translated from a contribution to culture into a marketplace commodity. *Finnegans Wake* discloses Joyce's attitude toward this whole process, for it is a book that records its own making. Both text and meta-text, it spins out a vision of human cultural history transmitted (and transmuted) through books that is as broad and encompassing as Blake's dark vision of the corrosive printing house in hell.

He knew he was not the first writer to think about the importance of printing. The *Wake* is, among many other things, an encyclopedia of printing history, printing terms, and printing practices. Joyce always acknowledged his debts. In the same way that we can collect the languages of death from the "Hades" section of *Ulysses,* by noticing Dublin's dead letter office, Bloom's mortal agony, and those who drink like the devil, we can glean references to the entire world of the book in *Finnegans Wake:* books have a visual appearance, a format, and a life in industry that is populated by journeymen, compositors, proofreaders, master printers, booksellers, and authors. Some Joyce scholars have pointed out that the *Wake* is a compendium of writing forms. Others, still, have shown us the "structural books" and the incidental references to Joyce's published predecessors that underlie the text. Joyce's central precursor is acknowledged to be Giambattista Vico (1668–1744), whose cyclic view of history gave Joyce the recursive structure of both his book and the fates of his characters. In *Scienza Nuova* (Naples, 1744), Vico envisioned history in three categories: the age of the gods, the age of heroes, and the age of man; and to each reign, he ascribed corollary forms of law, religion, and language. Years ago William York Tindall noticed that the three types of language used by gods, heroes, and ordinary men are used in the *Wake*—the hundred-letter thunderwords representing the voice of the gods, heraldic shields and hieroglyphics representing heroes, and anything composed from alphabets representing the languages of man. It is here that we should note that Joyce used these mimetic devices to locate his own book in history, to remind us that in his eyes, scribal and printing cultures both belong to a fallen and vulgar world. Monastic and civic life are not contrasted in the *Wake* but are made to share the same ignoble category within a larger cosmic scheme. Whereas scholars of the *histoire du livre* try carefully to distinguish between scribal and typographic cultures, noting the social changes that occurred in the Renaissance with the advent of printing technology,[2] the distinction was meaningless to Joyce. The writing on the wall in the Old Testament, the hand-rubricated ornamentation of *The Book of Kells,* the Gutenberg Bible were all part of the same conceptual category, sharing more by virtue of their letter forms than their difference might lead other scholars to believe.

But it is also the case that Joyce was most interested in the lowest, most vulgar form of written communication and that the *Wake* recapitulates the history of the book within which it is itself embedded. It does this by containing passages about the origin of the alphabet and the innumerable artifacts created from letter forms. The passage following Mutt and Jute's conversation about the Battle of Clontarf in book 1 is a case in point:

> (Stoop) if you are abcedminded, to this claybook, what curios of signs (please stoop), in this allaphbed! Can you rede (since We and Thou had it out already) its world? It is the same told of all. Many. Miscegenations on miscegenations. Tieckle. They lived und laughed ant loved end left. Forsin. Thy thingdome is given to the Meades and Porsons. The meandertale, aloss and again, of our old Heidenburgh in the days when Head-in-Clouds walked the earth. In the igno-

rance that implies impression that knits knowledge that finds the nameform that whets the wits that convey contacts that sweeten sensation that drives desire that adheres to attachment that dogs death that bitches birth that entails the ensuance of existentiality. But with a rush out of his navel reaching the reredos of Ramasbatham. A terricolous vivelyonview this; queer and it continues to be quaky. A hatch, a celt, an earshare the pourquose of which was to cassay the earthcrust at all of hours, furrowards, bagawards, like yoxen at the turnpaht. Here say figurines billycoose arming and mounting. Mounting and arming bellicose figurines see here. Futhorc, this liffle effingee is for a firefing called a flintforfall. Face at the eased! O I fay! Face at the waist! Ho, you fie! Upwap and dump em, ⊓ace to ⊔ace! When a part so ptee does duty for the holos we soon grow to use of an allforabit. Here (please to stoop). (18.17–19.02)

The passage moves through God's warning to Belshazzar: "Me-Ne, Me-Ne, TeKel, uPHäR-SiN" ("God has numbered thy kingdom and finished it"), to the clay tablets of the Egyptian Ramses kings, to the inscription writing of the early Greeks and Romans which was called *boustrophedon* because it used both directions and reiterated the movements of oxen plowing (this form of writing, incidentally, explains the "⊓ace to ⊔ace" typography of this page, for as the direction of writing changed, the direction of certain asymetrical letters such as "ᕼ" and "Ⅎ," was changed, but symmetrical letters, such as "O" and "T," were not affected). "Olives, beets, kimmells, dollies" are the beginning letters of the Hebrew alphabet (aleph, beth, gimel, daleth), as "afrids, beatties, cormacks and daltons" are those of the Greek (alpha, beta, gamma, delta). Joyce punctuates the entire passage with the three stops characteristic of *The Book of Kells*—"(Stoop)," "(please stoop)," "(please to stoop)"—and passes through the runic alphabet used from about the third to the thirteenth centuries in Germany: "But the world, mind, is, was and will be writing its own wrunes for ever" (19.35–36) to arrive at letterpress printing: "A bone, a pebble, a ramskin; chip them, chap them, cut them up allways; leave them to terracook in the muttheringpot: and Gutenmorg . . . must once for omniboss step rubrickredd out of the wordpress" (20.05–09). What is most remarkable about this "muttheringpot" of information is that for Joyce all forms of writing are reiterative; that is, they provide analogies for each other so that the construction of the printing press is an inevitability rather than an invention that changed, as Francis Bacon claimed, "the appearance and state of the whole world."[3]

Joyce follows Gutenberg's press with a list of famous printers: William Caxton, who first printed Chaucer's *Canterbury Tales,* is mentioned (229.31); Isaac Jaggard and Edward Blount, the printers of Shakespeare's first folio, are listed (481.36; 39.08); Christopher Plantin, famous for his 1769 Polyglot Bible, is identified by the sign of the Golden Compasses ("Goat and Compasses") (275.16); Aldus Manutius, the fifteenth-century

Venetian printer who preserved so many humanistic texts in Greek and Latin, is also identified by his press mark, the dolphin (275.n6). Blake's Dragon-Man and his cave tell us that Joyce saw the printing press in *The Marriage of Heaven and Hell* as a precursor as well.

Joyce then places these giants of the printing world in the company of printers whose work was of more personal interest to him: James Blow and Patrick O'Neill of Belfast introduced letterpress printing into Ireland in 1696 (251.31; 534.18). Francis Joy was the first papermaker in Ulster and the founder of the *Belfast News Letter* (534.18). And everyone, inside and out of Ireland, who had anything to do with the publication of Joyce's own work parades through the *Wake*—from John Falconer of the *Dubliners* travesty (185.04), to Maurice Darantière, who printed *Ulysses* for Harriet Weaver (123.04), to Margaret Anderson and Jane Heap of *The Little Review* (389.10–11), Ethel Moorehead and Ernest Walsh of *This Quarter* (426.08; 290.17), and Bennett Cerf of Random House (113.11).

This list could be expanded, but the central critical task in the *Wake* is not simply to identify patterns, but also to establish why those patterns were significant to Joyce. In this case, I believe his concern with printing history grew out of a fascination with the issue of recension; that is, he understood that the critical revision of a text—whether it was his own correction of page proof or the corrections that each generation imposes on the texts of the past—can corrupt as well as correct. Blake's great vision of the task of the printing press was to "cleanse the doors of perception," to free the mind from the debilitating conventions of the past. Joyce's vision was of a past that could never claim or restrict one because it could only be known through the successive permutations wrought by the printing process itself. In a limited but intriguing way, typographic error can be considered to be the basis of Joyce's model of history. It provides us, at the least, with a way of qualifying the great Viconian sweeps of time that inform the *Wake*, for it provided Joyce with a conceptualization of the past that makes the records of the past analogous to, rather than the opposite of, gossip. In the same way that stories are told and retold in print (or set and reset in type), gossip places successive interpretations on events that recede further and further from verification with each retelling. The washerwomen who chatter on the banks of the Liffey, wondering about the sex lives of Humphrey Earwicker and Anna Livia, are not unlike the great historians whose printed accounts of events elicit our highest respect: the intervention of the press will ensure their narratives a similar fate: they will continue until they "finally . . . meet with the acquaintance of Mister Typus, Mistress Tope and all the little typtopies. Fillstup. So you need hardly spell me how every word will be bound over to carry three score and ten toptypsical readings throughout the book of Doublends Jined" (20.11–16). Movable type is as much an invitation to error as to fixity as Joyce tells us repeatedly in his personification of the individual letter forms that comprise his book. They never stay in place: "The movibles are scrawling in motions" (20.21–22). "The . . . words run, march, halt, walk, [and] stumble at doubtful points" (114.08–09). Later they do exactly what Tim Finnegan does on his ladder; they become "lines of litters slittering up and louds of latters slettering down" (114.17–18).

These notions of the continual, erroneous permutations of type constitute a radical attack on the qualities the printing press is usually thought most to engender: fixity, consistency, and efficiency. But at the same time that Joyce challenges the idea of typographic fixity, he also relies on our expectation of it: were it not for the conventions of typographic display, we would not be able to read the *Wake* at all. Typography is the convention against which all of Joyce's variations and word plays are carried out. H. D., one of Joyce's contemporaries and an analysand of Freud, used the phrase "the writing on the wall"—not as an allusion to the hand of God descending in judgment on King Balshazzar—but as a way of identifying a hard surface of collective, intersubjectively recognized reality against which idiosyncrasy or pathology can be recognized. In Joyce's work, the regularity of visual convention supports, absolutely, the irregularities of style; it provides a "wall" against which Joyce's writing can be judged. It is no accident that the limited edition presses that have published fragments of the *Wake* have resisted the embellishments often associated with superlative book craftsmanship and have, instead, provided Joyce with simplicity and luxurious spacing as a fitting couch. Joyce's typographers have recognized that *mise-en-page,* the arrangement of the page, must remain absolutely classic if readers are to deal adequately with the "soundsense" of the words.

Their neutrality has also, I think, dealt with another issue that we must recognize: that the very form or appearance of the printed page provided Joyce with an emblematic visual representation of his own creative task. For the same text, printed at different times, in different countries and according to variations in national taste and technology, looks different: The Gutenberg Bible (Mainz, c.1455, fig. 1), printed in Gothic textura and arranged in double columns with rubrication, is only distantly related to the King James version and even further removed from *The Oxford English Bible* (Oxford, 1961). Caxton's text of *The Canterbury Tales* (Westminster, 1478?, fig. 2), printed in *lettre de forme* and *batarde* types, has an appearance not duplicated in any other edition. The original, Venetian edition of Euclid (Venice, 1482, fig. 3) has a character very different from the geometry book Joyce would have used as a schoolboy even though Ratdolt used the Roman letter forms that have come down to us for use in printing today. I think it was this sensitivity to the visual changes in letter forms, the different "clothing" that the same text can and does wear according to

1. Johann Gutenberg, Bible in Latin (42-line), Mainz, c. 1455, 11 3/4″ × 16″
(Photograph courtesy of the Houghton Library, Harvard University)

The Wyf off bathe

Here endith the Wyff of Bathes prologe.
And here begynnyth her tale.

In olde dayes of kyng Artur
Of whiche britous spekith gret honour
Al was this londe fulfilled of fayrye
The elf quene with her ioly companye
Daunced ful ofte in many a greue mede
This was the olde oppinion as I rede
I speke of many an hundrid yeris agoo
But now can noman se elphis mo
For now the grete charite and praiers
Of limytours and eke of othir freris
That serchen euery londe and euery streme
As thicke as motis in the sonne beem
Blissinge hallis chambris kechens and bowris
Citees Burghis castellis and eek touris
Shoppis bernys Shepens and deyries
This makith that ther be no feyries
For there as wont was to walke an elf
There walkith now the limytour hym self
In vndermelis and in mornyngis
And seith his matyns and his thingis
As he goth forth in his limytacion
A woman may go sauely vp and doun
Vnder euery busshe or vnder euery tre
There is none other incubus but he
And he ne wolde do hem ony dishonour
And so befil that this kyng Artour
Hadde in his hous a lusty bacheler

2. William Caxton, Chaucer: *Canterbury Tales,* Westminster, c. 1478, 7 1/2″ × 10″
(Photograph courtesy of the Houghton Library, Harvard University)

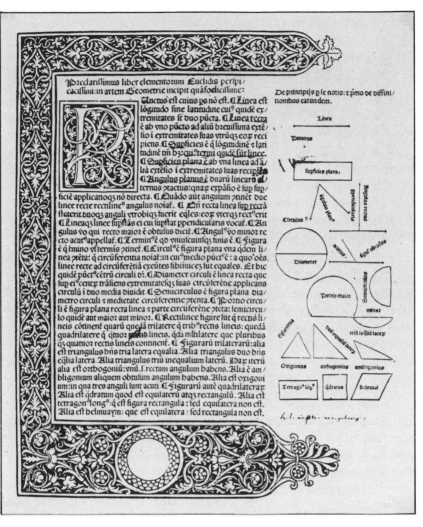

3. Erhard Ratdolt, Euclid: *Elementa Geometriae*, Venice, 1482, 8 1/8″ × 12 1/8″ (Photograph courtesy of the Houghton Library, Harvard University)

historical circumstances, that led Joyce to think of orthography, the printed symbols of the sounds of language, as a homologous and similarly variable system. *The Book of Kells* (fig. 4), with its "Weird and commanding beauty (and) . . . creeping undulations of serpentine forms that writhe in artistic profusion throughout the mazes of its decorations" (Sir Edward Sullivan 32), probably fascinated Joyce because it showed so clearly the possible disparity between the visual elaborateness of letter forms and page arrangement and the simplicity of the encoded message. He specifically mentions the "Tunc" page of the book:

TUNC CRU
CIFIXERANT
XPI CUM EO DU
OS LATRONES

(Then were there two thieves crucified with him [Matthew 27:38])

Joyce distantly imitates its erratic lettering on page 120 of his own book: "capItalIsed mIddle" he writes, following his typographical pun with a description that serves equally to describe the visual appearance of the old Irish manuscript and the verbal strategies of his own unprecedented text; each word is "as cunningly hidden in its maze of confused drapery as a fieldmouse in a nest of coloured ribbons" (120.05–06). The Polyglot Bible (Antwerp, 1569–72, fig. 5), with its synchronic babble of languages and types, can be seen as another visual predecessor to the *Wake.*

According to Joyce, cultural transmission from generation to generation involved inevitable error and it always occurred in visibly transfigured letter forms. As he put it on another occasion in the *Wake,* words are "as time went on as it will variously inflected, differently pronounced, otherwise spelled, changeably meaning vocable script signs" (118.26–28). We accept this drift as natural in the history of the printed book. Joyce considered his own text to be a similar permutation, his own characters within the text specific instances of the identity within change that evolving letter forms suggested. Humphrey Earwicker and Anna Livia, as male and female principles, are merely translated through the ages, their natures "variously inflected" in the same way that the Bible has been translated from language to language, from Gothic textura to Roman types, with more or less freedom from typographic error, while retaining its essential character as a sacred text.

If typography, the visual form of the printed book, provided Joyce with a paradigmatic way to embody identity within change, the press itself also showed him how to elevate these apparent disparities into a system where contraries are resolved and differences or "error" rendered irrelevant. We recall that Blake's printing house in hell was part of a dialectic process, the

inuenerunt sicut dixerat illis & pa.
rauerunt pascha .·

Vespere autem facto uenit
cum ·xii· & discumberabus eis &
manducantabus ait illis ihs

Amen dico uobis quia unus ex
uobis me tradet qui manducat
mecum

illi coeperunt contristari
& dicere ei singillatim num
quid ego sum

Qui ait illis unus de duodecim
qui intingit mecum manum in
catino & filius quidem hominis
uadit sicut scriptum est de eo
uae autem homini illi per quem
filius hominis tradetur .·

4. *The Book of Kells,* Iona, c. 800, 12 3/4″ × 9 1/4″; Trinity College Library, Dublin (Photograph courtesy of James H. Heineman, Inc.)

Hebrew text

וַיִּמַח אֶת־כָּל־הַיְקוּם אֲשֶׁר עַל־פְּנֵי הָאֲדָמָה כג
מֵאָדָם עַד־בְּהֵמָה עַד־רֶמֶשׂ וְעַד־עוֹף הַשָּׁמַיִם וַיִּמָּחוּ מִן־הָאָרֶץ
וַיִּשָּׁאֶר אַךְ־נֹחַ וַאֲשֶׁר אִתּוֹ בַּתֵּבָה ‏ וַיִּגְבְּרוּ הַמַּיִם כד
עַל־הָאָרֶץ חֲמִשִּׁים וּמְאַת יוֹם ‏

ח ‏ וַיִּזְכֹּר אֱלֹהִים אֶת־נֹחַ וְאֵת כָּל־הַחַיָּה וְאֶת־ א
כָּל־הַבְּהֵמָה אֲשֶׁר אִתּוֹ בַּתֵּבָה וַיַּעֲבֵר אֱלֹהִים רוּחַ עַל־
הָאָרֶץ וַיָּשֹׁכּוּ הַמָּיִם ‏ וַיִּסָּכְרוּ מַעְיְנֹת תְּהוֹם וַאֲרֻבֹּת ב
הַשָּׁמָיִם וַיִּכָּלֵא הַגֶּשֶׁם מִן־הַשָּׁמָיִם ‏ וַיָּשֻׁבוּ הַמַּיִם ג
מֵעַל הָאָרֶץ הָלוֹךְ וָשׁוֹב וַיַּחְסְרוּ הַמַּיִם מִקְצֵה חֲמִשִּׁים
וּמְאַת יוֹם ‏ וַתָּנַח הַתֵּבָה בַּחֹדֶשׁ הַשְּׁבִיעִי בְּשִׁבְעָה־ ד
עָשָׂר יוֹם לַחֹדֶשׁ עַל הָרֵי אֲרָרָט ‏ וְהַמַּיִם הָיוּ הָלוֹךְ ה
וְחָסוֹר עַד הַחֹדֶשׁ הָעֲשִׂירִי בָּעֲשִׂירִי בְּאֶחָד לַחֹדֶשׁ נִרְאוּ
רָאשֵׁי הֶהָרִים ‏ וַיְהִי מִקֵּץ אַרְבָּעִים יוֹם וַיִּפְתַּח נֹחַ ו
אֶת־חַלּוֹן הַתֵּבָה אֲשֶׁר עָשָׂה ‏ וַיְשַׁלַּח אֶת־הָעֹרֵב ז
וַיֵּצֵא יָצוֹא וָשׁוֹב עַד־יְבֹשֶׁת הַמַּיִם מֵעַל הָאָרֶץ ‏
וַיְשַׁלַּח אֶת־הַיּוֹנָה מֵאִתּוֹ לִרְאוֹת הֲקַלּוּ הַמַּיִם מֵעַל ח
פְּנֵי הָאֲדָמָה ‏ וְלֹא־מָצְאָה הַיּוֹנָה מָנוֹחַ לְכַף־רַגְלָהּ ט
וַתָּשָׁב אֵלָיו אֶל־הַתֵּבָה כִּי־מַיִם עַל־פְּנֵי כָל־הָאָרֶץ
וַיִּשְׁלַח יָדוֹ וַיִּקָּחֶהָ וַיָּבֵא אֹתָהּ אֵלָיו אֶל־הַתֵּבָה ‏
וַיָּחֶל עוֹד שִׁבְעַת יָמִים אֲחֵרִים וַיֹּסֶף שַׁלַּח אֶת־הַיּוֹנָה י
מִן־הַתֵּבָה ‏ וַתָּבֹא אֵלָיו הַיּוֹנָה לְעֵת עֶרֶב וְהִנֵּה יא
עֲלֵה־זַיִת טָרָף בְּפִיהָ וַיֵּדַע נֹחַ כִּי־קַלּוּ הַמַּיִם מֵעַל
הָאָרֶץ ‏ וַיִּיָּחֶל עוֹד שִׁבְעַת יָמִים אֲחֵרִים וַיְשַׁלַּח יב
אֶת־הַיּוֹנָה וְלֹא־יָסְפָה שׁוּב־אֵלָיו עוֹד ‏ וַיְהִי בְּאַחַת יג
וְשֵׁשׁ־מֵאוֹת שָׁנָה בָּרִאשׁוֹן בְּאֶחָד לַחֹדֶשׁ חָרְבוּ
הַמַּיִם מֵעַל הָאָרֶץ וַיָּסַר נֹחַ אֶת־מִכְסֵה הַתֵּבָה וַיַּרְא
וְהִנֵּה חָרְבוּ פְּנֵי הָאֲדָמָה ‏ וּבַחֹדֶשׁ הַשֵּׁנִי בְּשִׁבְעָה יד
וְעֶשְׂרִים יוֹם לַחֹדֶשׁ יָבְשָׁה הָאָרֶץ ‏
וַיְדַבֵּר אֱלֹהִים אֶל־נֹחַ לֵאמֹר ‏ טו
צֵא מִן־הַתֵּבָה אַתָּה וְאִשְׁתְּךָ וּבָנֶיךָ וּנְשֵׁי־בָנֶיךָ אִתָּךְ ‏ טז

Latin text

Et deleuit omnem substantiam quæ erat su
per terram, ab homine vsque ad pecus, tam re-
ptile, quàm volucres cæli: & deletæ sunt de
terra. Remansit autem solus Noe, & qui cum
eo erant in arca. Obtinueruntq; aquæ terrã
centum quinquaginta diebus. CAP. VIII.

A Recordatus autem Deus Noe, cunctorum-
que animantium, & omnium iumento-
rum quæ erant cum eo in arca: adduxit spiri-
tum super terram,& imminutæ sunt aquæ:
Et clausi sunt fontes abyssi,& cataractæ cæli: & prohibitæ sunt pluuiæ de cælo. Reuer-
sæque sunt aquæ de terra, euntes & redeuntes:
& cœperunt minui póst centum quinquagin
ta dies. Requieuitque arca mense septimo,
vicesimoseptimo die mensis super montes Ar-
meniæ. At verò aquæ ibant & decrescebát
vsque ad decimum mensem. Decimo enim
mense, prima die mensis, apparuerunt cacu-
mina montium. Cumque transissent qua-
draginta dies, aperiens Noe fenestram arcæ
quam fecerat, Dimisit coruum, qui egre-
diebatur & reuertebatur, donec siccarétur a-
quæ super terram. Emisit quoque colum-
B bam post eũ, vt videret si iam cessassent aquæ
super faciem terræ. Quæ cùm non inue-
nisset vbi requiesceret pes eius, reuersa est ad
eum in arcam. Aquæ enim erant super vniuer
sam terram. Extenditque manum suam, & ap
prehensam intulit in arcã. Expectatis autẽ vl
tra septé diebus aliis, rursum dimisit columbã
ex arca. At illa venit ad eũ ad vesperã, portans
ramũ oliuæ virentibus foliis in ore suo. Intel-
lexit ergo Noe q̃ cessassent aquæ super terrã.
Expectauitq; nihilominus septé alios dies, &
emisit colũbã, quæ nõ est reuersa vltra ad eũ.
Igitur sexcentesimo primo anno, primo men
C se, prima die mensis, imminutæ sunt aquæ super terram. Et aperiens Noe tectum arcæ, a-
spexit, viditque quòd exiccata esset superfi-
cies terræ. Mense secundo, septimo & vicesi-
mo die mésis, arefacta est terra. Locutus est au
té De° ad Noe, dicens: Egredere de arca tu, &
vxor tua, filij tui, & vxores filiorũ tuorũ tecũ.

תרגום אונקלוס

וּמְחָא יָת כָּל יְקוּמָא דְעַל אַפֵּי אַרְעָא מֵאֱנָשָׁא עַד בְּעִירָא עַד רִחְשָׁא וְעַד עוֹפָא דִשְׁמַיָּא וְאִתְמְחִיאוּ מִן אַרְעָא וְאִשְׁתְּאַר בְּרַם נֹחַ וְדִעְמֵיהּ כג
בְּתֵיבוֹתָא ‏ וּתְקִיפוּ מַיָּא עַל אַרְעָא מְאָה וְחַמְשִׁין יוֹמִין ‏ כד

ח ‏ וּדְכַר יְיָ יָת נֹחַ וְיָת כָּל חַיְתָא וְיָת כָּל בְּעִירָא דְעִמֵּיהּ בְּתֵיבוֹתָא וְאַעְבַּר יְיָ רוּחָא עַל אַרְעָא וְנָחוּ מַיָּא ‏ וְאִסְתְּכַרוּ מַבּוּעֵי א ב
תְּהוֹמָא וְכַוֵּי שְׁמַיָּא וְאִתְכְּלִי מִטְרָא מִן שְׁמַיָּא ‏ וְתָבוּ מַיָּא מֵעַל אַרְעָא אָזְלִין וְתָיְבִין וַחֲסַרוּ מַיָּא מִסּוֹף מְאָה וְחַמְשִׁין יוֹמִין ‏ ג
וְנָחַת תֵּיבוֹתָא בְּיַרְחָא שְׁבִיעָאָה בְּשִׁבְעַת עַסְרָא יוֹמָא לְיַרְחָא עַל טוּרֵי קַרְדּוּ ‏ וּמַיָּא הֲווֹ אָזְלִין וְחָסְרִין עַד יַרְחָא עֲשִׂירָאָה בַּעֲשִׂירָאָה בְּחַד לְיַרְחָא אִתְחֲזִיאוּ רֵישֵׁי טוּרַיָּא ‏ ד ה
וַהֲוָה מִסּוֹף אַרְבְּעִין יוֹמִין וּפְתַח נֹחַ יָת כַּוַּת תֵּיבוֹתָא דִּי עֲבַד ‏ וְשַׁלַּח יָת עוֹרְבָא וּנְפַק מִיפַּק וְתָאִיב עַד דִּיבִישׁוּ מַיָּא מֵעַל אַרְעָא ‏ ו ז
וְשַׁלַּח יָת יוֹנָה מִלְּוָתֵיהּ לְמִחְזֵי אִם קַלּוּ מַיָּא מֵעַל אַפֵּי אַרְעָא ‏ וְלָא אַשְׁכַּחַת יוֹנָה מְנָח לְפַרְסַת רַגְלַהּ וְתָבַת לְוָתֵיהּ לְתֵיבוֹתָא אֲרֵי מַיָּא עַל אַפֵּי כָל אַרְעָא וְאוֹשִׁיט יְדֵיהּ ח ט
וְנַסְבַהּ וְאָעֵל יָתַהּ לְוָתֵיהּ לְתֵיבוֹתָא ‏ וְאוֹרִיךְ עוֹד שִׁבְעָא יוֹמִין אָחֳרָנִין וְאוֹסִיף שַׁלַּח יָת יוֹנָה מִן תֵּיבוֹתָא ‏ י
וְאָתַת לְוָתֵיהּ יוֹנָה לְעִדָּן רַמְשָׁא וְהָא טַרְפָא דְזֵיתָא תְּבִיר בְּפוּמַהּ וִידַע נֹחַ אֲרֵי קַלּוּ מַיָּא מֵעַל אַרְעָא ‏ יא
וְאוֹרִיךְ עוֹד שִׁבְעָא יוֹמִין אָחֳרָנִין וְשַׁלַּח יָת יוֹנָה וְלָא אוֹסִיפַת לְמֵיתַב לְוָתֵיהּ עוֹד ‏ וַהֲוָה בְּחֲדָא וְשִׁית מְאָה שְׁנִין בְּקַדְמָאָה בְּחַד לְיַרְחָא נְגוּבוּ מַיָּא מֵעַל אַרְעָא וְאַעְדִּי נֹחַ יָת חוֹפָאָה דְתֵיבוֹתָא וַחֲזָא וְהָא נְגוּבוּ אַפֵּי אַרְעָא ‏ יב יג
וּבְיַרְחָא תִנְיָנָא בְּשִׁבְעָא וְעֶסְרִין יוֹמָא לְיַרְחָא יְבֵישַׁת אַרְעָא ‏ וּמַלִּיל יְיָ עִם נֹחַ לְמֵימַר ‏ יד טו
פּוּק מִן תֵּיבוֹתָא אַתְּ וְאִתְּתָךְ וּבְנָךְ וּנְשֵׁי בְנָךְ עִמָּךְ ‏ טז

---

5. Christopher Plantin, Bible, Polyglot, Antwerp, 1569–72, 11" × 16 5/8"
(Photograph courtesy of the Houghton Library, Harvard University)

synthesis of partial, limited modes of experience into a new vision of plenitude. Joyce's printing press comes to participate in a similar dialectic, or perhaps we should say that it initiates and resolves that dialectic. In book 2, chapter 1, Joyce describes the *Wake* as the "book of the opening of the mind to light" (258.31–32). This is his version of Blake's goal of cleansing the doors of human perception, and this enlightenment is couched in the language of "the tree" and "the stone," those contraries of inanimate and animate nature that remind us that life and death underlie the least manifestation of change: "Till tree from tree, tree among trees, tree over tree become stone to stone, stone between stones, stone under stone for ever" (259.01–02). Joyce's printing press embodies both contraries; for in early letterpress printing, the impression was always made between wood and stone. The press stone is the bed on which the letter forms lie locked into a frame, and the braces of the press that bring the platen down for the impression on paper are themselves made of wood. Joyce calls our attention to the identity of book, tree, and stone many times, but perhaps his clearest rendering of the printing process occurs when he tells us that "the elm . . . whimpers at the top [to] the stone that moans when stricken" (94.04–05). This describes the making of a letterpress book on an early platen press. As page after page is rendered in the press, Joyce reminds us that such leaves are "pages of nature's book" (57.31) as well as incidents in cultural history, that the work that issues from the composing stone of his imagination issues, finally, in the tree of life.

Notes

1. For an excellent discussion of this, see Morris Eaves, "Blake and the Artistic Machine: An Essay in Decorum and Technology."

2. See Lucien Febvre and Henri-Jean Martin, *The Coming of the Book: The Impact of Printing 1450–1800,* and Elizabeth Eisenstein, "The Advent of Printing and the Problem of the Renaissance" and "Some Conjectures about the Impact of Printing on Western Society and Thought."

3. "We should note the force, effect, and consequences of inventions which are nowhere more conspicuous than in those three which were unknown to the ancients, namely printing, gunpowder, and the compass. For these three have changed the appearance and state of the whole world" (Eisenstein 1).

Works Cited

Blake, William. "The Marriage of Heaven and Hell." In *Blake: Complete Writings,* ed. Geoffrey Keynes. London: Oxford University Press, 1971.

Bloom, Harold. "Dialectic in *The Marriage of Heaven and Hell.*" In *English Romantic Poets,* ed. M. H. Abrams. London: Oxford University Press, 1960.

Eaves, Morris. "Blake and the Artistic Machine: An Essay in Decorum and Technology." *PMLA* 92.5 (October 1977): 903–27.

Eisenstein, Elizabeth. "The Advent of Printing and the Problem of the Renaissance." *Past and Present* 45: 19–89.

———. "Some Conjectures about the Impact of Printing on Western Society and Thought." *The Journal of Modern History* 40 (1968): 1–56.

Febvre, Lucien, and Henri-Jean Martin. *The Coming of the Book: The Impact of Printing 1450–1800*. Tr. David Gerard. London: NLB, 1976.

Kenner, Hugh. "The Computerized *Ulysses*." *Harpers* (April 1980).

Sullivan, Sir Edward. *The Book of Kells*. London: The Studio Publications, 1914.

Finnegans Wake: The Passage toward Pentecost

Beryl Schlossman

From the first leap of *pesah* beginning the wandering of the Jews, the paschal celebration can be read as a nocturnal passage. The language of Passover and Easter makes a biblical entrance into infinity, by passing toward eschatology, that is, the visionary, prophetical dimension brought about by the apocalyptical break with the temporal world. As with the Four Last Things, the apocalypse determines the relation between the speaking subject and God—the rupture with the temporal has eternally infinite consequences. Pentecost, which falls fifty days after Passover or Easter, institutes the return of the Holy Spirit as God's gift to man: thus the intransitive passage, rather than ending, culminates in a passing on, a transmission. This *passing on* gives Pentecost its specific symbolic dimension, crowning the paschal cycle.

The Judaic Pentecost constitutes a condensation of multiple meanings. Consequently, the holiday had many names: the Festival of the Fiftieth Day, the Harvest Festival, the Feast of Weeks, the Day of First Fruits (*The Jewish Encyclopedia* 592–94). Pentecost ends the paschal period. In the process of Judaic adaptation of pre-Judaic ritual, Pentecost became the anniversary of the giving of the Law on Mount Sinai. In the apocryphal book of Jubilees as well as in the biblical book of Chronicles, Pentecost is again associated with the Alliance of Mount Sinai. After the second century A.D., official Judaism considered Pentecost as the festival of the giving of the Law (Delcor 865–67). According to the *Zohar,* the time between Passover and Pentecost constitutes "the courting days of the bridegroom Israel with the bride Torah."

According to rabbinical commentaries and apocryphal writings, Pentecost plays an important role as festival of revelation. The dramatizations of this revelation underline the importance of the voice of God giving the Law: his word is multiplied, disseminated, in a plurality of languages. The holy word is given to a multiple, universal ear. Rabbinical literature records a tradition stating that when God gave the Law on Mount Sinai, his voice was heard by all nations, dividing itself in as many languages as there were peoples. Rabbi Johanan writes: "Each word coming out of the mouth of the Almighty was apportioned into 70 tongues, such that each people heard the divine commandment in its own tongue" (*The Jewish Encyclopedia* 594).

Philo Judaeus recounts a midrashic tradition relating to the Revelation on Mount Sinai: "To their surprise, a voice was heard coming from the fire flowing from the sky: the flame became words articulated in the language familiar to the hearers, and what was said was so clear and distinct that they seemed to see it rather than hear it" (*De Decalogo* 46–47, quoted by Delcor). The voice heard on Mount Sinai becomes visible at Pentecost: according to the *midrash*, the Revelation takes the form of tongues of flame. The voice aflame with infinite languages, the luminous word, becomes a multiple illumination, a dream-image in which language unfolds as poly-theophany, as mystical vision. Philo Judaeus evokes the articulation and clarity of the spoken word which exceed the invisibility of hearing. But what would a visible voice be? An illumination of darkness, jubilation of the ineffable verb, heard by the infinite ear of the subject. From language singular to the infinite plurality of languages, sublimated enjoyment or *jouissance* is displaced toward the visible: the flames in which God voices his appearance, the creation of the Word written in fire function as divine signatures. It is written in the *Zohar* (literally, "the Book of Splendor") that the word in its infinite dimensions shines with a holy light (Scholem). The mystical word resonates with the mysteries of the letter and of signification.

The Christian Pentecost as described in Acts 2 appropriates the tongues of flame of the *midrash*, the descent of the Holy Spirit, the plurality of tongues. It is thought that Luke knew Philo's *midrash*. In the *Supplément au Dictionnaire de la Bible*, Delcor quotes Elbogen: "The festival of Weeks was surely known as festival of Revelation, and the effusion of the Holy Spirit in the Acts of the Apostles is merely a return to the Old Revelation" (875–76). In the New Testament, Pentecost takes place on the same day as the Jewish Pentecost, a festival of thanksgiving: fifty days after the Re-demption, the evangelical harvest takes effect. The gift of the Law on Sinai is repeated in the gift of the New Law. The church begins in Jerusalem the apostolate foreseen by Christ. Pentecost is second only to the Resurrection in liturgical importance, and concludes the Easter cycle.

Its liturgy overflows with joyous exclamations, hallelujahs, evocations of light and of the wonders of the Holy Spirit. Tertullian writes that Pentecost records God's *exaltation*, and "the pascal gift of Christ" (*De Baptisma* 19 in Casel 41–43). Hippolytus defines Easter as the memory of *immolation* and Pentecost as the mystery of *exaltation*, related to the Ascension (*Sur Elcana et Anne* in Casel 50). While indicating the link between the two Pentecosts, patristic tradition relegated the Judaic Pentecost to the status of *figure*.

Formerly, Pentecost was celebrated as a night watch. According to Tertullian, parousia is the object of Pentecost; the second coming of Christ operates as gift, message, excess of love, overflow of language singular into languages plural. In the early church, Pentecost was dramatized: during the Sequence, masses of red roses were spilled down from the vault; a dove flew, a trumpet was sounded, as reminder of the shofar on Mount Sinai and the great noise at the descent of the Holy Spirit on the Apostles ("Exposé liturgique: Pentecôte" in Lefebvre 1200–1201). Pentecost is the *presence* of the Word, reunited with the Father: this presence is transmitted by the tongues of fire. The form taken by the Holy Spirit is the pluralized gift of languages.

In Joyce's writing, the transmission of tongues in the offering of grace assures the symbolic experience of *passage*. Joyce's reading of the Judeo-Christian tradition focuses on Pentecost as its symbolic core: as a paschal culmination, enabling him to position himself within the plurality of tongues. Joyce's Judaic wandering through what was previously an *impasse*, the Red Sea of languages, leads him toward a personalized multiple language spoken in tongues, *given:* "sprakin sea Djoytsche" (*FW* 485.10), "speaking Joyce."

Joyce's Pentecost is anchored in Judaic symbolism. At nightfall, at the end of the "Mime" chapter, Joyce marks a return to nocturnal language with two pages of allusions to Jewish holiday and liturgy. The chapter is compared to a *fable* which is "lissaned out, the threads simwhat toran and knots in its antargumends" (245.9 10). The text is a woven net of knotted threads, a fishnet to catch names with: *simchat Torah,* literally, the "Rejoicing of the Law," is the Jewish holiday related to Pentecost. Joyce names himself as Torah, Law and text, the reading of which ends and begins again on this holiday. The gift of the Law to Moses is celebrated; and Joyce displaces this celebration toward his own gift of tongues in the evocation of the *targum,* Aramaic translations of the Torah, poetic variations on the Holy Text (Epstein 150–68). Joyce's writing, like the Kabbalists' reading of Torah, is a weave of names, a living network of the different names of God.

The Jewish context of Pentecost is named as "Yuddanfest" (*FW* 82.36) in book 1, chapter 4, and then doubled by its Christian repetition, that is, *tripled* in the J. J. and S. desired by the cad. The Pentecost described in Acts is a trinitarian production: Joyce's position in the eucharistic formula of John Jameson and Son is displaced to Shem, who pronounces a series of names of the pubs in which he will spend the money given him by HCE. The shofar, or ram's horn, of the Revelation on Mount Sinai can be heard. Shem's mystical enjoyment goes beyond the affirmative meaning of a single language: he is heard "remarxing in languidoily, seemingly much more highly pleased than tongue could tell" (83.15). He speaks in tongues: "in the Nichtian glossery which purveys aprioric roots for aposteriorious tongues this is nat language at any sinse of the world"(83.10). The tongues of fire sent to the apostles after the Resurrection are "aposteriorious tongues": the "aprioric roots" of the Word, the hebraic roots of Shem's "root language," become infinite, eucharistically divided into the seventy tongues of the Revelation.

Shem's "Nichtian glossery," his "nat language" indicate Shem's refusal of the community of messages, the community of institutions, as well as the community's negative reply: like the mocking witnesses of the apostles' Pentecost in Acts 2, the community, personified by Shaun, excludes Shem's "root language" from its dictionary (424.17).[1] But Shem's strategy of negativity operates in his nocturnal language: and here Joyce stresses a dual liturgical reference, from the pillar of fire in the desert and the light of Exodus to the night watch of Holy Saturday and Pentecost: "daylit dielate night of nights" (83.27).

In this text, we hear the negativity of a language in *passage,* its confrontation with "sins of the world." The Jews break with paganism, expel themselves from Egypt; they enter a symbolic night, the Holy Name calling them toward the Torah: night language in any sense of God's Word. That other world, without end. Joyce played on this in *Ulysses,* when "word" slipped to "world," bearing the darkness of sexuality, as far as Bloom's passage was concerned (*U* 77). In the *Wake,* the Word bursts forth from darkness, "sins of the world," in Shem's discourse.

Shem's negative language speaks the underside of the gift of tongues, and dissolves the world's abjection: *felix culpa.* Joyce dissolves his language as well: eclipsed, it will spring forth as the gift of tongues, as the multiple voices of the pentecostal enunciation. The nocturnal language is a mosaic of the Word, a space in which flaming luminous bursts of languages work their passage into writing.

Shaun's sermon focuses on the Judeo-Christian Pentecost: "what a lawful day it was, there and then, for a consommation with an effusion" (*FW* 432.13–14). Shaun as priest explicitly refers to the Trinitarian Pentecost: the revelation of the Law, the consummation of the Word, and the effusion of the Holy Spirit. Undone by his own desire, Shaun betrays the Catholic preoccupation with concupiscence: Whitsuntide is specified as "several sindays after whatsintime" (432.33). Sin exceeds the limits of language; however, grace, the only possible Catholic absorption of sin, functions as an excess of languages, and entrance into their infinity, an effusion echoing that experienced by the apostles. Joyce celebrates Shaun's sacred and comic effusion, in the exclamations of wind, *ruah,* glory and voice; Shaun's "breadth," both breathing and eucharistic bread, echoes the beginning of Hopkins's "Wreck of the Deutschland": "Thou mastering me / God! giver of breath and bread."

The passage of Pentecost is located at the meeting point of flesh not yet sublime and the poetic word of love. After Shaun's sermon Joyce echoes the end of *Giacomo Joyce,* in Shaun's condemnation of Shem and the seductions of his writing: "the wring wrong way to *wright woman.* Shuck her! Let him! *What he's good for.* . . . Could you wheedle a staveling encore out of your imitationer's jubalharp, hey, Mr Jinglejoys?" (*FW* 466.15, italics mine).[2] At the confluence of sexual *jouissance* and scriptural sublimation, Joyce signs his holy name of transmission, in the figuration of Giacomo become Shem.

HCE's paschal death is announced in connection with Pentecost in order to suggest that Joyce's languages are being crucified. His obituary reads: "after a lenty illness the roeverand Mr Easterling of pentecostitis" (130.8–9). His pentecostal death is prelude to the Resurrection in tongues, actualized in a thousand and one ways in the Joycean text—and particularly in book 4. The writing of the Letter is Shem's operation of the resurrection in tongues. Shem functions in the *Wake* as the metaphorization of Joyce's relationship to his own textual act: *his written version of the gift of tongues.* From Easter to Pentecost, Shem is the holy parody, the "divine comic Denti Alligator" (440.6) of the Judaic, Irish writer: in Hebrew, *name;* in Gaelic, *James:* Shem.

Joyce transforms language into tongues of flame: Shem's writing functions as a Pentecost of language. In book 1, chapter 7, of the *Wake* Joyce emphasizes the paschal character of Shem's writing. As symbol of resurrection, spiritual nourishment eaten in thanksgiving and blessed on Easter Sunday, Shem's Easter eggs become the symbol of his writing: "chanting . . . his cantraps of fermented words . . . (his oewfs a la Madame Gabrielle de l'Eglise . . . his soufflosion of oogs . . . his Frideggs a la Tricareme" [184.24]). The Annunciation, Good Friday, and the effusion of the Holy Spirit on Pentecost are evoked in connection with Shem's fermented words. This catalogue of scriptural cuisine follows a description of Shem's floors, walls, gate posts, and lintels, covered with writing like those in Exodus. This writing traces the leap of the Exterminating Angel through the Word, "alphybettyformed verbage," and the Holy Spirit, "puffers" (183.13, 12). This disguised holy presence raises the question of the Trinity within monotheistic language: "imeffible tries at speech unasyllabled" (183.14). The triune God is evoked via *shem,* the name as divine and messianic. This name, encoded by the Tetragrammaton as the one true name of God, plays a mystical role in Judaism. Gershom Scholem writes: "the name with which God designates Himself and with which he can be invoked removes itself from the acoustical sphere and becomes unpronounceable." This name "returns to the domaine of the ineffable" ("Le Nom de Dieu" 66). From the third century on, the newly unpronounceable Tetragrammaton is paradoxically called *Shem ha-meforash,* the *pronounced* yet *hidden* name, the *secret* name. As *Shem ha-meforash,* The Name of God vacillates between the virtual infinity of the name as ineffable, forbidden, and the creative identity of the name as signifying condensation which bursts forth in a Pentecostal revelation. According to *haggadah,* the Torah was written in black fire on white fire: before the tongues of fire there was the Law traced in fire, an infinite nomination. Its revelation is always to come, for the mystical Torah is written in the invisible forms of white light ("Le Nom de Dieu" 77–78 and Scholem 51, 62, 63). Writing itself approaches the ineffable as the invisible Revelation of forms, letters, names, significance.

It is in writing that Shem is named: the infinite Name is written as the virtuality of tongues. Shem covers the walls with fragments, souvenirs of *passage*—Exodus, the crucifixion, the Eucharist: "lees of whine," "broken wafers" (*FW* 183.32–34). The Eucharist echoes the ineffable name of the Kabbalists in that it acts as an invisible gift of infinity, which the sacrament renders metaphorical. Saint Augustine writes on the subject of "daily bread" that one should "ask for the bread necessary to the body, the visible consecrated bread, and the invisible bread of the Word of God" (*De Sermone Domini in monte* 2:26). This invisible mystery of the Eucharistic word can be observed through another of Shem's possessions: "Magnifying wine-glasses" (*FW* 183.21). Wineglass lenses, spectacles of the *Magnificat,* allude to the Annunciation: in receiving the Holy Spirit, the Virgin exalts God. And the "magnifying wineglasses" evoke the Pentecost of the Apostles, speaking in tongues of God's magnificence: they are accused of being drunk on sweet wine. Shem's "cantraps of fermented words," his naming in tongues and his magnification of God, stem from a reading of *invisibilia* through the magnifying drunkenness of the tongues of flame.

The reading/writing of consecrated wine as the radiant body of Christ, of the gift of tongues rendered visible, is summed up by Saint Athanasius: Pentecost is "the new wine that is the Holy Spirit" ("Première lettre pascal" in Casel 84). Shem's Pentecost, his scriptural passage toward art, is the eucharistic excess of languages.

Shem writes on his own body as *accident,* or species of the Eucharist: he is "transaccidentated." He is "writing the mystery of himsel in furniture" (*FW* 186.3–4; 184.9–10). The "el" of himself is heard later as an Old Testament name of God: and the *mystery* locates Shem's writing within the dimensions of the Catholic sacrament. According to Saint Augustine, the sacrament of the Eucharist is the result of "mystical prayer": the mystical dimension of the ritual word is due to "transformations of matter" into body and blood of Christ. These changes occur only because discourse opens out toward what Aquinas will later call the "infinite agent" of eucharistic conversion. Augustine emphasizes the invisible, immutable power of the Holy Ghost, an extension of the ineffable Tetragrammaton. In *On The Trinity,* Augustine writes: "when human hands have taken its visible appearance, the consecration which makes of this appearance such a great sacrament, comes only from the invisible action of the Spirit of God" (L.III, C.IV 10). Joyce writes this mystery as "something supernoc-tural" (*FW* 598.17). Shem's "mystery of himsel in furniture" is the writing of this mystery in the furnishings of language, the "persianly literatured" interior of the exile. Languages named in affirmation counterpoint the holy passage through negativity: "seedy ejaculations," "fresh horrors from Hades," with an ecstatic gesture, recalling Penelope: "ahs ohs ouis sis jas jos gias neys thaws sos, yeses and yeses and yeses" (183.23, 35; 184.1–2). The only gift we can receive as exiles: languages. And the tetragrammatic subject reveals itself as the mystery to be written, in the tongues appropriated as art: "his usylessly unreadable Blue Book of Eccles, *édition de ténèbres*" (179.26–7), darkness bringing forth light.

Shem rewrites this passage toward language of *Exodus*, named in Hebrew: *Shemot*, or "Names." Joyce turns to mysticism when he creates the Name as the center of language, the heart of sacred textuality. According to Nachmanides, Torah "is not only composed of names of God but in reality forms as a whole the single sublime name of God" (Scholem 52). According to Josef Gikatilla, Torah is the *explanation* of the Tetragrammaton (Scholem 55); the Torah is *woven* of the name of God.

The Torah is the text of the Tetragrammaton, the visible and invisible signifying leitmotif—like the name of Joyce, passing through all of *Finnegans Wake*. One could attribute this mystical quality to a whole series of names in the *Wake:* the invisible, ineffable proper name lends its subjective presence to multiple inscriptions. As a condensed form of the subject's symbolic power, the permutations of the proper name in the *Wake* maintain the relationship between the subject's language and its infinitely signifying revelation, which exceeds any closed reading. Joyce enters this realm of revelation in the act of multiple naming: Art, the gift of tongues, is also, according to Shem, the gift of names, "shemeries," fabricated by the "alshemist." He copies signatures, he *transnames,* making his passage through names: "In the name of" (*FW* 185.34; 187.35; 181; 145.21; 147.9). For Joyce, the name indicates the irreducible presence of the subject able to say "I AM," with a tetragrammatical gesture; this sets off the weaving of the Torah. The Pentecost of *Finnegans Wake* delivers the Torah of the name of Joyce in tongues. Shem's Letter is the figure of this text: gift, missive, amorous excess, overflow of language singular into the plural *jouissance* of the symbolic.

The subject of the Name is singularly sacred: he is vocatively present, in the performative act of naming. But what generates the divine, infinite quality of the Name? For John Stuart Mill names are "meaningless marks" (*System of Logic,* in Gardiner 1). A. H. Gardiner develops this hypothesis, insisting on the importance of the *referent* of the proper name and eliminating the signified. The privileged signifier remains, and the identification it accomplishes: "A proper name is a word or group of words which is recognized as having identification as its specific purpose, and which achieves, or tends to achieve, that purpose by means of its distinctive sound alone, without regard to any meaning possessed by that sound from the start or acquired by it through association with the object or objects thereby identified" ("Retrospect," in Gardiner 73).

Whereas most words "directly convey information," that is, function as *message,* proper names refer back to the *code,* or language as system, virtuality, structure. Gardiner writes: "Proper names merely provide the key to information" (Gardiner 75). The name is the key, source, warranty of language: Kabbalists would say that the Holy Name is the origin of language. The proper name anchors the subject in linguistic virtuality with a signifier, a mark, a letter: the name takes on the virtuality of language as an excess of symbolic meaning; what it signifies is the singular being, incommunicable outside of the proper name. The Kabbalists say the proper name goes beyond meaning yet makes meaning possible: bereft of a specific significance, the proper name is comparable to the divine word of mystical revelation, to the holy letter of the signature of the finger of God—an infinite "I AM," echoed by Bloom on the beach in "Nausicaa."

At Pentecost, the tongues of the Holy Spirit are rendered *visible;* for Joyce, Pentecost implies the visibility of the *Name.* When Shaun condemns Shem's "root language," he evokes the hundred-lettered Holy Name, the Kabbalists' culmination of *Shem ha-meforash.* The name withdrawn from pronunciation is infinitely serialized as the last name of a hundred letters rejoins the first name, the Tetragrammaton: "yav hace not one pronounceable teerm . . . to signify majestate." "Thor's for yo!—The hundredlettered name again, last word of perfect language!" (*FW* 478.11–12; 424.22–4). The infinitized name, last "wholly words" of Shemese (424.33) brings into relief the dissemination of the letter, dispersing its Mallarméan trace across the pages of *Finnegans Wake.* The "root language" suggests Hebrew, the language of revelation: in the passage toward Pentecost, Joyce sends his Name, his Letter, in the writing of a new tongue of Revelation. The roots hce and alp, the "trilitter"s, make of this Joycean enunciation a language of proper names, figured in illuminated monograms: art, the gift of tongues.

Notes

1. See *FW* 415.29–31, the Ondt's exclusion ("Nixnixundnix") of the Gracehoper: "he is not on our social list."
2. See *GJ* 16: "Write it, damn you, write it! What else are you good for?"

Works Cited

Augustine. *De Trinitate.* Paris: du Cerf, 1966.
Delcor, M. "Pentecôte." *Supplément au Dictionnaire de la Bible* 7. Paris: Letouzey et Ané, 1966.

Epstein, I. *Le Judaisme*. Paris: Payot, 1959.

Gardiner, Sir A. H. *The Theory of Proper Names*. 2nd Ed. London: Oxford University Press, 1954.

The Jewish Encyclopedia 9, 592–94. New York: Funk & Wagnalls, 1905.

Lefebvre, Dom G. *Missel quotidien et vesperal*. Bruges: Apostolat Liturgique, 1942.

"Le Nom de Dieu." *Diogène* 79. Paris: Gallimard, 1972.

Scholem, G. *La Kabbale et sa symbolique*. Paris: Payot, 1975.

Tertullian. *De Baptismo* 19. In O. Casel, *La Fête de Pâques dans L'Eglise des peres*. Paris: du Cerf, 1963.

"Mixing Memory and Desire": The "Tristan and Iseult" Chapter in *Finnegans Wake*

Margot Norris

A discussion of theme in *Finnegans Wake* raises a number of theoretical questions at the outset, and I therefore think it best to begin by putting my own particular critical biases on the line. If by "theme" we mean more than just "topic"—if we extend the term to encompass the donnée of a text—then I would argue that in a dream work like *Finnegans Wake,* the themes are perforce ontological and psychological. They are statements not only about what it *means* to be human, but also what it *feels* to be human. Sigmund Freud himself announced the grand theme of all dreams: since all dreams are wish fulfillments, their theme is *desire.* In *Finnegans Wake* we can see this shifting play of desire readily enough. The four chapters of book 2, for example, reflect the numerous permutations of desire among young and old, among parents, children, and siblings. It would be only a little reductive to argue that chapter 1, the "Mime," depicts the desire of children directed toward other children; chapter 2, the homework chapter, the desire of children toward adults or parents; chapter 3, the tavern episode, the interactions of adult desire; and chapter 4, the Tristan and Iseult chapter, the desire of adults directed toward the young. But I believe the predominant focus of *Finnegans Wake* is old age, and that Joyce's books follow the arc of Vico's cycles of personal history, with *Portrait,* the book of youth, corresponding to Viconian birth; *Ulysses,* the book of maturity, corresponding to Viconian marriage; *Finnegans Wake,* the book of old age, corresponding to Viconian burial; and *Dubliners*—with its careful trajectory through all the ages and conditions of its citizens—representing the recorso. I will therefore focus on book 2, chapter 4—the Tristan and Iseult chapter—in order to explore themes indigenous to old age, the theme of loss and dispossession, and of the imperishability of desire.

Now if this section were really about Tristan and Iseult—or at least presented a romance of passion, love potions, betrayals, ruses and entrapments—think what an anomaly that would represent in Joyce's *oeuvre!* Like it or not, we don't get much romance in Joyce's work (although we cherish what we get). The two unforgettable instances in the earlier works—Michael Furey under the dripping tree outside Gretta Conroy's window, and Molly and Bloom amid the rhododendrons on Howth Head—are both historicized events, distanced by time and restored to us as nostalgic memories erupting into the mid-life crises of prosaic and domestic marriages. Furthermore, in the *Wake,* as in "The Dead," the lover's point of view is usurped by an outsider, a jealous husband like Gabriel Conroy or King Mark, or by voyeurs whose coign of vantage is curiously like our own as readers—"their pair of green eyes and peering in, so they say, like the narcolepts on the lakes of Coma, through the steamy windows, into the honeymoon cabins" (395.7–9). Wakean romance is mediated by time and perspective; it is historicized and vicarious, reclaimed as a negative value—as something lost, something desired, something elusive.

The theme of loss in the "Tristan" chapter is expressed in the maudlin rhetoric of pity and self-pity dispersed throughout the discourse—"there was poor Matt Gregory" (386.13), "poor Johnny of the clan of Dougals, the poor Scuitsman" (391.4), "and poor Mark or Marcus Bowandcourt" (391.13–14), and "Poor Andrew Martin Cunningham" (393.5)—and accompanied by the sentimental strains of *Auld Lang Syne.* But the matter lost can be specified more precisely if we collate the four accounts we received from "Mamalujo," and attend to the recurring elements. There are quite a number, but perhaps two of the most conspicuous are "colleges" and "auctions" of which William York Tindall writes, "Colleges and auctions, by which they are obsessed, imply collection and dispersal" (213). Roland McHugh provides us with a less abstract connection between colleges and auctions, which sometimes occur connected in the text as "the auctions of the valuable colleges" (*FW* 386.23). He glosses "Chichester College auction" (390.18) as "In 1700 the lands of Ir. Jacobites publicly auctioned at Chichester House, College Green (subsequently replaced by Parliament building)" (390), an explanation that provides a political and nationalistic variant to the theme of loss in this chapter. But I wish to recall another instance where college and auction occur contiguously—Simon and Stephen Dedalus's trip to Cork in chapter 2 of *Portrait*—to explore the more personal and psychological measure of loss at issue.

Joyce presents this trip to Cork entirely from the son's point of view—Stephen unmoved by his father's nostalgic sentimental journey and embarrassed by his boastfulness and weakness. But in one of the many remarkable instances where the *Wake* reinterprets the earlier work and gives us a new perspective on a familiar scene—the "Tristan" chapter encourages us to revisit Cork from Simon's point of view, and to drink with him (uncontaminated by his son's emotional aridity) the bittersweet cup of kindness and memory. Stephen is right, of course, to be bitter; the auction dispossesses him of his birthright. But Simon is stripped of far more than his worldly goods on this sojourn; the visit to Queen's College, the conversations at cross-purposes with old acquaintances—these divest him also of his youth. For Simon, unlike Stephen, college signified not education and learning, but "the pleasure of companionship" and "the vigor of rude male health" (*P* 96). The *Wake* reflects just these aspects of college life—memories of racetracks ("the whole yaghoodurt sweepstakings and all the horsepowers" [387.10–11]), fast horses, fast cars, and fast women (that is, Issy described as a thoroughbred, or a night*mare,* of sorts—"so and so hands high, such and such paddock weight" [396.8–9]). Among the memories of former glories, Simon can count a wholesome and lusty sexuality ("Your father," said the little old man to Stephen, "was the boldest flirt in the city of Cork in his day" [*P* 94]) that in later life degenerates into clumsy and ineffectual coquettry with barmaids like Mina and Lydia in the Ormond bar. The "Tristan" chapter contains numerous echoes of the trip to Cork, including references to Queen's College (albeit the one in Ulster), and "Queen's Colleges," presumably including the one in Cork which is Simon's alma mater. In the song's closing line, "Mick, Nick the Maggot or whatever your name is" (*FW* 399.26–27), the four old men's vagueness and imprecision in naming things, a serious handicap for historians, echoes Simon Dedalus's analogous forgetfulness—"Here, Tim or Tom or whatever your name is, give us the same here again" (*P* 95).

Simon Dedalus also provides a clue to the familial and marital ambiguities of the four old men, if not to their curiously androgynous epithets—"four dear old heladies" (*FW* 386.15–16), or "four (up) beautiful sister misters" (393.17), for example. The four are described throughout in contexts that augur familial and marital dissolution—"all now united, sansfamillias" (398.11), "the four middleaged widowers" (390.13–14), "they were all summarily divorced four years before, or so they say, by their dear poor shehusbands" (390.19–20), and so on. If we consider for a moment Simon Dedalus and his companions in the coach on the way to Glasnevin, we note that they are all family men trapped in a marital limbo—Dedalus widowed, Bloom impotent and cuckolded, Cunningham married to an unsuitable drunkard, and Power keeping a woman on the side. (Martin Cunningham is also mentioned several times in the "Tristan" chapter as a drowned man). I would argue that these men (in this and other combinations) function as plausible prototypes for the four old men in the *Wake.* They are solid burghers who chronicle Dublin gossip and history, render judgments, and appoint themselves (with some hypocrisy) the guardians of probity—as in the *Dubliners* story "Grace," where they conspire to save Tom Kernan's soul and family life. *Grace* is a major verbal motif in the "Tristan" chapter—"preventing grace, forgetting to say their grace . . . so pass the poghue for grace sake" (395.21–24).

As historians, evangelists, or witnesses, the four old men leave something to be desired. Instead of corroborating accounts—the very function of the synoptic gospels—their tales produce curious variations, if not outright contradictions and discrepancies. For example, there are three references to "sycamores" in the chapter, but they seem to mean something slightly different each time—first (383.1), a tree where birds gather, including the four old men who are introduced as birds of augury, like Stephen's in *Portrait;* second, the tree under which "scandalous and very wrong" love-making transpires (388.23–24); and finally, we hear "they were all sycamore and by the world forgot" (397.23–24), where the reference is no longer to a tree but to illness. I would like to hazard an interpretation of the "syca-more" that is difficult to corroborate philologically, but for which an interesting contextual case can be made that would link the old men's lust, voyeurism, censoriousness, hypocrisy, and unreliability as witnesses—par-ticularly as synoptic witnesses ("falling over all synopticals" [394.05–6]). Although the trees in question in the Biblical account are a mastic and an oak tree, the four old men in the *Wake* have much in common with the two Elders in the Book of Daniel, who, when they fail to seduce the beautiful young Susannah, accuse her of having lain with a young man in the orchard. This would make their function analogous with that of the four old felons of Bedier's version of Tristan and Iseult, who spy on the lovers for King Mark. Only their perjury as witnesses would be added to the "hesitancy" motif of the Pigott letter that recurs throughout the *Wake*— and the love-making of Tristan and Iseult ("a seatuition so shocking and scandalous" [385.30–31]) would be no more than a fantasy or a lie, pro-duced by their frustrated and impotent desire. During an earlier trial of HCE in chapter 4 of book 1, the same account is produced as a confession: "It was when I was in my farfather out at the west and she and myself, the redheaded girl, firstnighting down Sycomore Lane. Fine feelplay we had of it mid the kissabetts frisking in the kool kurkle dusk of the lushiness" (95.19–23). Yet the uses of "sycamore" by the four old men might yet have the consistency of dream logic. Perhaps the complaint of being more sick— "sycamore"—is simply another expression of desire, a call for the "nurse-tendered hand" (392.9) of the fair Iscult, perhaps of the white hands, whose tradition it is to nurse the wounded Tristan back to health.

The "Tristan" chapter is one of the shortest in the *Wake*, but it has a complicated poetic structure, as many commentators have pointed out, and, I believe, an equally complicated thematic and rhetorical aim. I would argue that Joyce used Arthurian romance (and there are numerous refer-ences to the Guinevere/Lancelot adultery as well) for the same psychological purposes that T. S. Eliot did in *The Waste Land.* Although we know Joyce preferred the Bedier version, Jessie Weston *did* also translate Gottfried von Strassbourg's *Tristan and Iseult* in 1899, and motifs from Wagner's libretto recur both in Eliot's poem and in Joyce's *Wake* chapter. In both works, the romance is intended to represent a gap or a lack in modern life—a spiritual malaise that manifests itself in the aridity of the waste land, or its opposite, the punitive floods in the *Wake.* The sexual impotence of modern fisher kings is expressed in the sexual ambiguity of the four old men, who, like Tiresias, appear punished for their voyeurism with androgyny and clairvoyance, although their memories are bad and their visions distorted. Like Eliot's figures, who suffer from colds and carbuncles, Joyce's old men are afflicted with "phlegmish hoopicough" (397.24), or (ironically) the ingestion of bad fish. And in neither work does hanged god or drowned man (Martin Cunningham or Dion Boucicault, in the *Wake*) appear to effect the spiritual healing, the return of fertility, and the end of vicarious sexuality and Tin Pan Alley romance (the "Tristan" chapter's leitmotif is not only Wagner's *Liebestod,* but also "by she light of the moon, we longed to be spoon, before her honeyoldloom" [385.28]). But *Finnegans Wake is* a country for old men, who may be dead in life, but yet, as historians, are capable of "mixing memory and desire" (*Waste Land,* lines 2–3).

Works Cited

McHugh, Roland. *Annotations to "Finnegans Wake."* Baltimore: Johns Hopkins University Press, 1980.
Tindall, William York. *A Reader's Guide to "Finnegans Wake."* New York: Farrar, Strauss & Giroux, 1969.

Narratology and the Subject of *Finnegans Wake*

Jean-Michel Rabaté

Can it be that most applications of narratology to *Finnegans Wake* result in self-defeating tactics? We generally agree that any theory, while covering a certain field, also designates by its elaboration a gap, an empty space which it attempts to bridge, to fill in, to recover. In the case of the *Wake,* however, the real object of narratology may prove to be the gap itself: in no other text are the indeterminacies of the speaking voice so dense and overwhelming that the reader has only a blurred impression that something is being told, though he cannot ascertain what or by whom. As soon as we try to pinpoint the "events" of a story, it trails off elsewhere, and we have to discover to our surprise that we are in the middle of another narrative. Nevertheless, we retain a constant and insistent feeling that some kind of storytelling is going on in a text which relies so much on speaking voices to tie up all the fragments of such a huge mosaic. In the struggle between the vocal and the visual media, both voice and look destroy or cancel each other out in the end, achieving not a dialectical synthesis, but the most monstrous hybridization of a "soundsense" masquerading as a dream.

True, we know that Joyce originally drafted the early episodes of his *Work in Progress* as simple narratives. Does this imply that a genetic approach may disclose a key to the actual text and not only to the history of its composition? Do the earliest drafts of straightforward stories, those easy pieces around which the rest was slowly to coalesce, contain a kernel of sense, a conceptual mode, which would not only give us an insight into the general design of the book, but also provide a series of relatively fixed meanings, stably anchored behind further proliferation and obfuscation? It was precisely with such questions in mind that I chose a passage which encapsulates a little "story" of a slightly different kind, one which I came across in a notebook dating from 1926. The story remains relatively undeveloped in the draft, and though there are traces of some rewriting, the tentative alternatives do not condense in the final version:

genderless man embraces woman
traderep
orsemarines in an idingplace
orseriders in an idingplace
an idinole

iwood idingole
iroad. (Notebook VI.B.19, 95–96)

When we find this vignette on page 581 of *Finnegans Wake*, it remains recognizable, and the first problem which arises is the extent to which its being framed by a narrative of some sort modifies it, adds new characteristics to it, and more broadly allows it to function as a microunit within the text. In order to understand how this comes into play, it is necessary to situate the whole section taken as its context (*FW* 581.01–582.27). This is the end of the longest cinematographic sequence of book 3, chapter 4, which affords a general overview of the sexuality of Earwicker's family, called Porter here. The chapter heralds the dissolution of human age before the ricorso of book 4, which sees the coming of daylight. It exhibits a strange mixture of uncomplicated language, at times closer to conventional English than any other part of the *Wake,* and of really obscure scenes told from different perspectives, clothed in a juridical idiom, which present a bleak view of love-making but also propose a matrix capable of generating all stories.

This passage is not just another recapitulation of all the characters; it is also an elaborate digression bearing on the fictive nature of the text as such. The reader is no doubt ill at ease, unable to find his "zingaways" among constantly shifting personal pronouns which nevertheless retell the same hackneyed story. The reader must then confront a pure structure, with gaps to be filled and with an accompanying commentary on the sad fate of our incapacity to escape from identity:

> Bloody certainly have we got to see to it ere smellful demise surprends us on this concrete that down the gullies of the eras we may catch ourselves looking forward to what will in no time be staring you larrikins on the postface in that multimirror megaron of returningties, whirled without end to end. So there was a raughty . . . who in Dyfflingsborg did . . . With his soddering iron, spadeaway, hammerlegs and . . . Where there was a fair young . . . Who was playing her game of . . . And said she you rockaby . . . Will you peddle in my bog . . . And he sod her in Iarland, paved her way from Maizenhead to Youghal. And that's how Humpfrey, champion emir, holds his own. Shysweet, she rests. (582.16– 27)

The spaced-out pattern is a direct echo and continuation of "In Amsterdam there lived a . . . But how?" (565.09) in which a narrator is obliged to stop because of the fear he elicits from his auditor who trembles—this is a scene of homosexual seduction, turning the tables on the Cad, no longer Earwicker's attacker, but his friend or son to be won over. The same song marks the opening and the end of the second "position" of discordance in the musical pattern of book 3, chapter 4.[1] Unfinished sentences had already started proliferating in the previous chapter, in which they mimicked the floating voices of a mediumistic trance (486.17–18, 23–25), presented easy riddles (514.18), or provided the corrupted text of an old manuscript (481.2–3). In the instance of the bawdy song quoted here, the gaps can simply be filled in (a raughty tinker / did dwell . . .)[2] since the song is hardly modified.

I started with a story which might have been a conceptual nexus, and I will now deal with a formal matrix, almost devoid of "content," which is only used as a reminder that the reader must do some deciphering in order to make sense of it. *Finnegans Wake* appears hinged between a perpetual recapitulation of what is never fully told, and the anticipation of yet another more complete disclosure. Professor Jones gives a precious hint in an early passage as to the completion of the text by the reader: "This genre of portraiture of changes of mind in order to be truly torse should evoke the bush soul of females so I am leaving it to the experienced victim to complete the general suggestion by the mental addition of a wallopy bound . . ." (165.17–20). In our passage, the wallaby bound cannot help rebounding in the same place, a place in which "shysweet, she rests." This important, humorous transformation of MacMahon's celebrated phrase during the Crimean war, "J'y suis, j'y reste," states the dominant theme of "semper-identity." Yet the expression revealingly modifies the verbal aspect of the sentence, replacing a first person pronoun by a third person one, and in the feminine.

The entire passage is made up of such transformations of subjects. It starts as a report explaining how the population of Dublin—referred to as "they," with a name given now and then "(Big Reilly was the worst)" (581.7)—criticizes a "him" and his family. The anonymous narrator does not reveal an identity but a position in the grammatical scheme when he says "I": "Ah ho! Say no more about it! I'm sorry! I saw. I'm sorry to say I saw!" (581.24–25). The dialogue already implicit in the collective "we" with moving boundaries and mediating between "they" and "him" natu-rally enough creates a second person, implied by the invocation "say no more!" The game the text plays with readers is to have them adopt every subjective position sequentially, moving their places all the time, so that they become Earwicker's fighting sons or schizoid daughter(s): ". . . we may catch *ourselves* looking forward to what will in no time be staring *you* larrikins on the postface in that multimirror megaron of returningties" (582.18–20; italics mine).

I would like to pause a little and reflect on this weird multimirror, which changes "us" into "you." This is no doubt an apt metaphor of the complex textuality of the *Wake,* founded, as we know, on the circularity of history and of matter—in a mixture of Vico, Einstein, and Dunne's serial and reversible universe, which is condensed by "returningties." My contention is that such an apparatus frames the divided subject of desire, a divided subject which becomes the locus of a disjuncture between voices and events.

A firm narratological axiom is the link between voices and events: it has to be used as the basis for the identification of intra- or extra-diegetic narrators, positioned in such and such a way relative to their story. In *Finnegans Wake,* we cannot help asking the old question: "Who speaks there?" but it would be begging too many answers to affirm that the voices we have learned to distinguish are real narrators. This grants them too much continuity and substance, and in the above-quoted passage, it would be of no great help to decide that this is Mark the Evangelist who is acting as narrator. Indeed, the whole second section or "position" seems to belong to him, but we must admit that he is either split up into different sub-narrators, or just a facet of a more composite figure, able to sum Mark up with the other four in "they were all there now, matinmarked for lookin on" (581.21–22).

What is fundamentally at stake behind the ascription of any passage to a narrator is the question of the identity of the subject. If what we have seen in this particular passage does apply to the rest of the book, then we may have to replace the terms we still fondly use when dealing with texts, such as "point of view," "perspective," "narrator," "narratee," and so on, by more radical notions, possibly borrowed from philosophical discourse. The term "subject" will be the moot concept here, since it bears the onus of describing both a syntactical pattern, easily identifiable, and a moving instance of positioning, divided between writing and utterance, prone to becoming the object of its own speech, and the theme of a problematic self-questioning. The split subject tends then to fall back into being an object defined by the shift of verbal patterns, before merging into another voice.

Considered in this light, the narrativity of *Finnegans Wake,* which cannot be denied, becomes exactly what we, as readers, make up in order to escape from the impasses of self-cancelling or mutually excluding alternatives. Narrativity corresponds to our irrepressible effort to bridge the gap between the smaller units which at first appear very promising but which generally frustrate our expectations, and the overall sense of structure, a sense all the more pervasive as we realize that too many structures are superimposed onto a mosaic of discrete items, so that they tend to become all too rewarding for commentators, and, by their very proliferation, become one with the "matter" they were supposed to "inform."

Thus an "imaginary narrative" fulfills the function of mediating between the text and the reader already inscribed within it. The chaos facing us is a "complex matter of pure form" (581.29–30), echoing "the matter is a troublous and a peniloose" (581.01), and exceeds any meaning not predetermined by the Wakean patterns of guilt, trial, original sin as the sin of the origins, and so on. But at the same time, this chaos escapes from the control of first any narrator, then of even the author, since it is only found in an interaction between the structure of the text and our felicitous misreadings:

> Gives there not too amongst us after all events (or so grunts a leading hebdromadary) some togethergush of stillandbutallyouknow that, insofarforth as, all up and down the whole concreation say, efficient first gets there finally every time, as a complex matter of pure form, for those excess and that pasphault hardhearingness from their eldfar, in grippes and rumblions, through fresh taint and old treason, another like that alter but not quite such anander and stillandbut one notall the selfsame and butstillone just the maim and encore emmerhim may always, with a little difference, till the latest up to date so early in the morning, have evertheless been allmade amenable? (581.26–36)

All the "events" alluded to are always behind or before; they remain uncertain since the only certainty is that something happened—could it have been a sexual assault, a murder, a political insurrection, a foreign invasion? The reader can find elements which seem to corroborate each hypothesis in turn. The "events" must be contrasted with the "facts" which are the object of an inquiry, doomed in advance due to lack of certainty: "Thus the unfacts, did we possess them, are too imprecisely few to warrant our certitude, the evidencegivers by legpoll too untrustworthily irreperible . . ." (57.16–19). The "events" are not of the same nature as facts, ficts, and unfacts; they assert that something has happened and will happen again. The sense of a happening, always slightly deferred, is essential to promote the illusion of a performative action accomplished by the reader-in-the-text. It is closer to Heidegger's intuition that ontological difference is articulated by the bounty of the "be" contained in "Being": *Es gibt Sein,* "there-is-being" is a gift, a giving, a disclosure in language; this is here paralleled by the very German pattern of "Gives there not too amongst us after all events. . . ."

The "sameness" of such a pre-ontological giving underlies the recurrence of history, which, as Bloom's story of his encounter with Parnell in the "Eumaeus" episode of *Ulysses* shows, repeats itself with a difference (*U* 654–55). This statement acquires bleaker overtones in the *Wake,* since to "the way of all flesh" a *ricorso storico* adds yet another "age" and a perpetual war, which produces a "carnage." However, the opposites of "love and war" are implied in the theme of a bisexual "semperidentity" still explicitly stated by a first draft ("For there is scant hope to escape his or her semperidentity by subsisting upon variables" [*A First-Draft Version of "Finnegans Wake"* 262]), while our passage immediately sexualizes the opposites, and refers them back to ⊓ and Δ by way of their initials: "Scant hope theirs or ours to *e*scape life's *h*igh *c*arnage of semperidentity by subsisting *pea*semea*l* upon variables" (582.14–16; italics mine).

The slander and abuse leveled at Earwicker and his family is turned into a tongue-in-cheek commendation. The community is constituted by all speaking subjects who have inherited the story of the same, and who nevertheless tell it their own way. The tone is almost one of despair, as if the fate imposed by the cyclical scheme was unbearable, a negation of hope hinting at a sisyphean burden to be carried on. Here the solution lies not in a recourse to variation, but in the proximity of difference, still lurking at the core of identity. We find a sort of semantic chiasmus, since one would generally expect to find peace linked with identity, and carnage or battle with differences. The strategy of Joyce lies precisely in this reversal, which necessitates a deft manipulation of differences, even though sameness is outwardly predominant. These differences are shown at work in the "togethergush" which progresses through a series of expressions miming sameness ("fresh taint and old treason," fresh paint and old treason, as a history of human reason), and also subtly undermining it ("alteregoases"—with a pun on a *alter ego*, [576.33], and the Latin word for "other" blended with "age," or the "old man" in German—"but not quite such anander and stillandbut one not all the selfsame . . .").

We shift from a structure full of gaps to a series of little differences which introduce one to a chromatic language—as opposed to a diatonic language, which would be keyed in a normal way. All these musical metaphors are relevant here, for the passage also attempts to retell a history of music, with the "notables," "Sullivan," "betune," and several songs quoted. The question of difference within language is fundamental, for it turns out to be the real criterion for any judgment of Earwicker's "sin."

Earwicker is a "right renownsable patriarch," which means that he can be "renounced" and also "renowned"; he is "re-nouned" as well, his proper name being reborn through common names such as "father" or "ark," both contained in "patriarch." The "man from the nark" blends Earwicker as Noah and as Mark of Cornwall, and fuses this with the picture of a Viking invader who has replaced the ancient Gaelic hero Finn Mac Cool. His new stock plays on the senses of a new family originating a whole line of descent, and of a new vine plant. Noah, drunk with his wine, represents the mythical link between the eponymous hero and his substitute.

All this constitutes a commerce of nouns and of goods, as well as women (to use Lévi-Strauss's definition of society as a system of exchanges). The sons become tradesmen who profit from the original sin equated with perversion in general, or more precisely the homosexual incest when Noah, drunk and naked, exhibits himself to his sons: "shame, humbug and profit" (582.10). They have become "shareholders," thereby leaving behind the primitive times when they were merely smugglers of bootleg whiskey, or raiders living off bartered goods, and stealing women from native populations—as the Danes did, before they were to settle. Thus, Earwicker is described as having brought his wife from Cork county back to Dublin ("paved her way from Maizenhead to Youghal"). The link between "wine, women and song" is made explicit by the references to "find me cool's moist opulent vinery" and to the play on "wife" and "wine" ("zingaway wivewards"). This alludes to the discovery of Vinland (Newfoundland) by the Vikings, and to the pub as the place of the major events. The small traders who also play the customers are the converted descendants who accompanied the Vikings, settled instead of exploring other territories, took on the customs of the country, and helped to develop trade, coining in silver, cities, roads—which serve as a metaphor for the process of civilization: "carryfour," "asphault," "concrete," references to the Appian Way and Maida Vale in London. Civilization and traffic are associated, because both rely on linguistic transformation and exchange.

The "traders" thus oppose an aging autocrat, Freud's original Father, because he has refused to be converted either to the Lord's laws or to the law of a language which admits of difference. He is "unregendered," that is, "unregenerate" and "genderless," or even "un-engendered," since it is he who "begottom," begot them with his bottom as mythical father's arse. This is developed by the little story with which I began this paper. It tells us about "orsemarines in an idingplace" (cf. *FW* 581.20), just as it was drafted in the notebook. The shift from the legendary corps of the "horse-marines," to whom one generally alludes in a dismissive way because of some legpull ("tell that to the horsemarines!"), to "horseriders" without an "h" permits a series of interrelated puns on languages: ". . . then hemale man all unbracing to omniwomen, but now shedropping his hitches like any maidavale oppersite orseriders in an idinhole" (581.18–20). The man in question is "genderless" only because his language does not distinguish between the masculine and the feminine: "whose sbrogue cunneth none lordmade undersiding, how betwixt wifely rule and *mens conscia recti*." This is derived from the use of a Scandinavian language, which only possesses common and neuter to express gender. A letter to Miss Weaver states this reference very explicitly and links it to inversion: "Tristan on his first visit to Ireland turned his name inside out. The Norwegian-Danish language has neither masculine nor feminine; the two genders are common and neuter" (*SL* 306).[3] The same notebook which holds the draft of the little story has another reference to this linguistic trait, and attributes it to the two brothers: Shaun is "common," while Shem is "neuter."[4]

The Norse are hidden beneath the sea-horses and are also Greek soldiers crouching inside the Trojan horse. Such an idiom lends itself very well to perversion, moving from unrestricted Donjuanism which denies women any access to a desire dividing them as subjects, since it alludes to them only as wholes or holes, towards homosexuality, considered as the absence of difference ("undersiding" mixes *Unterschied* in German with "unde-cided" and "understanding"). When the two brothers are united as ⟨⟩ there is indeed no place for the feminine, except when it looms through the metamorphoses of bisexuality.[5]

All the sexual terms denoting coition are thus fundamentally ambiguous in pages 581–82: "peniloose" hints of "perilous" but suggests "penis loose" or "penislos" ("penisless" in German). "As long as ever there's wagtail surtaxed to testcase on enver a man" (*FW* 582.11–12) can mean "as long as every man has a penis and testicles" as well as "as long as there is intercourse involving the scrotum" ("wagtail," intercourse; "tail," feminine pudenda; "case," female pudenda in slang). Such an absence of distinction and sexual difference, although wallowing in sexual allusions, leaves any subject "undecided" as to his sexual role; sexuality is predetermined by language patterns, for sex and gender are linked, as was already shown by the passage on bisexuality (523–25) which utilized the same term of "excess" as here (*FW* 524.1 and 580.30).

The community requires laws to "assist them and ease their fall" (579.26); they want to be free of the guilt attached to perversion and finally to sexuality in general. They indeed wish to replace sex, with its attendant array of anguish and doubt, by grammatical gender which can more easily be controlled. Such laws become in turn the laws of fiction, a fiction whose collective nature is stressed. This is why the rowdy ballad ("There was a raughty tinker / Who in London did dwell / And when he had no work to do / His meat axe he did sell") offers blank spaces for any name to be inserted: what really matters is the structure which distributes the roles. The beginning of the "second position" of discordance is marked by a male voice suggesting homosexual contact to a frightened child; he is in fact asleep, dreaming a scene of seduction between his father and himself. "In Amsterdam there lived a . . . But how? You are tremblotting, you retchad, like a verry jerry!" (565.9–10). In the first occurrence, the sentence is merely interrupted, whereas in the second, the ballad yields nothing but a pattern of gaps which will accept any noun. Difference as such is constantly confronted with the ghost of sexual indifference or undifferentiation; thus "every man" is *enver à man* in Danish, but also *homme à l'envers* ("inverted," "reverse," "wrong man") in French. In the same way, the series of terms defining difference, "another," "alter," "anander," culminate on an undecidable word, mixing *einander* (one another) and *anander* (unmanly). Besides, the fourfold anaphoric *v* is heard as the voice of the four old men attempting to place a wedge between "u" (you and us, readers) and "double yous": "*v*ehmen's *v*engeance *v*ective *v*olleying, in*w*ader and *u*itlander. . . ."

The juridical nature of the whole episode rests on such a play on sexual difference: ". . . second position of discordance . . . Mark! You notice it in that rereway because the male entail partially eclipses the femecovert" (564.1–3). The juridical vocabulary shows that the matter is a question of pure form only if we see it as a play on shifting positions and displacement related to difference (pointing towards "toth's tother's place" in 570.13). Discordance is not limited to "sodomy" here, since the three notes played are "meseedo" (564.4), but takes in the generalized incest described by the

Honophrius passage (572–73). The hesitation between Mark the Evangelist and Mark the cuckold, Mark of Corn-wall (*corne* is "horn" in French), is an oscillation between witnessing (cf. *Zeuge* in German, related to generation and male organs) and watching, which leads to voyeuristic and onanistic satisfaction. What is seen then? A series of signs and numbers which come down to a "monomyth" (581.24): either a "single discourse," or a monolith, like Wellington's monument erected in Phoenix Park. For the park is the locus of all these perversions, acted out by shadowy figures.

The turning point in the text is then manifested through the shift from two juridical terms, "amenable" and "venue." "Amenable" means "liable to be brought to judgment," while "venue" is not simply the issue of Earwicker's stock, but the place as such: "venue" means the place from which a jury is drawn, the locale of an event brought to jurisdiction, the ground or position of someone in a discussion. It becomes in the end a statement showing that the residence of the parties is such that the proper court or authority is established. What stands out, then, is the relationship between place and authority, and the web of stories produced in the course of a long trial.

Such a trial is the trial of descendance rather than that of paternity: "we" represent(s) all men and women since "We have to had them whether we'll like it or not. They'll have to have us now then we're here on theirspot" (582.13–14). One cannot avoid having parents, however unpleasant that admission might be to someone intent on becoming his/her own father or mother. Death may play a key role here, since the question is that of a "demise" which turns "smelly." Demise hints of death and transmission of a heritage, both being committed "willy-nilly," or rather "willynully" (582.8), in the same process nullifying differences. As soon as one reaches the place where all the stories are generated, differences start proliferating again. Since the collective discourse hesitates between "mock indignation" and "mock praise" ("mock indignation meeting," [581.2], and "preposterose a snatchvote of thansalot," [582.2–3]), it will have to turn a "deaf ear" to the song of desperation contained in its universal idiom, its "esperanto" ("turn a deaf car clooshed upon the desperanto of willynully" [582.07–08]). We realize then how faithful Joyce was to be to his original project as sketched in the *Scribbledehobble*: "Arabian nights, serial stories, tales within tales, to be continued, desperate story-telling, one caps another to reproduce a rambling mock-heroic tale (L. G.) Scharazad's feat impossible" (*James Joyce's Scribbledehobble* 25 and Notebook VI.A.23).

Finnegans Wake appears therefore as the consistent realization of this program, as a machine containing matrixes of matrixes of stories, capable of narrating everything, and thus never really narrating one story. This machine will not allow us to gain knowledge or information, no matter how long we ponder the text. On the other hand, this lucid epic of disillusion exploits the pleasure we still take in expecting stories to be told to help us lose our knowledge, shed it gloss after gloss in the bottomless structure of perforated stories. The daring and committed loss we experience brings us back to our division as speaking subjects, facing a text which looks more and more like another speaking subject, formidable, inscrutable, but silently and intently peering into our bewildered and fascinated eyes— each contemplating the other in both mirrors of the reciprocal flesh of therehisnothis fellowfaces.

Notes

1. See Jack P. Dalton, "Music Lesson," in *A Wake Digest,* ed. Clive Hart and Fritz Senn.
2. See the reference to the complete song in Roland McHugh, *Annotations to Finnegans Wake* 582.
3. This letter is dated 27/1/1925, thus slightly anterior to the VI.B.19.
4. ∧ Common
    ⊏ Neuter (Notebook VI.B.19, 127).
5. I develop these points in an article on "Bisexuality in *Finnegans Wake,*" *Cahiers de l'Herne, James Joyce,* Spring 1985. I have written a summary of it under the same title in *Eigo Seinen / The Rising Generation, James Joyce Special Number,* Kenkyusha, Tokyo, June 1983, 64–67.

Works Cited

Dalton, Jack P. "Music Lesson." In *A Wake Digest.* Ed. Clive Hart and Fritz Senn. Adelaide: Sydney University Press, 1968.
A First Draft Version of "Finnegans Wake." Ed. David Hayman. Austin: University of Texas Press, 1963.
The James Joyce Archive. Notebooks VI.A. and VI.B.19. New York: Garland, 1978.
James Joyce's Scribbledehobble: The Ur-Workbook for "Finnegans Wake." Ed. Thomas E. Connolly. Evanston: Northwestern University Press, 1961.
McHugh, Roland. *Annotations to "Finnegans Wake."* Baltimore: Johns Hopkins University Press, 1980.

4.   Joyce's Consubstantiality

Joyce's Consubstantiality

Sheldon Brivic

Stephen Dedalus predicts *Finnegans Wake* on the tenth page of *A Portrait* when he presents a definition whose importance grows throughout Joyce's career: "It was very big to think about everything and everywhere. Only God could do that." Men can generalize, but only the concept of God defines a being aware of every detail of the universe. This concept, which Joyce persistently used to define his role as artist, was a central principle guiding the techniques that organized Joyce's creations. Many writers have believed in God more strongly than Joyce, but few have believed more strongly in their roles as gods, the creators of universes. And no writer has developed his godhead more systematically than Joyce, the theologian of fiction, who responded to Yeats's interest in peasant culture by saying that his own mind "was much nearer to God than folklore" (*SH* 5).

Understanding of how Joyce operated in creating his work and of how his work continues perpetually to create itself has been hindered by the critical tradition that an author should be absent from his "product." The idea of fiction as a craft that creates finished works or inanimate objects is related to the Deist notion that God can only appear in his world as a mechanism. It is alien to Joyce's sacramental view of art, which came from a medieval culture that saw God as a living being capable of uniting with his creatures. Daedalus, Joyce's favorite craftsman, made artifacts that contained living beings.

When a peasant sees Daedalus and Icarus flying in Ovid's *Metamorphoses,* he cries out that they must be gods (188). He is right in that they qualify for immortality by transcending the limits of ordinary experience. Joyce believed that every person had the ability to transcend the restrictions of ordinariness, but in order to draw out what was extraordinary in his characters, he had to introduce himself into the text as an active force, something beyond their factual world that could put them in contact with immortality.

The doctrine of authorial absence has led us to see Stephen in *A Portrait* as saying that an author disappears *from* his work rather than *into* it. But Stephen says, "The personality of the artist passes into the narration itself . . ." and in the dramatic form, that personality "fills every person with such vital force that he or she assumes a proper and intangible esthetic life" (*P* 215). The author's vitality here is a substance that he injects into the work: there it becomes a life that is unique to each character ("proper") and indefinable ("intangible"). Yet this vitality remains the substance of the personality of the artist.

When this personality "refines itself out of existence," the creator does not disappear: "The artist, like the God of the creation, remains within or behind or beyond or above his handiwork . . ." (*P* 215). If he is "indifferent," he lacks selfish interest because he invested his personality *in* a number of *different* figures when he attained the dramatic form. He has not subtracted his empathy, but multiplied it, and the reader is aware of Joyce as a presence high above his world and a mystery deep within it.

The much-vexed problems of how many narrators there are in *Ulysses* and exactly whom given phrases represent may be clarified by recognizing that the voices of *Ulysses* are parts of one being who projects many personalities. This multipersonal mind not only takes the features of different narrators, but he fuses with the minds of his characters: their thematic references often express his ideas as well as their own. And he speaks not only for people, but for atmosphere, for spirit: his techniques express the soul of his world.

Joyce had to face the consequence of Stephen's esthetic theory: that Joyce's characters live in a world in which God exists. It is a world in which essence precedes existence, for the details of this world were ideas in Joyce's mind before they were imprinted. Moreover, Joyce had the temerity to press the minds of readers around the world for all future generations into service to the structure constituted by his mind. He arranged that structure to accommodate all humanity and virtually every possible interpretation.

Aquinas says, "To make something the nature of which is simply to exist, is a contradiction in terms, for subsistent existence is noncreated existence" (*Summa Theologiae* I, Ques. 7, Art. 2, 120). The power that gives anything form must of necessity inform it with a purpose. Thus, the objects of the Joyce world must be informed with the ideas and will that created them.

Stephen and Leopold Bloom, for example, are meant to meet, and this meaning suffuses their existence. They not only meet five times by accident, but they have mental contact with each other at least seventy times before they meet, communicating through the mind of Joyce. When Stephen calls upon "Clan Milly" (*U* 393) to return or when Bloom thinks, "*Hamlet, I am thy father's spirit* . . ." (*U* 152), they express a purpose within themselves of which they are not aware. Because Stephen and Bloom are the opposing poles of Joyce's mind, the contact between them is defined as the action that constitutes their author. Thus, the eucharist they share when they drink cocoa is the substance of Joyce, for their communion is the principle that generates their world, their first cause.

Of course, Joyce effaced his godhead and surrounded the meeting of Stephen and Bloom with irony and misunderstanding. He had to negate the surface level of their communion in order to make their world a real world, a fallen world separated from him, but this does not erase the underlying impulse that created them. The deconstructive function of Joyce's work, powerful as it is, is only one side. One can no more deconstruct without constructing than one can exhale without inhaling.

In fact, of all the purposes Joyce can instill in his creatures, the most divine ones are the ones with the greatest latitude. Therefore the strongest expression of the desire to be God is the creation of a world of deconstruction, a world in which all fixed principles overcome themselves. One of the main sources from which Joyce derived the conception of such a world of flux was Nietzsche's *Thus Spake Zarathustra,* an extremely intense expression of the desire for divinity. Zarathustra longs to go "where all becoming seemed to me the dance of gods and the prankishness of gods, and the world seemed free and frolicsome and as if fleeing back to itself—as an eternal fleeing and seeking each other again of many gods, as the happy controverting of each other, conversing again with each other, and converging again of many gods" (309).[1] To create such vitality is to assume deity.

Joyce's continually avowed purpose was to create life, an activity reserved for God in Judeo-Christian tradition. He created perhaps the most complex cosmos and the most fully realized people ever created by man. He knew, however, that he could not make them live without assuming responsibility for being the beginning and end, alpha and omega, of the world he created. He had learned from Aristotle's *Metaphysics* that an object must have a cause of being and an end or purpose to exist fully: and he realized that the cause and end appropriate to the human soul require an imitation of God. So he gave the subjects of his world full causal dimensionality by building his personality into his narrative in the form of a series of substructures that constantly add external reference to the world of the text, like a sound track coming from another sphere.

Whenever the text leaves its established surface, it always refers to Joyce. All of the Homeric references, the literary allusions that do not arise from the action, the manifold references to the author and his biography, the coincidences and supernatural signs, the ironies that are not seen by the book's speakers, and the deferences of the meanings of words—all of these are organized by Joyce's mind, which is the most specific intellectual structure to which they can be referred. Whenever a phrase in the book is given such opacity, it speaks for Joyce as well as for its subject: and thereby it gains a significance that is indeterminate, the kind of suggestive aura things have in life because they go beyond any known system. This is the resonance of poetry, traditionally derived from divine inspiration. In Joyce this resonance refers to an invisible Joycean mental world "within or behind or beyond" the world of Bloomsday. Anthony Burgess has said that virtually every sentence in *Ulysses* contains a surprising word (Burgess 74). Therefore each sentence calls attention to the creative force behind it.

I'd like to consider briefly how Joyce's techniques work constructively in the "Oxen of the Sun" episode of *Ulysses*. Wolfgang Iser has pointed out that the various styles in the hospital scene undercut each other to demonstrate that no perception can ever be free of the imposition of stylistic convention (179–95). This is sound, but the denial of any particular truth always has to aim at a higher truth, and the styles of "Oxen" not only conflict, but work with each other supportively.

For one thing, they form an organic structure. A given phrase in "Oxen" will simultaneously represent a phase of the history of English prose style, an author in that history, a stage in the development of a fetus, and the feelings of the characters involved in the scene. These different functions make it resemble a cell that relates to several physiological systems (such as those of digestion, respiration, and movement) at once. By hiding such structures of meaning in his work, Joyce expands our faith, training us to believe in the presence of what is not immediately visible.

Moreover, the juxtaposition of fifteen hundred years of prose styles in "Oxen" produces a tremendous density—exactly the density needed for the scene in which Bloom makes the strange decision to follow Stephen. A Biblical feeling of casting perception through distant ages contributes powerfully to the evocation of something being born. And the elaboration of a unified mental construct that includes vast stretches of history serves to draw out what is really being born here: a transcendent mind that includes two personalities. This episode activates the process that leads to what Joyce, in the Linati schema, calls the "Fusion of Bloom and Stephen" in the last three episodes.[2]

Finally, if each style in "Oxen" is selected as the right one for its moment, then Joyce, by taking upon himself a power to change styles that extends virtually beyond human ability, actually eliminates the interference of style. That is, the total vision constituted by all of the styles is free of stylistic limitation, a pure representation of the ultimate reality of the scene. Readers who object that "Oxen" hardly seems free of stylistic imposition are expecting to see an ordinary human subject, a matter of convention; but what are portrayed are spiritual depths perceivable only by omniscience, a subject that can only be portrayed by exactly these words. Joyce believed that every discrete definition of human personality was a part of something larger, and one of his main concerns in bringing Stephen and Bloom together is to embody this larger something. In presenting God's outlook through style, one of the first aims Scholasticism would dictate would be to show the falseness of any particular style: for God would be bound to see beyond any specific system or set of values.

In representing the viewpoint of God stylistically, "Oxen" is parallel to "Wandering Rocks," which represents that viewpoint spatially. When "Rocks" is acted out across Dublin, even someone in a helicopter can't take it all in because he can't hear. An attempt to capture the action with a panel of nineteen video screens would only illustrate how God's viewpoint has to appear in fragmented form to mortals, who would still not be capable of watching it all at once. "Circe" develops God's view in psychological terms by creating beings who embody subconscious impulses, thus turning omniscience into omnipotence. And "Ithaca" renders God's viewpoint scientifically, as a catechism should. This episode of homecoming evokes such a breathtaking expansion of outer and inner space as to establish powerfully that the home from which the characters come and toward which they go is cosmic. This home is Joyce's mind.

By projecting himself as a spiritual undercurrent that expresses a divine perspective in his work, Joyce generates for his subjects the mystery and potentiality of actual being, the ability to continually surprise readers with new meanings. He is realistic in recognizing that nothing can exist without a submerged dependence on what created it. Many of the best novelists, from Cervantes to Pynchon, have rebelled against the incredible pretense that a novel is written objectively—that is, written by no one at all. Because Joyce was the most thoroughly self-conscious of novelists in designing the operation of his deity, an understanding of how he functions as first principle can help us to delineate the cosmogonic activities of many other writers.

To describe how Joyce functions, as Robert Day has pointed out, one must consider the relation between his two images of his divinity. On the one hand, there is the exalted figure whom Stephen refers to as "lord and giver of their life" (*U* 415), the aspect that led Joyce to say, "My art is not a mirror held up to nature. Nature mirrors my art" (*JJII*.677n). On the other hand, there is the debased image of the artist as forger, Satan, the sham who must imitate a prior Creator. The crucial distinction between the debased Joyce god and the exalted one may be located at the interface between the man and his work, the point of writing at which Joyce sacrifices his actual life to create his imaginary world.

To understand this process, we must focus on the substance of Joyce that goes into his work, the measure of being he withdraws from the external world and invests in his creation. This proportion of Joyce increased through his career as he grew more absorbed in his work, giving up such external distractions as jobholding, eyesight, and all but the most controlled social relations. Within the canon, as he progresses into his creation, things grow more personal and less bound to external models, more transformed by technical innovations into what is uniquely Joycean.

The portion of Joyce sacrificed to create his cosmos takes on ideal qualities from the point of view of the created world because it comes from a larger realm of possibilities and is shaped by an unknowable will that gives to its products a superabundance of purpose. But at the same time that Joyce is totem or sacred in relation to his world, he is also taboo or despised. The artist figure is subject to irony throughout Joyce's work because Joyce can only enter his work as a specific person by falling into a negation of his own totality. The artist is mocked by the mentality of Shaun just as Christ was mocked by those who belonged to the world. But this mockery is Joyce's way of enhancing his power by controlling it. He has to keep himself from overwhelming the free reality of his world, its essential right to its own illusion of independent existence. By mocking Joyce, his world tries to bring him down to its level, but he remains transcendent. The appearance of freedom in his creation, its inability to include him, ultimately expresses his own largeness.

Outside his work, Joyce was fallible and uncertain, but as a creature function seen from within it, he has absolute authority: he is the ineluctable origin and goal of every point in the novel. Every being in the book is derived from him, and their numerous references to his biography constitute efforts to apprehend their common source. But none of the characters can catch more than indirect glimpses of the totality of the Joycean mental world in which they participate. As Dante puts it in canto 19 of the *Paradiso*, ". . . the creating Word / would still exceed creation infinitely" (217).

Joyce's readers are in a situation similar to that of his characters in that they relate to his work as his creatures. He endows them with the ability to imagine interpretations more wide-ranging than what they would formerly have been capable of, and thereby he grants them psychic life. But the more they learn about his world, the more they realize that their interpretations do not come close to covering the text. Thus they are impelled toward the infinite creating word behind the text.

Stephen's continual discussion of the artist as god in *Ulysses* is an examination of Joyce's role. In fact, all references to God in Joyce's mature fiction are references to Joyce. And we can clarify how Joyce operates in his text by a brief analysis of one of Stephen's statements about his relation to Joyce. He is speaking in "Scylla and Charybdis" about the survival of an author in his work and also about the passage from present identity into the future: "In the intense instant of imagination . . . that which I was is that which I am and that which in possibility I may come to be. So in the future, the sister of the past, I may see myself as I sit here now but by reflection from that which then I shall be" (*U* 194). Stephen believes that he will become his own creator in the sense that what he is will not be clear until he looks back on it. This notion is related to Joyce's definition of personality in the 1904 sketch "A Portrait of the Artist" as a continuum of which only a part is visible at any one time (Anderson, ed., 257–58). And this may well be based on the idea Augustine expresses in the *Confessions* (IV.10) when he says that only God can see the whole of anything because only he can see all times at once. In this passage Stephen transcends and expands himself by glimpsing the larger totality of which he is a part.

Stephen would like to become Joyce and write *Ulysses*—in fact, he is determined to—but he doesn't know what Joyce or *Ulysses* are. These ideals are potential in him, but their specific forms lie beyond his consciousness in the realm of destiny. By using Stephen to refer outside of the text, Joyce makes this passage indicate on one level the inevitability of his becoming Joyce and creating himself beyond his own accessible imagination. But Stephen is already created beyond his imagination; this passage reveals an enormous potential in him of which he has only an intuition.

Joyce generally aimed to show what is beyond consciousness, including not only the Freudian unconscious, which he developed skillfully, but spiritual potential such as Stephen shows here (the Jungian unconscious) and a large range of other possibilities. To reveal such elements, he had to assume a god-like role, for Augustine says that the part of a man that he does not know is occupied by God (X.5–8). To describe the disclosures he aimed at, Joyce used the term *epiphany,* which means a revelation of God. Perhaps the central method for developing the divine possibilities of the mind that Joyce evolved through his career was to multiply its parts and to give each the independence of a personality.

Joyce's transformation from mortality to deity takes place when "the personality of the artist passes into the narration." And the crucial process in this transmission of Joyce into his work is self-division or dismemberment. After all, God enters the world by dividing himself, for he is most effectively seen from life as a multiple being such as the Trinity or the Eucharist. As Joyce multiplies himself, the personality of his work expands.

Joyce's canon represents a continuous development of the idea of mind, which grows more powerful and complex from one work to the next and within each work. *Dubliners* shows the minds of its characters controlled by society, and *Portrait* shows a young man opposing such control in order to develop an individual mind. In *Ulysses,* two people come in contact with an extra-individual or multi-personal mind that unites them. The realization that mental process involves more than one person leads to a larger totality.

After having been distant from his creation in *Dubliners* and ambivalent toward it in *Portrait,* Joyce entered his world by dividing himself between Stephen and Bloom in *Ulysses.* This duality was expanded to a trinity at the end of *Ulysses* by Molly. And in the *Wake,* the trinity becomes a quaternity and then a quincunx. The interplay of active forces in the last two works gives them self-sufficiency and vitality because the mind of Joyce is fully present as a living being in them. One of Joyce's steadiest aims throughout his career was to expand the mind by multiplying its parts, progressing toward an infinite intelligible being. He could do this only in personal terms because, as he once remarked, he could never understand any mind but his own (*JJII* 265).

The family of the *Wake* is composed of the parts of the mind of the dreamer who generates them. A number of authorities, including Father Boyle, have identified the dreamer of the *Wake* as Joyce. The mind of the author is the inaccessible finality of Finn. His created ego is drawn into the dream by an alluring projection of desire, ALP, the "ondrawer of our unconscionable" (*FW* 266.30–31). This feminine part of the mind motivates perception in the masculine part: but each new perception competes with an existing image in its effort to grasp the object of desire. The need for a male competitor against whom to define oneself sets up the Shem-Shaun polarity in the mind. And the contrast between the female who is known and the ideal feminine that is unknown results in the division between ALP and Isabel. Thus, the mind of the author of the dream unfolds into a series of conflicting parts to expand into a creatively complete psychological metabolism.

Freed from the strategic need to maintain unity by its dreaming or fictional state, this mind can unleash its constituents. The permanence of these family functions throughout Joyce's history of humanity suggests that they make up a mental structure inherent in human life, the fully realized form of the mind. Each of these persons, by pushing in his or her own direction, expands a dimension of the *Wake* world and works to define the others by opposition, as functions in a psychic apparatus modify each other. But because each function in the *Wake* mind is a living being, the total mental structure is capable of more complex interactions than any mechanical psychic apparatus.

The *Wake* is filled with recognition that the creatures who inhabit it are projections of a primal mind beyond their knowing. With every word he writes, the author is finished as a unity and wakes as a partial being. Lost in the confusion of his dismemberment, the characters strive to reconstitute him. Their learning, for example, is an epistemological effort devoted to "establishing the identities of the writer complexus (for if the hand was one, the minds of active and agitated were more than so)" (*FW* 114.33–35). By defining the minds of their author, they hope to identify themselves. But his real existence, the unity behind the multiplicity of his manifestations, is in another world that they can only reach by leaving their lives behind.

The religion of these creatures aims at serving this mind containing minds that precedes and follows all of their history and includes their entire universe. Yet they have an underlying fear of his waking because if he united, he would stop projecting them, as Augustine says God projects all beings constantly, and they would be reabsorbed into him. They urge him to rest in his position as alpha and omega (*a* and *z*): "Now be aisy, good Mr Finnimore, sir. And take your laysure like a god on pension . . ." (*FW* 24.16–17). Like Freud's totem sons, as the agents and beneficiaries of his demise, they have high stakes in his death even while they feel him as the absolute source of life within themselves.

The mind they worship is Joyce's most essential creation, elaborated with steady progress through his career. Out of the multiplicity of this being, first identified by David Hayman as the Arranger, the fullness of Joyce's world springs. Only a mind composed of a family of minds can provide the complex perspective needed to fill Joyce's universe with the vital interactions that make up the dancing of its gods. The most productive feature of this expanding mind is its ability to divide itself, to hold several visions at once. Joyce associated this ability with the feminine, perhaps because it is through the feminine that a man can pass out of himself. And if others suggest that Joyce's god is feminine, it may be in this crucial principle that the femininity Joyce worshipped is to be located.

Notes

1. Earlier Zarathustra, who is clearly autobiographical, says, "*If* there were gods, how could I endure not to be a god" (198): but in the passage quoted above and elsewhere, he presents gods as central features of his universe. He is continually deifying his spirit and describing himself in divine terms. For example, he trembles with "godlike desires" to unite with the sky (276), and he awaits the hour when he is to go down and redeem mankind (308–10). In July 1904 Joyce sent a postcard to George Roberts which he signed, "James Overman" (*Letters* I:56).

2. The Linati schema appears in Richard Ellmann, *Ulysses on the Liffey,* between pages 187 and 188.

Works Cited

Burgess, Anthony. *Joysprick: An Introduction to the Language of James Joyce.* New York: Harcourt Brace Jovanovich, 1975.

Dante Alighieri. *The Paradiso.* Tr. John Ciardi. New York: New American Library, 1970.

Ellmann, Richard. *Ulysses on the Liffey.* New York: Oxford University Press, 1972.

Iser, Wolfgang. *The Implied Reader: Patterns of Communication in Prose Fiction from Bunyan to Beckett.* Baltimore: Johns Hopkins University Press, 1974.

Joyce, James. *"A Portrait of the Artist as a Young Man": Text, Criticism, and Notes.* Ed. Chester G. Anderson. New York: Viking, 1958.

Nietzsche, Friedrich. *The Portable Nietzsche.* Ed. Walter Kaufmann. New York: Viking, 1954.

Ovid. *Metamorphosis.* Tr. Rolfe Humphries. Bloomington: Indiana University Press, 1955.

Saint Thomas Aquinas. *Summa Theologiae I: The Existence of God.* Ed. Thomas Gilby. Garden City, N.J.: Doubleday Image, 1969.

Joyce's Goddess of Generation

Elliott B. Gose, Jr.

Earth mother or goddess of wisdom, fallen woman or mysterious muse, the images of woman which are often seen as restrictive today reach back into the roots of western culture. Artists express them as inevitably as they seek contact with the dark hidden sources of their creativity. For a man these feminine images are likely to represent all that he has repressed or longed for, the Other which is potential in him, the soul which he wants to integrate. Such was certainly the case with James Joyce. In this essay I shall investigate some of the many female forms that he embodied in *Ulysses*.

In the Butcher and Lang translation of *The Odyssey*, the invocation to the muse ends, "Of these things, goddess, daughter of Zeus, whencesoever thou had heard thereof, declare thou even unto us." However much they sound like a Joycean parody, these lines do admit a dependence on the muse which I believe Joyce also acknowledged. Stephen Dedalus may be determined to make the son consubstantial with the father, but Joyce had come to understand the consubstantiality of a mother goddess. In making this assertion, I am of course going against abundant evidence that Joyce mistrusted women. *Ulysses* contains obvious examples of this mistrust: the treatment of Gerty as Nausicaa, of Bella as Circe, and of Molly as Penelope. Why not, then, conclude that Joyce picked *The Odyssey* for its treatment of women as limited characters rather than for its presentation of the muse and Athena as inspiring helpers? The answer, as usual, is that Joyce chose his model for both its affirmative and its ironic possibilities. I see the conventional virgin-whore dichotomy transformed by Joyce's imagination into a more creative balance of feminine energy.

That the traditional dichotomy was part of Joyce's conditioning is, however, evident from his letters to Nora from Dublin in 1909. As Ellmann comments in his introduction to the collection in which the Dublin letters appear, Joyce felt "compelled to set up images of purity against images of impurity" and asked Nora to "share in shame, shamelessness, and un-ashamedness" (*SL* xxv). In his earlier biography, Ellmann noted that Joyce not only showed an awareness of the polarity of two related views of Nora, as mother and as wife, but declined "to confuse the two images" (*JJI* 305). This clarity of vision in his personal life was, of course, carried over into his fiction. Attracted to the cult of the virgin when young, Joyce made fun of it in the "Nausicaa" episode. Mark Shechner views the attack on the cult as a tribute to its emotional power (chap. 4). He claims that the primary source of what Joyce called the "namby-pamby jammy marmalady drawersy" style of "Nausicaa" was "Joyce himself," specifically the "embarrassing prose of his romantic youth" (176). This acute insight needs tempering.

Just as Flaubert said that the Madame Bovary whose romanticism he exposed was himself, so I would argue that Joyce was conscious of his connection to Gerty MacDowell, whose sensibility determines the style of the first half of the episode. His calling that style "drawersy," for instance, might remind us that Joyce was a fan of ladies' drawers (Budgen 319). His letters to Nora also testify to his general concern with women's dress and the details of its materials and construction. My claim is that Joyce was well aware of feminine urges within (cf. my discussion in Gose 102–5); in fact, he cultivated them to serve him as muse, soul, and goddess.

Sensitive to the meaning of words, Joyce commented that his last name contained *joy* and would obviously have been aware that it was also a woman's first name. He insisted to his first biographer that his middle name had been recorded by the parish clerk as Augusta. Such an emphasis would align Joyce with one of his early literary heroes, Ibsen. In his first published essay, in 1900, Joyce praised the Norwegian dramatist for the "curious admixture of the woman in his nature" (*CW* 64). Stephen, in *A Portrait* and *Ulysses*, shows an awareness of the woman in himself. In the "Proteus" episode, he thinks, "Our souls, shamewounded by our sins, cling to us yet more, a woman to her lover clinging, the more the more" (*U* 48). In "Oxen of the Sun" Joyce placed the soul in a more positive context. Although many earlier passages in the episode purvey a medico-cynico view of women, beginning with the nineteenth-century styles that view is replaced by a more affirmative one. "What is the age of the soul of man? As she hath the virtue of the chameleon to change her hue at every new approach, to be gay with the merry and mournful with the downcast, so too is her age changeable as her mood" (*U* 412–13). I take this to be one of several points in this episode at which Joyce is commenting on its technique. His style could be said to change its hue in every section, moving from gay to mournful, its changes of mood accompanying changes in the successive ages from which the styles are drawn.

This mutability of style and mood may be connected with an important dream Joyce had of his mother while he was in Paris in 1903. In it she delivered a heartening message: "I am susceptible of change, an imaginative influence in the hearts of my children" (Scholes and Kain 44). Like the soul in the passage quoted above, this female is responsive to male needs, needs of feeling and imagination. In fact, even before the dream, Joyce had come to a conscious appreciation of such a maternal figure. As his essay on the Irish poet Mangan indicates, as early as 1902, Joyce was aware of the importance of "imagination" as "the mother of things, whose dream are we, who imageth us to herself, and to ourselves, and imageth herself in us"

(*CW* 78). The dream message can be seen almost as prophecy in view of the rush of creativity which Shechner has shown followed the death of Joyce's mother (Shechner 238–40). The most important product of that period is the opaque but stimulating sketch, "A Portrait of the Artist." In a passage which seems to describe a sexual encounter that engaged the hearts as well as the loins of the participants, the narrator takes a religious view of his partner: "Thou wert sacramental, imprinting thine indelible mark, of very visible grace. A litany must honor thee; Lady of the Apple Trees, Kind Wisdom" (Scholes and Kain 66). Shechner offers this passage as an example of the early romantic Mariolatrous prose that Joyce later turned against. But what these sentences demonstrate is that even at the age of twenty-one Joyce had begun to rebel against the cult of the Virgin. In making up a sacred litany to a profane prostitute, he might be seen as crudely blaspheming. But a closer look at the two epithets will uncover a more profound intention.

To honor the Lady of the Apple Trees is to value Eve over Mary, sinning over purity, "the ways of error and glory" in "the fair courts of life"[1] over ingrown virginity and enforced orthodoxy. Eve is the mother of generation. The model of creativity she represents is explicit in Stephen's view of the artistic process in *A Portrait of the Artist as a Young Man:* "artistic conception, artistic gestation and artistic reproduction" (*P* 209). As Ellmann claims, in *A Portrait* the "creator is not male but female . . . a goddess" (*JJ* 306).

Joyce's preference for Eve over Mary reverses the traditional view, which Stephen alludes to in "Oxen of the Sun." He cites Augustine's contrast of Mary who bore the Redeemer with Eve who introduced original sin. A few lines earlier, however, Stephen implicitly offered another view, a contrast closer to Ellmann's elevation of the female as creator. "In woman's womb word is made flesh but in the spirit of the maker all flesh that passes becomes the word that shall not pass away. This is the postcreation" (*U* 391). On a first reading, the "but" followed by "word that shall not pass away" suggests that God's spiritual creation is higher than woman's physical one. But this suggestion is qualified by the succeeding sentence. Taking Joyce's "this" to refer to the previous clause, I apply "postcreation" to that clause and see "maker" as *writer* and "word" as *literature*. Writing literature is a postcreation because it takes Eve's creation as its model.

In her monograph on *Finnegans Wake*, Grace Eckley emphasizes that "the creative qualities for Joyce logically belonged to the female figure," and cites his letters to Nora as evidence of his "dependence on feminine inspiration" (161, 163). In addition she notes a corroborating passage from the library scene in *Ulysses.* "As we, or mother Dana, weave and unweave our bodies, Stephen said, from day to day, their molecules shuttled to and fro, so does the artist weave and unweave his image" (*U* 194). The assumption here is clearly in harmony with Joyce's early Aristotelianism: "the artistic process is like the natural process" (*CW* 145). Although connected with the Irish mother goddess, Dana, the weaving image contains an allusion (presumably unconscious in Stephen) to Penelope, who not only wove during the day but unwove at night. Like Nora Joyce, Homer's Penelope remained true to her mate through many trials. Weaving is creative work, woman's work, a connection between gestating children and creating art. For the artist to "weave and unweave his image" may mean to imagine and then revise his work, or it may indicate, by analogy with the process of physical growth, a transformation: the "artistic conception, artistic gestation and artistic reproduction," suggested earlier. The image does not remain static after conception; it grows during gestation and changes as the artist produces the work until the original image may disappear through the process of artistic evolution. In any case, here as elsewhere in *Ulysses,* the reference to a physical process connected with a mother goddess adds to the evidence that Joyce equated creation with the female principle.

The umbilical cord, which connects a pregnant woman to the child within her, provided Joyce with a symbolic indication of her fitness for a role in his imagination. In "Oxen of the Sun," for example, we find the following characterization of Augustine's attitude to Eve: "our grandam, which we are linked up with by successive anastomosis of navelcords sold us all, seed, breed and generation, for a penny pippin" (*U* 391). Anastomosis, a joining together through canals (whether of exterior rivers or interior blood vessels), is an apt symbol for the cord which connects each man to a woman; more importantly it connects all mothers not only back through their mothers to past generations but also forward through their daughters to future generations. Augustine's negative valuation can be changed to a positive one to suggest the connection of humanity with all the past and all the future. Whether through soul or body, the female is the vehicle.

In his usual thorough way, Joyce used anastomosis to reinforce not only his theme but also his technique. Anastomosis thus becomes a classical rhetorical device, the insertion of one word in another. Stuart Gilbert, with help from Joyce himself, provided an example in the list of "rhetorical forms" in the "Aeolus" episode: *underdarkneath*. Applying the sense of the passage in which Joyce introduced the word "anastomosis," we could see *under-neath* as feeding the growth of *dark*.

Another example of anastomosis brings together more clearly the rhetoric of insertion and the theme of joining and feeding: *Rosevean*, the name of the schooner Stephen saw at the end of "Proteus." The rose is the symbol of Mary. Anna was her mother, and Eve is the ultimate mother of humanity. Mary and Anna are not so much separated as connected by Eve: she serves as the originator of that canal through which all women are joined. Eve's maculate gendering is officially balanced by Mary's immaculate conception of Christ. But in Joyce's vision, just as Anna conceived Mary by the same means Eve did her offspring, so Mary's conception has that honorable tradition behind it. Thus between Anna and her daughter stands the original progenitor, a reminder of the human condition, or as Joyce phrased it in the "Portrait" essay, of "the beauty of mortal conditions" (Scholes and Kain 65). Those same conditions produced the actual ship with the name that Joyce read about and adopted, a name that has beauty and a secret meaning. The natural process produced an image exemplifying that constant change which Stephen praised in the library. Mary as rose has, of course, subsequently been transformed in a variety of works of art, much of it ethereal. Joyce's belief that "the artistic process is like the natural process" meant that his art would not aim at the intense inane but would rather draw its strength from nature, particularly from the natural process of generation.

The most blatant examples of thematic and rhetorical anastomosis both occur on the same page of "Proteus." In his usual witty and impious way, Stephen develops the theme by imagining the umbilical cords that have linked successive generations as a continuous canal through which he may try to place a long distance phone call to his original parents. "The cords of all link back, strandentwining cable of all flesh. . . . Hello. Kinch here. Put me on to Edenville" (*U* 38). Consideration of Eden leads him to think of Eve's womb of sin and thence his own conception. He then speculates on "the divine substance wherein Father and Son are consubstantial." Finally he asks, "Where is poor dear Arius to try conclusions? Warring his life long on the contrasmagnificandjewbangtantiality. Illstarred heresiarch." That overweighted word is Joyce's rhetorical contribution to a long-standing debate. The doctrine of consubstantiability was promulgated in the Nicene Creed (325 A.D.) and asserted that Christ was "begotten not made, of one substance with the Father." The rest of creation God made but did not beget. This view was opposed by Arius who held that Christ also was only created. Stephen sympathizes with Arius, having thought at the beginning of the paragraph, "I was . . . made not begotten." The use of anastomosis, as I read it, is an expansion of the *sub* from "consubstantiality" into a longer phrase that indicates some of the implications of a prefix that means "under," or that which supports.

What *sub* connects with and feeds into this concept are four difficulties: "transmagnificandjewbang." As glossed by Joseph Campbell, "trans" suggests "transubstantiation," the doctrine that the bread and wine wholly become the body and blood of Christ during the Eucharist (11). This belief could be taken as an extension of God's substance from Christ to man, an anastomosis of Christ through the divinized substance into man as physical-spiritual creature. Campbell connects the next term, "magnificand," with "magnificat," the canticle taken from Mary's hymn of praise at being singled out by God. "My soul doth magnify the Lord. And my spirit hath rejoiced in God my Saviour. Because he hath regarded the humility of his handmaid; for behold from henceforth all generations shall call me blessed" (Luke I:46–48, Duoai translation). I shall comment on "generations" below.

Campbell takes "jew" to refer to Christ's being a Jew. A further clue appears at the end of Mary's hymn. "He hath received Israel his servant, being mindful of his mercy: As he spoke to our fathers, to Abraham and to his seed for ever." The idea of seed can be connected with the anastomosis passage in "Oxen of the Sun": Augustine insisted that Eve "sold us all, *seed,* breed and generation" (italics mine). Mary, like Joyce, implicitly corrects a too-great emphasis on Christ as only begotten son by acknowledging the importance of generations, the continuity that links God to man going back as far as the patriarch Abraham in her understanding, and as far as the matriarch Eve in Joyce's.

Campbell connects "bang" with God's thunder which frightens Stephen in "Oxen of the Sun" (*U* 394; cf. 34). Robert Boyle suggests that "jewbang" could refer "to the destruction of the Jewish doctrine of the unity of God" (since the Magnificat celebrates "the Incarnation") or "to the imagined intercourse between Mary and the Power" (28). Accepting all these possibilities, I read the whole phrase as a balance made up of two contrasting parts: the first two are multisyllabic, abstract, theological terms contradicting Arius's views, extending God's substance even to humanity, while the second two are monosyllabic, shifting the focus to a more specifically physical concern with generation. My conclusion is that Joyce wished to demonstrate a process going on in man through history, with an emphasis on the mother figure who was the connection between father and son.[2] The distortion of "magnificat" to "magnificand" bears out this suggestion of an internal balancing, the "and" connecting "jewbang" as a second pair and a supplement to the first pair, "transmagnific."

The most obvious place to look for the fallen woman in *Ulysses* is the "Nighttown" episode, set in Dublin's red-light district. At the beginning of this episode, Stephen delivers a delayed response to the quotation from the mass with which Mulligan opened the novel: *"ad deam qui laetificat juventutem meam"* (*U* 433). Stephen here invokes Georgina Johnson as the goddess who gives joy to his life. His distorting *deum* to *deam*, masculine to feminine, so as to refer to a prostitute, probably suggests Stephen's need to blaspheme. But there is evidence that Joyce here intends an invocation more in Homer's manner than in Mulligan's. The clue comes later in the episode when Stephen discovers that Georgina Johnson has left prostitution for marriage to a Mr. Lambe from London. Stephen comments, "Lamb of London, who takest away the sins of our world" (*U* 560). This

Lamb is obviously a stand-in for Christ who, far from idolizing virginity, gave sympathetic support to Mary Magdalen.

The other epithet applied to the prostitute in the early "Portrait" sketch was "Kind Wisdom." We know that the wisdom of the flesh helped send Joyce on his way out of the church, out of Ireland, and into his imagination and the world's. The Greeks personified wisdom as Sophia; Joyce knew her through Giordano Bruno's *Expulsion of the Triumphant Beast* and as the fallen goddess of Gnosticism. Sophia figured prominently in the philosophy of the Gnostic Valentine, who is mentioned in "Telemachus" (*U* 21). According to the eleventh edition of the *Britannica*, "the Mother-goddess stands . . . at the center" of Valentine's system. Even in her fallen state, Sophia "is a world creative power" who can be invoked and known. Valentine preached her redemption through marriage to "her Higher celestial brother," and man's redemption through a sacrament modeled on that marriage. Joyce's 1909 letters to Nora suggest such a relation.

Sophia appears in *Ulysses* as part of an ironic parody of theosophical writing that runs through Stephen's mind during his dispute with AE (George Russell) in the library. Here as elsewhere, I believe that Joyce, while sympathetic with Stephen's animus against the inanities of such writing, obtained more imaginative stimulation from them than Stephen's anxious consciousness could. "The Christ with the bridesister, moisture of light, born of an ensouled virgin, repentant sophia, departed to the plane of buddhi" (*U* 185). The source of most of this seems to be *Isis Unveiled* by H. P. Blavatsky, a theosophist we know Joyce read: "As soon as Jesus was born, Christos, uniting himself with Sophia (wisdom and spirituality) descended through the seven planetary regions . . . When on the cross, Christos and Sophia left his body and returned to their own sphere. . . . Sophia-Achamoth, the half-spiritual, half-material LIFE [is] the *sister* of Christos, the perfect emanation, and both are children or emanations of Sophia, the purely spiritual" (2:186, 226–27 [Blavatsky's italics]).[3]

Neither here nor in *The Secret Doctrine* can I find Blavatsky referring to a *"repentant* sophia." But Joyce would have found in the National Library a book that did develop that side of the goddess. *The Gnostics and their Remains* by Charles William King was Blavatsky's cited and quoted source for a recently discovered Gnostic text, the *Pistis Sophia*, in which Sophia "having once caught a glimpse of the Supreme Light was seized with a desire to fly upwards into it" (15). Unfortunately a jealous god of her own level lured her with a false light down into matter. The *Pistis Sophia* is mainly composed of Christ's repetitious descriptions of "the successive steps by which she ascends through all the Twelve AEons by the Saviour's aid, and *the confession* she sings at each stage of her deliverance out of chaos. Each confession is proposed by Jesus to a disciple for explanation. . . . A remarkable peculiarity is that all throughout[,] Mary Magdalene is the chief speaker, and the most highly commended for her spiritual knowledge" (15; [King's italics]). The parallel between the redemption of Sophia and that of Mary Magdalen would not have been lost on Joyce. In his concern with Sophia (and with Eve) Joyce found in Gnostic thought support for the fallen goddess of generation who desires and will achieve spiritual enlightenment.

I have already suggested that the Magdalen theme receives its most thorough treatment in the "Circe" episode. The goddess Circe is usually seen as reducing man to an animal. The negative valuation that accompanies this accurate perception was reversed by Giordano Bruno in a manner Joyce approved. In *The Heroic Frenzies,* a book Joyce owned, Bruno characterized Circe as "the generative matter in all things. She is called the daughter of the sun because from the father of forms she has inherited" an ability to transform all being through "glorious afflictions" (*Heroic Frenzies* 75, 263). Circe's counterpart in the "Nighttown" episode is the whore-mistress, Bella Cohen, who will afflict Bloom.

As indicated earlier, the Christian model for the reformed prostitute, Georgina Johnson, is Mary Magdalen who figured in Joyce's imagination as part of an important pattern in this episode. The only mention of her in "Circe" is indirect ("Rescue of fallen women Magdalen asylum," [*U* 443]). In the British Museum notebooks, however, there is a more revealing entry: "Left hand = Mary of Magdala" (Herring 433). This equation not only relates her to the Christ who sits on God's right hand; it also fits into an important left-right pattern in the episode.

In "Magic on the Notesheets of the 'Circe' Episode," Norman Silverstein twenty years ago investigated the importance of the left in that episode. On its first page an idiot "lifts a palsied left arm" in answer to the children's command, "Kithogue! Salute" (*U* 429). As Silverstein noted, the Gaelic *kithogue* means "lefthanded" and has two connotations, either "of sinister (in both senses) or of awkwardness" (19–26). The term sets "the spirit of the Circe episode where the upsidedown and perverse dominate the universe. . . . Tied up with Satan, the left is also the direction toward evil and toward Hell" (24). Thus one of the celebrants of the Black Mass late in the episode has "two left feet" (*U* 599). We shall discover, however, that the left also has a more positive function in "Circe."

Silverstein listed only one use of the word "right." Bloom's saying "Keep to the right, right, right" (*U* 436) is his way of reminding himself of the Masonic "fidelity of virtue" (Silverstein 24). An earlier appearance of "right" provides an even clearer opposition to Silverstein's characterization of "left." Stephen's first words in "Circe" come from the Antiphon for Pascheltide, *"a latere dextro"* ("from the right side" [*U* 431]). Stephen's quotation also gives a context: welling from the right side of the temple, water brought salvation to those who stood in its course (see Weldon Thornton,

Allusions in "Ulysses"). This church liturgy connects "right" with salvation, the orthodox aim of Christianity. But Stephen as he chants flourishes his "ashplant in his *left* hand" (*U* 431, italics mine). This is the same ashplant with which, in denial of his mother's right arm pointing at him in a Christian plea, he will later smash the chandelier in the brothel (*U* 582–83).

The overt goddess of this episode is not Circe but Shakti. She is mentioned by Mananaan MacLir, a Celtic god whom AE had invoked in his play *Deirdre*. As many critics have noted, Joyce uses Mananaan partly to make fun of AE the mystic poet in contrast to George Russell the bicycling editor of a dairy periodical. This contrast comes to a focus in Mananaan's two hands: *"His right hand holds a bicycle pump. His left hand grasps a huge crayfish by its two talons"* (*U* 510). Here the right is public and down to earth, the left hidden and of the ocean. Soon the dominance of the right becomes clear, as Mananaan *"smites with his bicycle pump the crayfish in his left hand"* (*U* 510). Since Mananaan was a sea god, he thus repudiates his own nature and origin. It is therefore both understandable and a sign of serious limitation that Mananaan should warn "beware the left, the cult of Shakti."

As Gifford and Seidman point out, Hindu Shaktism involves the worship of various goddesses. Traditionally it is a cult of the left hand, while the worship of Hindu gods is associated with the right hand. Mananaan's warning may be against imbalance toward the left, but his self-punishing action suggests rather a fear causing (or caused by) an imbalance toward the right. The larger implication for this episode and for Joyce's theology is that God in the macrocosm is an androgynous being that differentiates itself into the symmetrical sexes only in its lower (manipulative?) functions, the left and right hands of this world (Magdalen and Christ in the Christian version). In the microcosm of the human individual, there is also a left and a right; incarnation in one sex naturally causes onesidedness until balanced by the other. What a man needs is, so to speak, a right relation to the left.

Both Stephen as perverse left hand and Bloom as undextrous right are faced with their wrong relation in "Circe." Although Bloom is demeaned by the sensual Bella, as Circe she also offers him the "glorious afflictions" that result in his purging the negative potential of the internal female. Shaktism includes goddesses who represent a full spectrum of this female potential, thus putting it in harmony with the evocation of the soul in "Oxen of the Sun," as well as with the view of the archetypal goddess offered to our time in the unconscious anima of Carl Jung or the White Goddess of Robert Graves. There is a lot of personality splitting in "Circe," but there is also some fusion, as when Stephen the left-leaning blasphemer and Bloom the right-speaking Mason blend in the mirror late in the episode (*U* 567). This important fusion is not the male-female one my approach has pointed toward. That fusion is most strongly indicated in the "Ithaca" episode: in the Linati scheme, "fusion" is the word Joyce used to describe both the technique and the thematic coming together of Bloom and Stephen (Ellmann, *Ulysses,* unnumbered pages following 187).

We come finally to the muse and the earth goddess. On the last page of "Ithaca" Molly Bloom is called "Gea-Tellus" (*U* 737), the Greek-Roman goddess of earth and fertility. As characterized by the young Joyce's hero, Giordano Bruno, "our earth" is "the divine mother who hath given birth to us, doth nourish us, and moreover will receive us back" (*On the Infinite Universe and Worlds* 257). Similarly Joyce follows his reference to Molly as earth with the description, "fulfilled, recumbent, big with seed" (*U* 737). He ends the paragraph with a reference to Bloom as "the manchild in the womb." An earlier description connected earth with Molly's buttocks in evoking Bloom's mood of "Satisfaction at the ubiquity in eastern and western terrestrial hemispheres . . . of adipose posterior female hemispheres, redolent of milk and honey" (*U* 734). These images obviously should be linked with that process of conception, gestation, and reproduction that I have connected with Joyce's mother and his view of Eve and the imagination.

Only a writer who was in deep contact with his feminine side could have written the "Penelope" episode. I do not, of course, mean that Joyce there plumbs the female psyche. "Penelope" is a man's picture of a woman, but is drawn from inner perceptions as well as outer observations and various theories. One of these theories, as Joseph Voelker has argued, comes from Giordano Bruno (39–48). Molly in her self-contradictions represents the inexhaustible divine in nature, a version of God fuller and more real than man's logical definitions of Him.

Molly is referred to by O'Madden Burke as "the vocal muse" (*U* 135), a tribute not only to her voice but to her inspiring beauty.[4] The reader, who has access to her mind in "Penelope," may take her as the vocal muse in a down-to-earth but ultimately-divine way. Since we know how much her monologue and nature owe to Joyce's wife, I propose to conclude this investigation of Joyce and the goddess by a brief consideration of Nora as muse, goddess and fallen woman. The most obvious indication of her importance is that Joyce set *Ulysses* on the day of their first tryst. In one of his 1909 letters to her, he wrote, "It is perhaps in art, Nora dearest, that you and I will find a solace for our own love" (*SL* 165). *Ulysses* and *Finnegans Wake* could be taken to fulfill that hope.

The most revealing indication of Nora's artistic function for Joyce is in the notes he made for *Exiles.* We can see her there as the original for Molly, the earth goddess of "Ithaca." "She is the earth, dark, formless, mother, made beautiful by the moonlit night, darkly conscious of her instincts." Thinking of the youthful lover who died for her, Nora in Joyce's imagi-

nation sheds "tears of commiseration. She is Magdalen who weeps remem-
bering the loves she could not return" (*JJI* 335). This picture of Mary
Magdalen sublimates the prostitute in the feeling woman. Joyce's letters
to Nora in 1909 make clear, however, his insistence that both he and she
had fallen but that she would continue to redeem him.

Although Nora as dark earth may be the original of Molly as Gea-Tellus,
earth as divinity, it is the forms of the goddess in *Ulysses* that have been my
focus. Guilty of infidelity as a wife, Molly is true to Joyce's larger conception
of woman as hemispheric world, as receptor of seed, as bearer of the
generational canal, as the matrix of creation. Aware of the feminine within
as an unconscious reality, the suppressed half of an androgynous creator,
Joyce resolutely moved through shame and guilt to an imaginative expression of wholeness. Whether looking within or without, he seems to have
seen an Eve or Magdalen or Sophia desiring atonement but caught in the
dirt from which our earth is continually created. Repudiating religious
orthodoxy, Joyce immersed himself in the darkness of the senses as the
only observable habitat of the spirit. Violating literary orthodoxy, he
plunged his reader into the dark underside of social and psychological
reality, insisting that in that repudiated realm lay salvation. In his effort to
bring about a balance of the denied and accepted, he brought together
dark with light, left with right, fallen with redeeming, female with male.
As a male himself, he recognized a submerged, complementary nature, the
female as his soul and muse, the consubstantial goddess of generation who
can be discerned behind the revealing-concealing words of *Ulysses* as the
divine principle of creativity in Joyce's world.

Notes

1. This is Stephen's reaction to the bird girl in *A Portrait of the Artist as a Young
Man* (172). For a more detailed appraisal of Stephen's early relation to the feminine,
see my article "Destruction and Creation in *A Portrait of the Artist as a Young Man*,"
James Joyce Quarterly (Spring 1985): 259–70.

2. See Robert Boyle's study of the dove as female third person of the trinity,
"Worshipper of the Word: James Joyce and the Trinity" (128–35).

3. In her discussion of the Cabala in this section of her book, Blavatsky frequently
refers to the androgynous nature of God.

4. The tribute is made equivocal by his adding "Dublin's prime favorite," as
though she were a roast of beef (or as Lenehan suggests, a sexual favorite.)

Works Cited

Blavatsky, Helen P. *Isis Unveiled*. 2. Pasadena, Calif.: Theosophical University Press,
    1960.
Boyle, Robert. *James Joyce's Pauline Vision*. Carbondale: Southern Illinois University
    Press, 1978.

———. "Worshipper of the Word: James Joyce and the Trinity." In *A Starchamber Quiry,* ed. E. L. Epstein. New York: Methuen, 1982.

Bruno, Giordano. *The Heroic Frenzies.* Tr. Paul Memmo. Chapel Hill: University of North Carolina Press, 1965.

———. *On the Infinite Universe and Worlds.* Tr. Dorothy Singer in *Giordano Bruno: His Life and Thought.* New York: Henry Schuman, 1950.

Budgen, Frank. *James Joyce and the Making of "Ulysses."* Bloomington: Indiana University Press, 1960.

Campbell, Joseph. "Contransmagnificandjewbangtantiality." *Studies in the Literary Imagination* 3.2 (Oct. 1970): 11.

Eckley, Grace. ". . . The Tree and the Stone in *Finnegans Wake.*" In *Narrator and Character in "Finnegans Wake,"* ed. Michael H. Begnal and Grace Eckley. Lewisburg, Pa.: Bucknell University Press, 1975.

Ellmann, Richard. *Ulysses on the Liffey.* New York: Oxford University Press, 1972.

Gose, Elliott B., Jr. *The Transformation Process in Joyce's "Ulysses."* University of Toronto Press, 1980.

Herring, Phillip F. *Joyce's "Ulysses" Notesheets in the British Museum.* Charlottesville: University Press of Virginia, 1972.

King, Charles William. *The Gnostics and their Remains.* Minneapolis: Wizards Bookshelf, 1973.

Scholes, Robert, and Richard Kain, eds. *The Workshop of Daedalus.* Evanston: Northwestern University Press, 1965.

Shechner, Mark. *Joyce in Nighttown: A Psychoanalytic Inquiry into "Ulysses."* Berkeley and Los Angeles: University of California Press, 1974.

Silverstein, Norman. "Magic on the Notesheets of the 'Circe' Episode." *James Joyce Quarterly* 1 (1965): 19–26.

Voelker, Joseph. " 'Nature it is': The Influence of Giordano Bruno on James Joyce's Molly Bloom." *James Joyce Quarterly* 14 (1976): 39–48.

5. Biographical Studies

"Thrust Syphilis Down to Hell"

J. B. Lyons, M.D.

I

Willard Potts, the editor of a widely distributed study of Joyce in exile, recalls Edna O'Brien's question, "Was he neurotic?"—remarking that recently the chief question seems to be, "Was he syphilitic?" "Such questions," Potts writes, "have their interest but are limiting and in any event have been explored adequately" (xiv). If I venture to revive matters which might have been tactfully avoided it is because I believe that one of these questions still lacks an authoritative answer.

Was he neurotic? The short answer "yes" is unlikely to be contested, and I shall not discuss it further other than to remark how commonly psychoneurosis is creativity's burdensome, albeit fruitful, companion. Was he syphilitic? The question, I suspect, is ill-mannered, and because those who pose it seem determined to prove that Joyce suffered either from congenital or acquired syphilis, or preferably both, I am glad to say he had neither.

My diffidence in discussing clinical matters before a literary audience is diminished by the fact that syphilis, the unwelcome gift of the last years of the quattrocento, has notable literary associations. The term itself derives from a sixteenth-century poem in Latin hexameters, *Syphilis Sive Morbus Gallicus,* by Hieronymous Fracastorius. This work in the manner of Virgil's *Georgics* was published in Verona in 1530 and is not to be dismissed as a piece of doggerel by a Renaissance physician toying with letters, for it was admired by Scaliger. Fracastorius was a poet, doctor, mathematician, and astronomer; his verses were praised by John Addington Symonds, and more recently an American critic described his dialogue on poetry (*Naugerius, Sive de Poetica Dialogus*) as a work of consummate art. Nahum Tate, the Dublin-born poet laureate, translated it in 1686, and the following are its opening lines:

> Through what Adventures this unknown Disease
> So lately did astonished *Europe* seize,
> Through *Asian Coasts* and *Libyan* Cities ran,
> And from what seeds the malady began,
> Our Song shall tell: To Naples first it came
> From France, and justly took from France its Name
> Companion of the War—
> The Methods next of cure we shall express,
> The wond'rous wit of Mortals in Distress . . . (337)

In the third book of *Syphilis Sive Morbus Gallicus* the dire punishment of a young shepherd, Syphilus, who has raised an altar to false gods, is described:

> A Shepherd once (distrust not ancient Fame)
> Possest these Downs, and *Syphilus* his Name.
> A thousand Heifers in these Vales he fed.
> A thousand Ewes to those fair Rivers led:
> For King Alcithous he rais'd this stock,
> And shaded in the Covert of the Rock . . . (369)

Eventually the prejudicial appellation "French disease" (it was also called "the Spanish scabies," "the Neapolitan disease," and, by the Turks, "the Christian disease") was replaced by the inoffensive name of Fracastor's shepherd.

Shakespeare has catalogued some of its nastiest manifestations in *Timon of Athens:* "Consumption sow in the hollow bones of man . . . Crack the lawyer's voice . . . Down with the nose, down with it flat . . . Make curl'd pate ruffians bald. . . ." Ibsen's *Ghosts* gives a misleading portrayal of congenital syphilis which may have influenced Joyce.

The roll-call of the victims of syphilis is answered by distinguished voices, including those of Henry VIII of England and Francis I of France. It destroyed Baudelaire, Guy de Maupassant, and Lord Randolph Churchill with a fury that is relevant, for it commonly claims a heavy debt.

Do Joyce's traducers believe his hubris deserved chastisement? Do they equate his adolescent desecration of the family's lares and penates with the blasphemy of Fracastor's shepherd, that they so casually attach a demeaning diagnostic label? Dr. F. R. Walsh's recollection in the *Irish Medical Times* of how John Stanislaus Joyce told a group of Dublin medical students in 1920 that he had acquired a syphilitic chancre in Cork in 1867, his sole treatment a local application of carbolic acid, prompted Hall and Waisbren, the latter a Milwaukee internist, to say "that Joyce's father was a profligate who may well have passed on syphilis to his son" (963).

This, however, is the flimsiest of evidence—the boastful comments of an elderly man whose magnificent constitution and survival to the age of eighty-two hardly suggest that he had harbored a major infection. Those who practiced medicine when syphilis was common did tests on even the most unlikely patients, knowing that a denial of exposure to risk meant nothing. But if a person actually boasted that he had been poxed, he too was probably to be disbelieved.

The classic stigmata of congenital syphilis—deafness, interstitial keratitis, and Hutchinson's teeth—are ineradicable. There is no question of James Joyce's having had any of them, nor was any of his siblings thus affected. Incidentally, the pro-congenital syphilis lobby conveniently exclude Poppie and Stannie and the other children from their accusations.

Those who argue that Joyce acquired syphilis stand on firmer ground. It may well be that he was lucky to have escaped it, for Oliver St. John Gogarty's letters to Joyce, and to Dr. Michael Walsh, indicate that Joyce was treated for a venereal infection in 1904 (Lyons, *Oliver St. John Gogarty— The Man of the Many Talents*). This appears to have responded to the meager therapeutic resources then available. Within six months he had left Dublin with Nora Barnacle in a partnership the least gallant lover would hardly have contracted had he harbored a persisting infection. There has never, to my knowledge, been the slightest hint that he transmitted an infection to his consort, though we have abundant evidence of their erotic fervor.

As a youth, Joyce was healthy and active. His only physical blemish was the myopia for which Dr. A. H. Benson prescribed spectacles, the famous glasses broken on the cinder track in Clongowes. Dental decay became bothersome in 1905—"My mouth is full of decayed teeth, my soul of decayed ambitions"—and the abdominal symptoms which caused Nora, in Pola, to pray, "Oh my God, take away Jim's pain," may have been an early manifestation of the duodenal ulcer which killed him in 1941.

His first serious illness (other than the infection [gonorrhea?] referred to above) was that for which he was treated in Trieste's Ospitalo Civico in 1907, from mid-July until September. Alarming rumors reached Dublin. "I heard you were stricken with a grievous distemper," Gogarty wrote, "and that you were paralysed. You can understand that the sight of your handwriting rejoiced me, as it disproved the statement that your right arm was paralysed" (Lyons, *James Joyce and Medicine*, 65). Joyce's uncle assured Gogarty that the disease was "altogether ethical" and in his next letter Gogarty refers to it as rheumatic fever. That explanation is almost certainly incorrect. The combination of acute rheumatic symptoms with iritis suggests today either Reiter's syndrome or sarcoidosis, neither of which could have been diagnosed in 1907. Hans Reiter, a German army doctor, described the details of the disease which bears his name in 1916 in the case of a German lieutenant serving on the Balkan front. Acute arthritis as a manifestation of sarcoidosis has been recognized much more recently. There was a relapse of the iritis in 1908, and in a letter to his sister, Joyce wrote: "I feel a little better of the rheumatism and am now more like a capital S than a capital Z" (*Letters II* 226).

Writing to his wife from Dublin on 1 November 1909, and presumably referring to a genital discharge, Joyce thanks her for inquiring about "that damned dirty affair of mine. It is no worse anyhow. I was alarmed at your silence first. I feared you had something wrong. But you are all right, are you not dearest? Thank god! Poor little Nora, how bad am I to you!" (*Letters II* 259). Ellmann sees this as "a minor complaint probably contracted from a prostitute" (*Letters II* 259n) but one cannot say whether it was a new infection or a relapse of the "dose" picked up in Nighttown in 1904. Circumstances favor the latter, for, with the exception of unconsummated affairs with a young pupil in Trieste and with Marthe Fleischmann in Zurich, he does not appear to have been a philanderer.

Joyce's clinical history contains further low-key references to pains in limbs and back, but the continuing problem was what he described to Forrest Read in May 1917 as "rheumatic iritis complicated with synechia and glaucoma" (Read 96). Such indeed was his plight that Ezra Pound wrote: "My dear Job: you will establish an immortal record. At what period the shift of terminal sound in your family name occurred I am unable to state, but the -yce at the end is an obvious error. The arumaic — b is obviously the correct spelling" (Read 121).

The features of this chronic eye disorder are unlike syphilitic iritis, which occurs in the secondary stage of the disease when other diagnostic signs abound. It can be confirmed or excluded by a blood test, the Wasserman Reaction, which became available in 1906 and would have been a routine procedure by the time Joyce had had his first eye operation. Actually Joyce himself, in a letter to Miss Weaver in 1930, provides an assurance that he did not have syphilis:

> Dr. Fontaine is also rather distant with me. I have the highest opinion of her and allowed her to bring me after Borsch's death (1929) to be seen by a young French ophthalmologist, Dr. Hartmann, who said the only possible solution of the case was that my eye trouble proceeded from congenital syphilis which being curable, he said the proper thing for me was to undergo a cure of I have forgotten what . . . I told this to Dr. Collinson and he dissuaded me strongly from undergoing it. He said that at the very beginning Dr. Borsch and he had discussed this possibility and that Borsch had excluded it categorically on account of the nature of the attacks, the way in which they were cured and the general reactions of the eye. (*SL* 348)

Lucia Joyce's doctors also excluded syphilis, and the final proof that the celebrated novelist did not have a treponemal infection was Dr. Zollinger's post-mortem examination which showed no suggestion of syphilis (Lyons, *James Joyce and Medicine* 221).

2

Sexually transmitted diseases inspire fear and remorse in those who contract them but are a rich source of amusement to others, who ask for nothing better that to hear that an acquaintance has come a cropper on such a banana skin. This comic element has been overlooked by some of *Ulysses'* unsmiling readers. Furthermore, idioms which use "poxy" as a general term of derogation or "GPI" (general paralysis of the insane) as a synonym for any form of eccentricity have been interpreted literally. Thus Hall and

Waisbren are led grievously astray by Buck Mulligan's light-hearted comment "that fellow I was with in the Ship last night says you have g.p.i." and because Stephen does not bother to reply they conclude that "he accepts what Buck says as a fact" (Hall and Waisbren 963), whereas Mulligan merely implies that Dedalus is an oddity.

John Garvin supplies another instance of this black humor. An obituary notice credited John S. Joyce as "late LGB" (Local General Board), but Garvin's friend Jim Tully said, "They should have put him down as 'late GPI'" (Garvin 38). And Joyce himself could refer to the disease in a spirit of levity. "Syphilis is for the French," he wrote to Harriet Shaw Weaver, "what God Save the King is for the English, when it is mentioned *tout le monde se decouvre*" (*SL* 348).

Hall and Waisbren see syphilis as a major theme in *Ulysses,* but Shen and Soldo believe they have overstated their case and accuse them of hunting wildly for symbols. They regard, for instance, every use of the letter *S* "as a code symbol" for syphilis, and Dr. Waisbren seems to have absolved himself of all restraint in attributing every clinical aberration in the book to syphilis. I can accept only six items from the seventy-five tabulated by Hall and Waisbren as evidence of syphilis, although I do agree that venereal diseases are well represented in *Ulysses,* and fifty or so quite convincing references can be readily mustered. I do not, however, see syphilis as a theme but as a reflection of environmental reality.

The ambiance of *Dubliners,* as I have argued elsewhere, is alcoholism ("Diseases in *Dubliners*"), but even a cursory reading of *Ulysses* reveals sufficient Hogarthian depictions of sexual mishap to terrify all but the hardiest of Don Juans. The "snares of the poxfiend" (427) generally result in "a hard chancre" (476); its treatment may end in "a dark mercurialised face" (456). Fortunately Stephen has "sheltered from the sin of Paris" (25) in the Bibliothèque Sainte Geneviève; back in Dublin he recalls a shawled prostitute soliciting in a dark archway: "A she-fiend's whiteness under her rancid rags" (47). Bloom cautions him on the dangers of Nighttown, "a regular deathtrap for a young fellows of his age" (614).

Syphilis was an occupational risk for servicemen. Bloom remembers how Arthur Griffith's *United Irishman* referred to "an army rotten with venereal disease" (73); Molly suspects that "the half of those sailors are rotten again with disease" (778). But its stigma, as the Citizen indicates, is not confined to any sect or class: "There's a bloody sight more pox than pax about that boyo. Edward Guelph-Wettin!" (330).

"God knows what poxy bowsy left them off" (6) is Buck Mulligan's disparaging comment about Stephen's second-hand trousers. Bloom thinks of the "quack doctor for the clap," Henry Franks, whose advertisements are read by "some chap with a dose burning him" (153).

The whores include Bird-in-the-Hand, "which was within all foul plagues" (396), and the surprisingly well-spoken Biddy the Clap (590). Bloom, in an altercation with Bella, speaks of a "kipkeeper! Pox and gleet vendor!" (554). It is Kitty Rickets who most clearly describes the appalling consequences of a syphilitic infection: "And Mary Shortall that was in the lock with the pox she got from Jimmy Pidgeon in the blue caps had a child off him that couldn't swallow and was smothered with the convulsions in the mattress and we all subscribed for the funeral" (520).

Joyce's account of the horrors of syphilis carries no moral implications but could serve well as a warning and deterrent. The reference to "civilisation" and "syphilisation" (*U* 325) echoes Krafft-Ebing's contention that G.P.I. was commoner in persons of some intellectual attainment than in the unlettered, but his own brief enrollment as a medical student did not bring him even to the threshold of clinical instruction, contrary to what Hall and Waisbren imply.

Clive Hart's *Concordance to "Finnegans Wake"* has no entry for "syphilis" but does include a synonym, "lues" ("or lues the day" [*FW* 347.14–15]); "poxed" ("Cursed that he suppoxed he did" [90.25]); "poxy" ("Gotopoxy" [386.31]); "an infamous private ailment (vulgovariovenereal)" (98.18); and "he suffered from a vile disease" (33.17–18).

There is no direct reference to syphilis in either *A Portrait of the Artist as a Young Man* or *Dubliners,* but it is likely that a number of laundresses in "Clay" had the disease. Others such as Corley, Jack Mooney, Bob Doran, and Ignatius Gallagher could fall under suspicion, and the amorous couples in Phoenix Park, whose "venal and furtive loves" were so disturbing to Mr. Duffy ("A Painful Case"), faced the prevailing risk.

Corley ("Two Gallants"), a calculating womanizer, knows that a former girlfriend is "on the turf now," in modern parlance "on the game." Jack Mooney "had the reputation of being a hard case" and one of his mother's lodgers ("The Boarding House"), Bob Doran, "had sown his wild oats"; Ignatius Gallagher ("A Little Cloud") "summarized the vices of many capitals" to the astonishment of Little Chandler.

The suggestion that Father Flynn's illness ("The Sisters") was general paralysis of the insane is, to my mind, unacceptable (Lyons, "Animadversions on Paralysis as a Symbol in 'The Sisters'"). It is a poor compliment to Joyce to imply a degree of incompetence which would provide a classic account of cerebral arteriosclerosis—"There was no hope for him this time: it was the third stroke" (*D* 9)—instead of the tragic features of G.P.I., a rapidly evolving dementia punctuated by convulsive attacks and paresis, inexorably progressive and seen in the middle-aged rather than the elderly.

In his essay "Ibsen's New Drama" (*CW* 47–67), written before he was eighteen, Joyce refers to the harrowing simplicity of *Ghosts.* It seems likely that his knowledge of syphilis is partly based on Oswald Alving's illness, actually an unrealistic portrayal of congenital syphilis, which is a truly baneful inheritance. When affected infants survive they may, as indicated above, display specific physical depredations—fissured lips, snuffles, and saddle nose—and there is a general stunting of growth and failure to thrive. "A considerable number," according to the leading British neurologist, S. A. K. Wilson, "are more or less defective from birth, in the sense that their faculties do not develop normally; but others are children of a promise that is never fulfilled; after a hopeful beginning at school, gradually a cloud creeps over the adolescent mind, obscuring its salient features and finally quenching its fertility" (Wilson 563).

Oswald Alving's robust physique and artistic sensitivity would have been unusual endowments in someone with congenital syphilis; moreover, congenital G.P.I., a rare condition, generally occurred between the age of nine and sixteen rather than at the later age that suited the dramatist. This clinical picture of "juvenile paresis" had not been clearly delineated when Ibsen wrote *Ghosts* in Sorrento in 1881, and his account of Oswald Alving's illness closely follows the features of acquired G.P.I. "Mother, it's my mind that has broken down," Oswald explains during his last evening of sanity, "I shall never be able to work anymore! . . . Never!—never! A living death! Mother, can you imagine anything so horrible?" (Ibsen 82).

Joyce's "Epilogue to Ibsen's *Ghosts*" (*CW* 271–73), written in 1934 ("Explain, fate if you are and can / Why one is sound and one is rotten" [*CW* 272]), confirms how imperfect his clinical knowledge was even then. The conundrum is solved when one realizes that the lapse of eight years between the conception of the diseased Oswald and the seduction of the servant had rendered the seducer uninfective. Regina's mother, Johanna Engstrand, and her infant remained healthy.

His inadequate knowledge may, indeed, have fostered temporarily in Joyce a degree of "syphiliphobia." This clinical entity, familiar to those who practiced medicine before, say, 1950, evoked an obsessional dread of syphilis in persons exposed, however briefly, to the risk of contact: thereafter they remained unable to accept reassurance of freedom from infection. Did Joyce's failure to see the details of *Ghosts* as unlikely fictions cause him to identify with Oswald Alving? Was he misled by Ibsen's portrayal of the promising and apparently healthy artist suddenly stricken by the sins of his father? In 1904, Stanislaus wrote in his *Dublin Diary:*

> He talks much of the syphilitic contagion in Europe, is at present writing a series of studies in it in Dublin, tracing practically everything to it. The drift of his talk seems to be that the contagion is congenital and incurable and responsible for all manias, and being so, that it is useless to try to avoid it. Heaven seems to invite you to delight in the manias and to humour each to the top of its bent. In this I do not follow him except to accept his theory of the contagion, which he adduces on medical authority. Even this I do slowly, for I have the idea that the influence of heredity is somewhat overstated. Yet I am rapidly becoming a valetudinarian on the point. I see symptoms in every turn I take. (51–52)

Little Stephen Dedalus was puzzled by the metaphors in the litany of the Blessed Virgin; his creator, given to what Stanislaus Joyce called "pseudo-medical phraseology," saw no incongruity in the misappropriation of technical terms to express disparagement. He called Hellenism "European appendicitis" and on 7 January 1904, in "A Portrait of the Artist" (the earliest version of *A Portrait of the Artist as a Young Man*) referred to "the general paralysis of an insane society" (Scholes and Kain 68), lumping together the innocent and the venal, the ascetic and concupiscent. His indulgence in jargon is not unprecedented. A supporter of Mrs. Josephine Butler, founder of the International Abolitionist Federation—its concerns were brothels and white slavery—believed syphilis to be "the punishment inflicted by nature on vicious men" and stated in 1902 that its eradication would result in the ruin of society and morality through "a moral syphilization even worse than that of the body."

This misapplication of medical nomenclature is less maladroit than it might first appear when one understands that in Joyce's youth, as in earlier times, the cause of syphilis was arguable. The horror-stricken Neapolitans and the besiegers, the army of Charles VIII of France, accepted that the epidemic of 1495 resulted from a conjunction of Jupiter and Mars in the previous year, and Fracastor, swayed by astrology, accepted that men were "Slaves to the very Rabble of the Sky" (Tate 341). The principal means of spread, however, cannot have been long in doubt, and Fracastor advised sufferers to avoid noxious winds, to remain active, but to

> Abstain however from the Act of Love,
> For nothing can so much destructive prove:
> Bright Venus hates polluted Mysteries,
> And ev'ry Nymph from foul Embraces flies,
> Dire Practice! Poison with Delight to bring,
> And with the Lover's Dart, the Serpent's sting. (354)

Accidental transmission is an occasional occurrence in every century and guilty burgesses have sought refuge hopefully in such a contingency. Thus, Joyce in his "Epilogue" writes:

> Olaf may plod his stony path
> And live as chastely as Susanna
> Yet pick up in some Turkish bath
> His *quantum est* of *Pox Romana*. (*CW* 272)

Syphilis has been called "a fever diluted by time," and Phillipe Ricord of Paris divided it into three stages—primary, secondary, and tertiary. A Dublin surgeon, Abraham Colles, formulated a proposition, now known as Colles's law, that although a diseased infant may infect a wet-nurse, it never infects its mother. Dr. William Wallace, an Irish physician who had made a similar and earlier observation, saw that this indicated that the mother was already infected: "You may say she was sound . . . but you have, in my opinion, a proof in her having given birth to an unsound child that she was unsound. . . ." His point is relevant to my argument. Those who favor the idea that James Joyce had congenital syphilis must realize that their contention carries the implication that his mother was infected. There is no evidence to support this suggestion; however, Stanislaus Joyce's diary entry may indicate that his brother was misled by a theory current at the turn of the century, and cited by Osler in the fourth edition of his *Principles and Practice of Medicine* (1901), that the disease could be inherited from the father ("sperm inheritance"), while the mother remained healthy. "It is, unfortunately," Osler wrote, expressing a now discredited theory, "an every-day experience to see congenital syphilis in which the infection is clearly paternal" (266).

The precise cause of syphilis was not established until 1905 when Fritz Schaudinn and Erich Hoffmann identified the *Treponema pallidum*. Meanwhile certain disorders, including G.P.I., were considered to be "not exclusively and necessarily caused by syphilis," an interpretation which increases the scope and lessens the offensiveness of Joyce's metaphor.

As Fracastor was aware, the disease affects humans exclusively, and Metchnickoff's transmission of syphilis to an experimental animal ("And to such delights has Metchnikoff inoculated anthropoid apes" [521]) was duly noted by Joyce in "Circe." The organ of this episode is the locomotor apparatus and, as Joyce credibly told Frank Budgen, it has the rhythm of locomotor ataxia, a form of neurosyphilis (Budgen 228).

3

I do not find it easy to accept John Garvin's assertion that the "knowledge" that Joyce's father had syphilis in his youth "was the kinetic factor that drove two of his sons into exile" (42). Surely Joyce's flight to Pola and Trieste is adequately explained as a lover's retreat from the general squalor of the family home in North Dublin and an evasion of the financial responsibility which an eldest son might have been expected to shoulder. More difficult still to credit, unless as a macabre joke, is James Joyce's alleged confidence in 1931 to Tom Kiernan, a member of the Irish diplomatic corps, that "his father was bedridden in Dublin, near death in the last stages of G.P.I." (Garvin 42). This is impossible to reconcile with his more characteristic statement to Miss Weaver after his father's death: "I knew he was old, but I thought he would live longer" (*Letters III*).

Two years later the "Epilogue to Ibsen's *Ghosts*" included an absolution applicable, I like to think, to John Stanislaus Joyce:

Blame all and none and take to task
The harlot's lure, the swain's desire.
Heal by all means but hardly ask
Did this man sin or did his sire. (*CW* 273)

By then, as we have seen, Joyce had his doctor's assurance that his eye disorder was not syphilitic, and later he learned that he had conveyed no luetic taint to Lucia.

Diagnosis is ordinarily a private matter between doctor and patient, and when it becomes a speculative free-for-all, as has happened in James Joyce's case, objectivity must not be obscured nor speculation permitted to run rife. In conclusion, therefore, echoing Joyce's "Thrust syphilis down to hell" (*U* 427), I submit that there is no acceptable evidence that John Stanislaus Joyce had tertiary syphilis, and affirm that there is ample proof that James Joyce escaped this infection.

Fracastor described a decision to make a placatory sacrifice to "the offended Sun":

> On *Syphilus* the dreadful Lot did fall
> Who now was plac'd before the Altar bound,
> His Head with sacrificial Garlands crown'd,
> His Throat laid open to the lifted Knife,
> But interceding *Juno* spar'd his Life,
> Commands them in his Stead a Heifir slay,
> For Phoebus' Rage was now remov'd away. (372)

Do we not owe the guiltless Dublin author the duty of a similar liberation from the damaging question "Did Joyce have syphilis?" by answering it, finally, with a resounding "No"?

Works Cited

Budgen, Frank. *James Joyce and the Making of "Ulysses."* Bloomington: Indiana University Press, 1960.

The Collected Works of Ibsen. New York: Greystone Press, n.d.

Fracastorius, Hieronymous. *Syphilis Sire Morbus Gallicus.* Verona: 1530.

Garvin, J. *James Joyce's Disunited Kingdom.* Dublin: Gill and Macmillan, 1976.

Hall, V., and B. A. Waisbren. "Syphilis as a Major Theme in James Joyce's *Ulysses.*" *Archives of Internal Medicine* 140 (1980): 963–65.

Hart, Clive. *A Concordance to "Finnegan's Wake."* Minneapolis: University of Minnesota Press, 1963.

Joyce, S. *The Dublin Diary of Stanislaus Joyce.* Ed. G. H. Healey. London: Faber, 1962.

Lyons, J. B. "Animadversions on Paralysis as a Symbol in 'The Sisters.'" *James Joyce Quarterly* 11 (1974): 257–65.

———. "Diseases in *Dubliners:* Tokens of Disaffection." In *Irish Renaissance Annual* II, ed. Zack Bowen. Newark: University of Delaware Press, 1981.

———. *James Joyce and Medicine.* Dublin: Dolmen Press, 1973.

———. *Oliver St. John Gogarty—The Man of Many Talents.* Dublin: Blackwater Press, 1980.

Osler, William. *Principles and Practice of Medicine.* 4th ed. London: Appleton, 1901.

Potts, Willard. *Portraits of the Artist in Exile*. Seattle: University of Washington Press; Dublin: Wolfhound Press, 1979.

Read, Forrest, ed. *Pound/Joyce: The Letters of Ezra Pound to James Joyce with Pound's Essay on Joyce*. New York: New Directions, 1967.

Scholes, Robert, and Richard M. Kain. *The Workshop of Daedalus*. Evanston, Ill.: Northwestern University Press, 1965.

Shen, W. W., and J. J. Soldo. "Symbol Hunting in James Joyce's 'Syphilizations.'" *Archives of Internal Medicine* 141 (1981): 691–92.

Tate, Nahum. *Syphilis: or a Poetical History of the French Disease Written in Latin by Fracastorius. And Now Attempted in English by N. Tate*. In J. Dryden's *Miscellany Poems*. Fifth Part, 327–73. London: Tonson, 1727.

Wallace, William. "Exanthematic Form of Syphilis." *Lancet*, 20 May 1837:282–86.

Walsh, F. R. *Irish Medical Times*. 9 May 1975.

Wilson, S. A. K. *Neurology*. 1. London: Butterworth, 1954.

Joyce's Early Publishing History in America

Ann McCullough, O.P.

Although Benjamin W. Huebsch cannot in any sense be said to have "discovered" James Joyce, it is almost impossible to overestimate the publisher's contribution in establishing and maintaining Joyce as a recognized literary artist in America. Huebsch was the first to publish *Dubliners* in the United States, and the first to publish *A Portrait of the Artist as a Young Man* anywhere. With the exception of *Ulysses,* Huebsch published all of Joyce's major work up to 1925 under his own imprint: *Dubliners* and *Portrait* in 1916, *Chamber Music* and *Exiles* in 1918.

Had not *Ulysses* been embroiled in a censorship controversy after its partial publication in the *Little Review* in 1919–20, Huebsch almost certainly would have added that Joyce epic to his list. Even though practical considerations forced the publisher to refuse *Ulysses,* a refusal that hurt and angered the author, Joyce placed *Finnegans Wake* with Huebsch in 1931, six years after Huebsch's firm merged with Viking Press in 1925. It seems in retrospect largely a matter of chance that Huebsch came to play the role he did in bringing Joyce before that small but intelligent and articulate segment of the American reading public which played so large a part in establishing recognition for the great writers of their time.

BWH: Person and Publisher

Even when one considers only his contribution with respect to Joyce, Ben Heubsch made a difference in publishing. He once compared being a publisher to being a poet: both were sacred callings and required complete dedication. If he made any money with his books, he was pleased, but the real point was that he had to consider a book worth publishing. His friends described Huebsch as calm and gentle, with a very hard core at his center. He could not be imposed upon and, with a deep and consistent sense of values, he never gave up strongly held convictions.

Ben Huebsch got into publishing by happenstance. He started out as a lithographer's apprentice, but hoped to become a musician. Huebsch attended Packard Business College and studied violin with Sam Franko before joining his uncle and brother in their small printing shop. Shortly after he entered the shop, they left it, and Huebsch found himself alone in the printing business, for which he had little formal preparation.

Within a very few years, Huebsch acceded to the wishes of Edward

Howard Griggs, a friend for whom he had been printing pamphlets, to promote and sell as well as to print his manuscripts. One of Griggs's manuscripts, entitled "A Book of Meditations," was the first book Huebsch printed. The year was 1902. Whether or not he recognized it at the time—and the likelihood is that the thought never crossed his mind—Huebsch was the first American Jew to enter general publishing in the twentieth century.

In 1905 Huebsch slowly began to publish books other than those by Griggs, each title in some way reflecting his idealism or highly principled social conscience. From even this early time, many of the most important books on his list were translations of Continental authors unavailable until then in America. Publishing some of these required finesse and courage, since censorship laws at that time were stringent and placed heavy restrictions on any publisher. In 1915, however, Huebsch displayed fearless determination in the face of that censorship by publishing D. H. Lawrence's *The Rainbow,* an earlier casualty of equally strict censorship laws in England. Were it not for an unfortunate misunderstanding,[1] Huebsch would also undoubtedly have published Lawrence's *Women in Love,* a fact which renders less surprising his subsequent willingness to publish Joyce's *Ulysses.*

Publishing the Early Joyce

As it was Huebsch's colleague George H. Doran who contacted him about publishing Lawrence, so it was that another associate introduced him in the summer of 1914 to James Joyce, this time the English publisher Grant Richards, who that year had brought out Joyce's short stories in England. Nearly two years elapsed, however, before Huebsch actually published Joyce in 1916 (it was not until 1915 that Huebsch had begun to correspond with the author). The connection between author and publisher throughout their long association was primarily professional, although they met once in Paris in 1920[2] and Huebsch responded frequently and loyally over the years to the needs of Joyce and his family.

In spite of his occasionally prickly and over-sensitive genius, Joyce inspired loyalty not only in his American publisher but also in a large coterie of friends and business associates. All of them concerned themselves, often independently of one another, with promoting Joyce's interests and with providing a channel for dealing with his publishers, a task Joyce rarely faced directly.[3] Their correspondence, which could form a literature of its own, presents a fascinating though often confusing backdrop for Joyce's literary achievement.

The occasionally misdirected devotion of Joyce's family and friends complicated Huebsch's work considerably. Joyce did business with Huebsch, particularly in times of illness, not only through family members—his wife,

Nora, and later his son George—but also through James Pinker, his literary agent in London; John Quinn, the New York lawyer who had appointed himself a kind of American agent for Joyce; and friends Ezra Pound and Harriet Shaw Weaver. Magnanimous toward Joyce as each of these persons was, one was frequently working at cross purposes with another, often leaving Joyce relatively in the dark and Huebsch with him, at least to the degree that he received conflicting, incomplete, or incorrect information. Huebsch learned rapidly, however, and his long, sometimes turbulent, relationship with Joyce proves almost more than any other his capacity for encouraging new voices in modern literature.

Grant Richards it was, then, who in 1914 offered Huebsch American rights to Joyce's *Dubliners*. Joyce had actually finished the book in 1907, but fear felt by two different publishers concerning Irish and English censorship[4] (Joyce had no such fear, of course) had delayed its publication until 1914 when Richards judged that the moral climate in England would allow him to bring it out with a minimum of risk. After he had read *Dubliners* Huebsch was drawn to Joyce, whose fresh style seemed to him to possess literary merit such as he had rarely before encountered. The book's earlier history of repeated rejections by other publishers did not deter him, for his philosophy had always been to bring out works of merit regardless of their immediate marketability, on the assumption that a good book will pay its way. A politically idealistic man himself, he was attracted by writers motivated by ideas of reform or radicalism. In Huebsch's judgment, Joyce seemed to be just such an author. But, impressed as he was by Joyce's work, its publication in America by his small and struggling firm required careful consideration.

In June 1915 Huebsch wrote Joyce that he had read "with keenest interest and appreciation" a copy of *Dubliners* given to him by Richards. He continued, "I wanted very much to accept his offer of the American rights but as my capacity is limited, and short stories in book form do not sell well in America I reluctantly abandoned the idea." But, Huebsch added, "If anything else of yours has been published in book form I should be very glad to read it" (*Letters I* 81). Joyce was only too glad to pursue the tentative overtures of the first American publisher who had shown a practical interest in his work. He wrote Huebsch in July 1915 about American publication not only of *Dubliners,* but also of *Chamber Music, Portrait,* and *Exiles* (7 July 1915, Joyce Collection, University of Buffalo Library).

Negotiations about publication of *Dubliners* dragged on, becoming inevitably entangled with discussion of publication of *Portrait,* which Joyce earnestly wanted to be published during 1916. In June 1916, almost exactly a year after he had begun corresponding with Joyce, Huebsch wrote to Harriet Weaver, offering his contract for *Portrait* and promising to give it his best efforts in spite of his belief that its success would be artistic rather than popular. It was, in Richard Ellmann's words, a memorable decision. Taking the line that would eventually endear him to Joyce as well as to Miss Weaver, he wrote in 1916, "I should be willing to print absolutely in accordance with the author's wishes, without deletions . . ." (*Letters I* 91). The contract specified that Huebsch would supply printed sheets from America for joint imprints for an English publisher, the cost then to be shared between them. Provided also in the contract was an arrangement for Huebsch to secure sheets of *Dubliners* from Richards.

Both books were ready for the fall season of 1916. Although *Publishers' Weekly* referred to "A Picture of the Artist" in its index to fall announcements, Huebsch ordered a full page in the 18 November 1916 *Publishers' Weekly,* where Joyce's *Portrait* and *Dubliners* were advertised for the first time, in the estimable company of D. H. Lawrence's *The Prussian Officer* and *Amores,* among others. Both of Joyce's books were ready for distribution by December 1916, and Huebsch promoted them as vigorously as he was able. As part of his campaign to advertise his new publications, the publisher took the entire back cover of the March 1917 issue of the *Little Review,* where he introduced "James Joyce, an Irishman of distinction whose two books *(Dubliners* and *Portrait)* compel the attention of discriminating seekers of brains in books." So it was that *Portrait* came before the reading public for the first time anywhere, because an American publisher was willing to gamble on an unknown author simply because he liked what he wrote.

Huebsch's later decision to destroy his publishing records leaves unclear the exact number of Joyce's books sold in America during this period. Although, as Huebsch predicted, *Dubliners* does not seem to have fared so well, *Portrait* sold briskly enough for Huebsch to make almost immediate plans to run a second edition. On 14 May 1917 he wrote Joyce optimistically, "Your two books are making friends for you in America, and the sale, though not yet large, is unquestionably such as to indicate a steady demand." Indicating in this letter his interest in further publication of Joyce, Huebsch wrote, "What may I say to people who are interested as I am, in a volume that will take us through the next period of The Artist's career?" (14 May 1917, Joyce Collection, Cornell University Library).

It was only a matter of time, then, before Huebsch published an American edition of *Chamber Music,* which had come out in England in 1908 under Elkin Mathews's imprint, and Joyce's new play, *Exiles.* Discussion of a possible American edition of *Chamber Music* had been going on for several years, but it was not until July 1917 that John Quinn offered publication of *Exiles* to Huebsch (5 July 1917, B. W. Huebsch Collection, Library of Congress). Since obtaining an accurate text of Joyce's work was, as always, a cause of delay for Huebsch, publication of *Exiles* did not occur until spring 1918, with the play published simultaneously on 25 May 1918 by Richards in England and Huebsch in New York. Although he had been urging Joyce to add poems to the original edition, Huebsch brought out *Chamber Music* on 30 September 1918, according to Joyce's wishes as it stood in the English edition.

Publication Negotiations—*Ulysses*

During this same period, Joyce, suffering from recurring eye trouble, continued unremittingly to labor on his longest work, *Ulysses,* which, in spite of opposition from John Quinn, had begun to run serially in the *Little Review.* Huebsch wanted to publish the book before the end of 1918, before the completion of the serial. He wrote to Harriet Weaver in spring 1918 in order to establish the date the book would be finished. Joyce projected completion by the summer of 1919, Miss Weaver replied, but the author had suggested to her that in order to keep his name before the few people who were reading what he wrote, Huebsch might wish to consider publishing as a cheap paperbound book the *Telemachia,* that is, the first three episodes under the title *Ulysses I.* Huebsch responded directly to Joyce that he did not favor a separate printing of parts of *Ulysses.* He wrote, "Your reputation here is sufficiently secure to make it unnecessary to publish part of the work merely for the sake of keeping you before the public" (16 July 1918, Joyce Collection, Cornell University Library). If Huebsch had agreed to publish the fragment of *Ulysses* at this time, before litigation involving the *Little Review* barred it from the United States until 1932, the "wanderings of *Ulysses*" and the course of literary history might have been dramatically different. As it was, however, Joyce followed Huebsch's advice about his epic novel, pushing as quickly as circumstances of ill health and poverty would allow toward completion of *Ulysses.* Ezra Pound wrote Joyce to encourage him, "I don't want to hurry you; and the slowness of making permanent literature is incomprehensible to all save the few of us who have tried" (Read, ed., 147).

In mid-June 1919 Huebsch and John Quinn were exchanging letters about the prosecution of the *Little Review* for obscenity because of its serialization of *Ulysses.* Quinn feared just this situation, in part because he knew he would be drawn into it, and he had warned Joyce not to agree to the serialization. At first, Huebsch did not appear to take the prosecution too seriously; he certainly did not foresee that the case would be the finish of his expectation eventually to publish Joyce's novel.

Not anticipating any trouble beyond that which he was accustomed to experiencing in publishing Joyce, Huebsch proceeded in the summer of 1919 with plans for his annual trip to Europe. Even though *Ulysses* was far from finished, Huebsch hoped by a visit to Miss Weaver to lay the groundwork for its American publication. She welcomed his visit as a sign of his good faith, but it was not until March 1920 that Joyce's work had progressed enough for him to think seriously about contract terms for publication of the novel. Joyce wrote Huebsch to alert him that the "Oxen of the Sun" episode of *Ulysses* was nearly completed, with only "Circe" and the close of the book remaining to be written, "so that in all probability it can come out in Autumn." With his customary concern for exactness in the printed text, Joyce added, "I suggest that the contract be made now with my agent because if convenient to you, I should like to have the first half of the book in proof early in summer. I shall ask you to let me have also a review as the book has cost me six years of exhausting labor" (14 March 1920, B. W. Huebsch Collection, Library of Congress).

Much as Huebsch personally desired to move ahead with negotiations for publishing *Ulysses* immediately, the pending *Little Review* trial was a cause for increasing uneasiness. A small publisher without financial backing from other sources simply could not afford the risk of a possible fine and imprisonment for violation of the anti-obscenity laws then in force. Moreover, the complete manuscript of *Ulysses* did not yet even exist, and Huebsch was experienced enough to request a reading before entering into any agreement with Pinker.

Neither Pinker nor Joyce seemed entirely aware of the ramifications of the fact that officials of the United States Post Office had already seized three issues—January and June 1919, and January 1920—of the *Little Review*. Quinn, on the other hand, drawn into the *Little Review* case against his will and better judgment, needed no such enlightening. He was becoming increasingly anxious about the effects of that litigation on Huebsch's decision to publish *Ulysses*. In a long letter to Joyce written in mid-August 1920, he laid out for the author the problems publication of a trade edition would inevitably bring to Huebsch: suppression of the text, arrest, trial. Still, he encouraged Joyce to hold firm on publication without alterations by having Huebsch print a private edition for subscribers only. "After the privately printed edition is exhausted," Quinn wrote, "then a trade edition can be published from the same plates if at that time Huebsch wants to run the risk of prosecution. But if Ulysses were published in a trade edition it is almost a certainty that sooner or later there would be complaints about it and it would be suppressed, and Huebsch prosecuted" (15 August 1920, John Quinn Collection, New York Public Library).

That fall Huebsch and Joyce met in Paris for the first time. From the point of view of both, the meeting was a disaster. In an all-out effort to convince Joyce of the difficulties of publishing *Ulysses* in America, Huebsch spoke frankly about the problems of inevitable censorship. Huebsch suggested deletions and alterations of the text to pacify authorities in the

United States, but Joyce would not hear of it, even though by that time he had received Quinn's letter. In spite of the truth evident in Huebsch's warnings, the two parted uncomfortably, with the author feeling that his trust in his New York publisher had been severely undermined.

Quinn, meantime, was struggling to delay the *Little Review* trial until after Huebsch had had time to publish *Ulysses* in book form. Although Quinn pushed him for a quick decision, Huebsch knew that he faced almost certain arrest, fine, and imprisonment should he agree to publish *Ulysses*. In spite of Quinn's insistence, he was determined to make up his own mind in his own time about whether he would risk his publishing firm and his entire career by publishing Joyce's novel.

With no decision from Huebsch, Quinn defended the *Little Review* during the trial of February 1921. With his defeat came the sickening realization that the possibility for Huebsch's publication of the novel in book form was likely to be irretrievably lost. Indeed it was. As a result of the *Little Review* case, Huebsch was more convinced than ever that, much as he wished to, for him to publish *Ulysses* without alterations was sheer folly.

From the vantage point of the sixty-plus years that have passed since this pivotal moment in Ben Huebsch's publishing career, with *Ulysses* now firmly established as a masterpiece of contemporary literature, it is easy to romanticize the decision facing him as one preceded by excruciating un-certainty. Uncertainty there surely was, but above all there was clear-headed knowledge of the factors which, on balance, indicated that Huebsch would have to choose the larger good of his freedom, financial solvency, and career over his loyalty to Joyce.

On 5 April 1921, reluctant but finally certain of what course he must follow, Huebsch sent Quinn his reply. He wrote: "A New York court having held that the publication of a part of *[Ulysses]* in the Little Review was a violation of the law, I am unwilling to publish the book unless some changes are made in the manuscript as submitted to me by Miss H. S. Weaver who represents Joyce in London. In view of your statement that Joyce declines absolutely to make any alterations, I must decline to publish it" (quoted in Gorman 280–81).

Nor was *Ulysses* published in the United States until Bennett Cerf at Random House in 1932, after clarifying through Huebsch that Viking Press (which merged with Huebsch's firm in 1925) did not wish to pursue the possibility of publication, made elaborate preparations with Paul Léon to import a copy of the Paris edition. The authorities were alerted and the book seized; the verdicts of the ensuing trials freed *Ulysses* for publication by Random House in the United States in 1934. Even though Huebsch and Viking regretted this single volume missing from their otherwise complete list of Joyce's works, rights to *Ulysses* remain with Random House.

Postscript: *Finnegans Wake*

In 1931, a year before Random House began its pursuit of *Ulysses*, Huebsch visited Joyce again in Paris and signed with him a contract for "Work in Progress," later published by Viking as *Finnegans Wake*. In the contract Joyce specified that this book was to be published by Huebsch, no matter to what firm he might be attached (*JJI* 655). Writing in 1949 to Stuart Gilbert, editor of the first volume of Joyce's letters, Huebsch referred to this clause as proof of the quality of his relationship with Joyce. Recalling his astonishment at this unusual provision in the agreement, "which could only have been inserted by the express direction of Joyce," Huebsch wrote, "It must be apparent that he had confidence in me personally if he made so extraordinary a stipulation" (20 January 1949, Library of Congress). Commenting on the clause in his *Oral History*, Huebsch said, "I don't think Joyce made that odd contract because he feared someone might tamper with his material or overlook his interests. It was simply that he had had unpleasant experiences with publishers, and he wanted to be sure of with whom he was dealing—that's all" (Huebsch 184).

Notes

1. Huebsch, confident as the author's American publisher that he had first publishing rights, knew Lawrence was writing *Women in Love*, but was apparently reluctant to push the author by asking if he had finished the novel. In the meantime, Lawrence had sent the manuscript to James Pinker, his English agent, who had received refusals from Methuen and Duckworth, and simply failed, for whatever reason, to submit it to Huebsch for his consideration. This absence of communication between author and publisher or agent and publisher was part of the reason for Lawrence's eventual move to another publisher.

2. Their meeting about *Finnegans Wake* occurred in 1931 after Huebsch had joined Viking Press.

3. In the introduction to the first volume of Joyce's letters, Stuart Gilbert notes Joyce's method of briefing meticulously those whom he was using as intermediaries, a method employing to the full his unusual gifts of memory and organization. Since a veritable round-robin of letters accompanied even the smallest transaction with Huebsch, Gilbert's point is well taken: "A full-length book could be compiled on his dealings with publishers, reluctant, timid or enthusiastic, and it would be well worth writing for the light it would throw on the *petite histoire* of modern literature" (*Letters I* 38).

4. A number of sources document these earlier publishing difficulties, the most detailed being "A Curious History" under the by-line of Joyce's close friend and mentor, Ezra Pound. Published in the *Egoist* of London in lieu of Pound's "biweekly comment upon books published during the fortnight," the article quotes a lengthy letter from Joyce printed originally in *Sinn Fein* of Dublin and the *Northern Whig* of Belfast. Huebsch later reprinted it with additions in New York as a promotional

broadside just after his publication of *A Portrait of the Artist as a Young Man* and *Dubliners*. Joyce's statement details the reluctance, then absolute refusal of Grant Richards of London and the Messrs. Maunsel of Dublin to publish *Dubliners* in unexpurgated form and Joyce's subsequent abrupt departure from Ireland. Joyce's letter first appeared in *Sinn Fein,* Dublin (2 September 1911), and the *Northern Whig,* Belfast (26 August 1911). Pound's article appeared originally in the *Egoist* (14 January 1914) and was published by Huebsch on 5 May 1917. This broadside and information relating to its publication history are in the Rare Books Division, New York Public Library.

Works Cited

Gorman, Herbert S. *James Joyce.* New York: Farrar and Rinehart, 1939.

Huebsch, B. W. *Oral History.* Oral History Collection. Columbia University Library.

Read, Forrest, ed. *Pound/Joyce: The Letters of Ezra Pound to James Joyce with Pound's Essay on Joyce.* New York: New Directions, 1967.

Shadow of His Mind: The Papers of Lucia Joyce

David Hayman

By this time we seem to have a plethora of witnesses to James Joyce's creative as well as his private life. To the biographies, memoirs, letters, and conversations recorded by friends, we can add the collected notes and manuscripts. We know about his flirtations, his foibles, his intense pre-occcupation with home and family, his anguish over health, finances, and reputation, and particularly his concern for the condition of his daughter, Lucia (1907–1982), with whom he was deeply involved on unspecifiable emotional levels. The account of Lucia's behavior, published in the *James Joyce Quarterly* by her cousin Bozena Delimata (54–57 and passim), and the remarks of Jane Lidderdale and Richard Ellmann in their biographies of Harriet Weaver and James Joyce have spread information, however thinly, concerning Lucia's behavior and her impact on the lives of others. But still, due to the understandable reticence and solicitude of friends and family alike, we have much to learn, especially since a major potential source of information, the letters from Joyce to Paul Léon, is destined to remain in the vaults of the National Library in Dublin till sometime in the 1990s.

Although Joyce invested his daughter with qualities that reappear in the female figures in *Finnegans Wake,* and perhaps even in the young Milly Bloom of *Ulysses,* we don't know nearly enough about the original for these portraits in which we detect a strange but powerful blend of quirkiness, tenderness, poignancy, and humor. The young/old Issy/Isolde, the "link-ingclass" girl, whose words and behavior constellate the pages of *Finnegans Wake,* may well be the plaintive yet appealing shade of a real girl/woman (an extension of the golden girl who shadows Bloom's Dublin day in *Ulysses* with flashes of nubile light). In her various lunar phases, she constitutes a strange projection of changeable, adorable, vulnerable youth, susceptible to schizoid shifts between generosity and malice, modesty and seduction, tenderness and rage.

Lucia Joyce was born in Trieste on 26 July 1907, during a period of Joyce's extreme impecuniousness, following his brief, unhappy stint in a Rome bank and at a time when he was engaged in the rewriting of *Stephen Hero* into *A Portrait of the Artist as a Young Man*. The impacts of her early years, of her father's shifting fortunes, of family relationships, and of their many moves are only vaguely present in the Lucia Joyce papers that were recently purchased at auction by the Humanities Research Center of the University of Texas at Austin. But Lucia herself is very much a presence, a figure paradoxically preserved and seemingly unchanged in the amber of her illness. In his summary of events occurring between 1920 and 1939, Richard Ellmann mentions the growing concern over Lucia's condition:

> But the principal family trouble came from his daughter, Lucia, who in 1932 showed signs of the schizophrenia which had presumably begun during her girlhood, but had been dismissed by her parents as childish eccentricity. The next seven years of Joyce's life were pervaded by a frantic and unhappily futile effort to cure her. . . . It seemed to him that her mind was like his own, and he tried to find evidence in her writing and in her drawing of unrecognized talent. (*Letters III* 6–7)

Between 1932 and 1958–61 (the latter being the period of these papers), Lucia spent most of her time in a series of asylums in France, Switzerland, and England.[1] Of her life in the asylums we have only the scattering of remarks in these papers, the remarks of those who visited her, and Joyce's comments in some of his letters, but it is fairly clear that her condition did improve somewhat under more modern treatments during the post-war years, and these documents bear witness to her sharp, if selective, memory, her sense of herself as at times irrational, and her remarkably gentle, if occasionally whimsical, nature. Taken together they constitute a portrait not only of her father, her friends, and her family relations but of a state of mind that finds its way, through the crazed mirror of Joyce's very much engaged prose, onto the pages of *Finnegans Wake*.

The Lucia Joyce papers consist of three distinct parcels composed over a period of approximately four years, at a time when Lucia seems to have been responding well to her treatments. The papers were apparently given to one of Lucia's nurses at St. Andrew's Hospital, Mrs. M. B. Burbridge, who subsequently retired and put them, along with a few letters, up for auction at Sotheby's in London in June 1981. Thirteen of the ninety-two pages are in typescript (typed perhaps by Harriet Weaver); the rest are written in pencil in Lucia's fairly legible hand in small notebooks (4 × 6-1/2 inches).

The typescript made from Lucia's manuscript (probably in 1959) is in five numbered installments. Richard Ellmann believes, and Jane Lidderdale affirms, that Miss Weaver got Lucia to write "The Real Life of James Joyce Told by Lucia Joyce" at the behest of Patricia Hutchins, author of two popularizing biograpical books (*James Joyce's Dublin,* 1950; *James Joyce's World,* 1957). Undoubtedly Miss Hutchins hoped to glean from them some fresh biographical insights, but I find no evidence that she used the information. The procedure indicated by Lucia's subdivisions and notes was a painful one. Each of the installments seems to have elicited fresh questions from Miss Hutchins which Lucia tried, usually unsuccessfully, to answer. The first three segments, written in November–December 1958, are punctuated by the word "end" and a note apologizing for the fact that they are in pencil. Section 4, dated July 1959, is also punctuated by "End." The final segment is followed by a slightly petulant note to Miss Weaver: "Here is a little more of the Essay for you. I don't think I will make it any longer as it would become boring. If you can't read it Tant Pis! [*sic*]. I'm sorry I had to do it in pencil as my pen is locked up." The date is 5 September 1959, and the manuscript that began as a "biography" had evolved into an autobiography. Though these pages were of decreasing value to Miss Hutchins, it is very likely that they served as good therapy for Lucia herself. For today's postbiography reader, they comprise a curious melange of precision and illusion, reality and dream, revealing a troubled but not unappealing spirit.

It was Richard Ellmann himself who requested and received the second document, an "Autobiography" entitled "My Life," which Lucia apparently saw as an extension of the earlier papers. She began writing on 24 November 1961, during the period Ellmann was preparing his volumes of the letters. Included at the end of this small notebook is a note addressed to Sylvia Beach, Ellmann's intermediary. It is followed by a postscript to Ellmann concerning Jane Lidderdale. In it Lucia expresses her concern about Miss Weaver's death in 1961 and speaks of her own relations with a Protestant clergyman named E. W. P. Langham and her subsequent "conversion to Catholicism."[2] Ellmann does not appear to have made much use of this document, which he barely recalls.

The final parcel, though mysterious and profoundly touching, is perhaps less revealing than it would at first glance appear to be. Entitled "My Dreams," it is prefaced on the verso of the cover by Lucia's version of "I'm Forever Blowing Bubbles." (In this case the bubbles are compared, probably as an afterthought, to her dreams.) If many of the entries have an authentic ring, others seem to have been concocted to please some unnamed person, perhaps one of the nurses. If some seem quite normal, others reveal a childish quirkiness, as does an extended meditation on the killing of insects. According to the Sotheby catalogue entry, this notebook was written in 1960. It was probably part of an informal therapy.

Although each of these items was written for a stated purpose, and though there is little in the way of coherent development in either the biographies or the dream notebook, they are best thought of as a triptych focusing upon Lucia Joyce primarily in relation to the world of her parents. This is true even though a number of the entries in the "Life" relate to Lucia's post-1935 existence in asylums. Each panel of this triptych is distinct in conception and character; each seems to respond to a different series of demands, both external and internal, but their content frequently overlaps. Details are compulsively repeated; approaches are dovetailed in such a way as to give these papers a coherence that derives no doubt from the limited nature of Lucia's obsessions.

Clearly, the study of Lucia's papers is a delicate operation. But taken together, they contain nothing shocking or objectionable, no stupendous revelations, few new facts, only many suggestive overtones about Lucia's condition from which only the most tentative conclusions could be drawn by a layman. On the other hand, much can be drawn from them concerning the preoccupations that helped shape Joyce's portrait of young womanhood in *Finnegans Wake,* Lucia's relations with men in the Joyce entourage, and the significance of certain figures to Joyce at given moments in the *Wake*'s development. It is also important to see the "Real Life" for what it was, a way of extracting from a disturbed woman specific information about events, people, and places. That the result is a touching human document, replete with accurately and inaccurately remembered details and distorted readings is inevitable, considering Lucia's condition and personality. It is the quality of her memory that should interest us most, however, given the evidence we possess for Joyce's use of her as an inspiration. It is the nature of her character and her relationship with her father that should attract the biographer of Joyce.

"The Real Life of James Joyce" begins *in medias res,* as would a biographical sketch written by a very young girl: "James Joyce was a real irish man. He was a humorist and would often make jokes with people. He used to have dinner at a Restaurant in Montparnasse called the Restaurant des 2 Trianons. You could see him there with his wife and daughter."[3] Very quickly, all pretense of chronological development fades. Time takes on the quality of Bergsonian duration and we move rapidly back and forth through time and space within a radically associative discourse which is at once surprisingly rational and predictably self-serving. For example, we move from a discussion of Joyce's travels to mention of his visits to Lucia's asylums, his gifts, his "wealth" since the publication of *Ulysses* at the rue de l'Odéon, to Giorgio's Talbot automobile. From all of this evolves, almost against the grain, an intimate, if very fragmentary, portrait of the family in the twenties.

What was implicit in the first fragment is made explicit in the second. Lucia is being primed with specific questions as she would be at an interview: "I remember my father writing *Ulysses* yes I saw the manuscript it was all striked [*sic*] out with red pencil," or again, "Yes, I wrote an article about the famous Charly [*sic*] Chaplin the Disque Vert which was published by Valéry Larbaud."[4] It is hard to say at times what questions were asked, but as we read, we become aware that Lucia interprets them freely, supplying the answers she wants to give. Thus, the remark about her Chaplin essay tells us nothing new. The questioner wanted details Lucia would not or could not supply. These questions seem on the whole to have acted as would visual stimulae on the mind of an eccentric and self-engaged stroller (a character from *Ulysses*, perhaps).

Lucia's mind is not well-stocked or well-developed. Her vocabulary of interest, her memories, and her store of images are severely limited. But her memories, spanning some fifty years, are numerous enough to make interesting conjunctions possible. Thus, a recollection that Stanislaus Joyce was confined during World War I in Felsenegg, Austria, recalls a traumatic thunderstorm experienced with her mother in a small boat on the Lago Maggiore in Switzerland. Joyce's friend Ottocaro Weiss's dark complexion brings to mind in typical Joycean fashion (the remark appears to have been his originally) his other friend, the "fair" Oscar Schwartz. But the dreams, predictably, provide us with far richer and more private associations.

All three documents are (unconsciously) organized around certain motifs and preoccupations. The first and most pervasive of these motifs relates to Lucia's references to friends, male and female, to names that have a way of reappearing as part of her personal landscape. Many of them are friends of Joyce's who became or were fancied to be Lucia's suitors; others were friends of Giorgio's, the brother with whom Lucia had strong emotional ties. One is struck by the number of men who were or are said to have been Jewish. Lucia's extreme sensitivity to Jewishness and her attraction to "Jewish" males approached the condition of fixation. This is true not only because she repeatedly mentions Jews by name but also and mainly because she labels Jews in ways that members of no other group are labeled. We may account for this in many ways. Richard Ellmann has pointed out to me that many of Joyce's friends were actually Jewish and that Giorgio married Helen Kastor, whose Jewishness is alluded to by Lucia. We may also note that Joyce, like Stephen Dedalus, tended to romanticize Jewishness as a component of character, even though he does not actually simplify the perceived Jewishness of Leopold Bloom. Drawn to Jews as outsiders, undoubtedly attracted by a sensitivity he noted in certain of his friends and transmitting that taste to both his son and daughter, Joyce seems to have had a determining impact on his offspring. More important, it is through the offspring that we find confirmation of his profound interest in and perhaps identification with Jews, this despite his inevitable ironic handling of the question. In this instance, Lucia's fixation becomes a litmus test for an aspect of Joyce's personality. It may well be that she is the admittedly distorting, but still adequate, reflection which Joyce felt her to be.[5]

Other Joycean behavioral traits are evident in these papers. Like her father, Lucia is socially reticent but warmly appreciative of friendly acts. Like him, she fears thunderstorms, and she persists in speaking of older people as "Mr." or "Miss." Like him, she loves music, although her favorite is Wagner, to whom she refers repeatedly, a taste she shares with her mother. In Paris in 1921, she "learned Wagner the Preludium of Tristan und Isolde on the piano." In June 1921, she attended a performance of that opera "at the Champs Elysées Theatre." The biography exhibits throughout a touching pride in her father's accomplishments and his fame, with which she clearly identifies. It projects at times a sense of herself as living in his shadow, as well as under his protection. However, Joyce actually plays a diminishing role as Lucia lapses into increasingly personal reminiscences. The narrative contains a generous sampling of Joycean trivia (some of which must be discounted): the Joyces had a dog and a cat in Trieste (despite JJ's canine phobia?); Lucia and Giorgio acted in the English Players' production of *Riders to the Sea* while Joyce sang from behind the scenes; Joyce used to make a salad of "salmon and garlick. It was rather nice." She quotes verses from songs Joyce sang; she claims Joyce was jealous of his friend Ottocaro Weiss's attentions to Nora; twice she refers to a tumor operation performed on Nora by Dr. Bergeret, "one of the best surgeons in Paris" (actually a hysterectomy performed early in 1929); and so on (*JJI* 619–20). What is most striking is not what Lucia reveals on this level but how much she represses, not only of the family life of the Joyces and of Joyce's story, but of her own. She does not tell us about her stay in Bray (1935) with her aunt Eileen, related in such colorful and depressing detail by her cousin Bozena (Delimata 54–57 and passim), nor does she relate her experience with Maria Jolas in Paris, or her rather tempestuous relationship with her mother, which figures among the causes for her confinement, or her experiences in England with Miss Weaver. Indeed, she glosses over several events which must have been traumatic. She mentions her airplane trip to England but speaks only in passing of a period spent in a *camisole de force* ("straitjacket": the words are left in French within her predominantly English text), though she does mention that the cause for that rather extreme treatment was her tearing off her clothes and breaking windows. She gives scant and belated attention to the circumstances of her father's death, and even as late as 1960, especially in her "dreams," writes of him as though he were alive. Still, her last word on the subject of both parents is particularly lucid, tender, and moving in its understated affection:

> My parents were neither big nor small but they looked very young and I never thought they were going to die so soon. My father had a duodenal ulcer and he had a blood transfusion but they could not save him. My mother had either pneumonia or arthritis and she died. She was like a sister to me and we were the best of friends. She never scolded me and allways [*sic*] wanted me to be happy and have a good time.

Lucia's relationship to her family is most poignantly revealed in her recorded dreams, written some twenty years after her father's death. Perhaps these dreams were stimulated by the pressure she was under to write down her memories. Certainly they reveal less that is abnormal than do the biographies, and nothing that could be construed as shocking in a post-Freudian era. They are in fact less revealing than the dreams Joyce himself included in his *Wake* notebooks. Yet the very first item is an anxiety dream recounting her departure from the hotel where the family was staying, getting lost, and being run over by a train in a place she did not recognize. Typically, in the early dreams she makes contact not only with her parents but also with Giorgio and Helen Joyce. Throughout the papers we find evidence of attachment to her first sister-in-law, whom she calls a "beautiful jewess." On occasion it seems that Giorgio has (somewhat inadequately) replaced her father. In one particularly engrossing dream, she imagines herself at tea with her brother, first in a tearoom and then in an apartment where he gives her sweets.[6] The dream continues, taking her to a place within sight of the Eiffel tower, as was one of Joyce's apartments. There she is frustrated in her attempt to get a taxi for home and is finally told that her father has died. A later dream is even more complex and dramatic, but it repeats in a subdued tone the basic pattern of dependence and severance. She is in a restaurant and can't get home. There she is shown a photo of her murdered father and of her mother. This is followed by an unpleasant personal encounter with a Mlle. Bontemps, a near accident in an automobile, and a return from the "mountains" concluding with the statement "I saved myself." Without attempting a detailed analysis, we can say that years after her father's death, his image is still a source of shelter. His presence is felt and his death is of deep concern, if not a motive for guilt, even in the penultimate dream where "they told me my father was dying."

There is evidence throughout these papers of extreme naiveté verging on childishness. Lucia persists in repressing her awareness of her present situation, her sense of herself as having been different for a long while. Her vague concern for appearances contrasts oddly with a rather matter-of-fact treatment of her position at the various asylums, of her relationship with the nurses and doctors who play such a predominant role in her life there, her accounts of the menial chores she performs with pleasure and satisfaction, her encounters with other patients, and of the seasonal excursions apparently made by the more tractable inmates. What is missing, perhaps understandably, is a view of herself as a person, a mature and fulfilled adult and not just an extension of her family, a marriageable young woman, or an inmate. The reader of Joyce has the eerie feeling of reading, in these notes by a person quite capable of appreciating the arts and of reading mature literature (books she is careful to list), the words of Joyce's eternally desiring juvenile, Issy/Isolde.

It is finally her relationship to Issy that I find most engrossing, that and her brief profiles of four of the men she thought of as suitors—the young Russian Alex Ponisovsky, Samuel Beckett, Alexander Calder, and Emile Fernandez.[7] Of the three, Fernandez, who is described in terms of his Jewish ambiance and in relation to a series of male friends, receives the most attention. He was the brother of Yva Fernandez, who was one of three translators of the 1926 *Gens de Dublin (Dubliners)*. It is perhaps important that Yva (Lucia calls her Iva) was among Joyce's earliest translators. She is alluded to in a letter to Stanislaus Joyce, dated 28 October 1920, in connection with the translations she had already completed. This suggests that Lucia's relationship to the Fernandez family may date from the very earliest Paris epoch. However, Lucia alludes to Emile as a friend of her brother Giorgio, which suggests that her own relation with him began somewhat later. Whenever it began, it may have been the longest lasting, if not one of the deepest, relationships. It seems all the more strange, therefore, that Ellmann notes him only briefly in a paragraph cataloguing (with some omissions, if we are to believe Lucia) her training and experience as a dancer between 1926 and 1929: "On April 19, 1928, she danced in the 'Prêtresse Primitive' at the Theatre du Vieux-Colombier, and on February 18, 1929, in another Lois Hutton recital at the Comédie des Champs-Élysées in Le Pont d'or, an operette-bouffe, with music by Emile Fernandez, a young man with whom she was briefly in love" (*JJI* 625). Lucia mentions Fernandez's gift as a pianist and credits him with having written the "Ballet Mecanique" in which she claims she played a small part.[8]

Lucia's account, one of the most elaborate in the initial "Life of James Joyce," suggests a much richer and more prolonged relationship, one that may have been years in developing. She returns to the subject in her "Autobiography," where she elaborates further on their friendship. Fernandez even appears in and dominates one of the last of her dreams in which her father and Giorgio also figure. Her memory is crowded with details about his house; his family; his aunts, whom she names and describes; his numerous relatives, among whom she numbers Darius Milhaud; and even his friends. One senses in reading the two pages of Miss Weaver's typescript, pages in which the details seem to pour out in profusion, constituting a rich cluster of exceptionally pleasant recollections, that Lucia is luxuriating in the memory of that warm Jewish context as much as in the thought of a former flame. She speaks of frequent teas and outings, names the restaurants they went to, and mentions Fernandez's proposal and her refusal, which she regrets in her 1961 account. It would seem that she kept up with the family for a long time, long enough to know that, like her, his sister Yva "went mad and had to be sent to a lunatic asylum" and that Emile eventually married an Italian girl from Livorno. She says she was invited to the wedding. It is perhaps significant that the paragraph immediately following that long exposition begins with the following disturbing account of events that happened a decade later during World War II: "Later I was in Ivry and we were bombarded by the Germans. Then we had a terrible thunderstorm. I nearly died of fear as the noise of the thunder was so terrific."

The account of her brief relationship with the sculptor Alexander Calder, mentioned only in the "Autobiography," is quite a different matter. Calder spent many years in France, arriving in 1926 and quickly making his reputation by putting on performances of his bent wire circus. Ellmann, who does not mention him in his published work, confirms that Lucia "did go with" him. He is apparently not the only American she went with. Her account of Calder is preceded by the following cryptic lines:

> Then I had another boyfriend who was american. He was also very nice looking but I was a bit jealous of him. He asked me if I would like to go to America with him but I said no since my parents did not like me to go so far away. I don't remember his name but he was very young at the time. Sandy Calder was an american also he was a jew I think he had curly hair and was sort of an artist. he had a strange kind of circus which he invented himself. We were in love but I think he went away. Anyway he never wrote to me and I don't know what became of him.

Calder spent a great deal of his life in France, but Lucia appears to have known him only during the relatively brief period of the circuses, which won him acclaim. It is entirely possible that she met him, as she did many other young men, through her brother, who seems to have had a fairly wide circle of artistic friends during the twenties.

The relationship with Beckett was even more ambiguous and far more protracted. Lucia probably met him in 1928–29 and they went out together occasionally over an unspecified period of time. Ellmann speaks of Beckett's feeling that "he should have more than a casual interest in this tortured and blocked replica of genius" and his later self-doubts because he could not manage that love (*JJI* 662). I have tried to show elsewhere that this frustrated and frustrating relationship (which on Lucia's part resulted in a loss of self-control) found a bitter, self-castigating, literary outlet in the story "Walking Out" from Beckett's first book of fiction, *More Pricks than Kicks*. It is a girl named Lucie who, while riding after her kinky fiancé, is hit by a car and incapacitated, a fact that makes her susceptible to becoming Belacqua's wife in the next tale. In short, Beckett's guilt feelings for having been unable to accept Lucia's advances are displaced and salved by his hero's nursemaidly relationship with her namesake ("A Meeting in the Park" 375). Beckett, who through the years has been among Lucia's most attentive friends, plays a surprisingly small part in these papers, appearing briefly (significantly in association with other names) in two dreams and only once in the "Autobiography." The portrait given in the latter is accurate and full of circumstantial detail, but curiously flat:

> Then I knew Samuel Beckett who was half Jewish he became my boy friend and he was very much in love with me but I could not marry him as he was too tall for me. He was a writer and pianist. He had a very beautiful cousin Peggy Sinclair she lived in Germany Cassel. They came to see us at the Square Robiac Peggy had a very nice dark blue coat on. Mr. Beckett and I had tea at the Pavillon Royal in the Bois de Boulogne and that day there was a thunderstorm. He lived in the Ecole Normale Superieure and gave me a copy of Dante La Divina Commedia as a present. He said I danced very well. He was a very good-looking young man.

It is also noteworthy that Lucia's memory jumps from this portrait, dating from the early thirties to the bombardment she experienced at the asylum in Ivry in 1941. Ponisovsky, who actually proposed, is mentioned only briefly, as a Pole, and referred to in passing by his first name.[9]

Critics and students of Joyce will be most interested in the literary implications both of Joyce's relationship with Lucia during the early years of *Work in Progress* and of the signs available in these papers of her role as a model for the multivalent ingenue, Issy/Isolde. Given Joyce's demonstrable love of associations, if not coincidences, we cannot discount the importance of Lucia's emphatic taste for Wagner's operas and particularly for *Tristan and Isolde*. It is also important that Lucia shared this taste not with her father, who was lukewarm on Wagner, but with her mother, and that the two would have been identified in Joyce's mind in relation to this taste. Like Milly for Leopold Bloom, Lucia was the young shade of her mother and a fragment of his own youth.

Whether Lucia's affection for Wagner's *Tristan* reflects either her character or her taste, whether that taste was stimulated by Joyce or Nora or both parents eager to find an outlet for their eccentric child, she was certainly associated with Isolde in Joyce's mind. He began working on the Tristan theme, which was to generate a major nodal system in his new book, soon after he completed work on *Ulysses* in 1922. Notes for a Tristan skit (now in chapter 2.4) were taken under the heading *Exiles* and partly inspired by certain undeveloped aspects of that curious piece of turn-of-the-century theater for which he had earlier prepared a psychoanalytical profile of his companion, Nora.[10] There it was Nora who was identified with the Irish princess, but in the *Wake* it is Lucia who provides a readily observable pattern for adolescent behavior. That pattern deepened as Joyce became aware of the implications of two Isoldes.

The earliest jottings suggest a broad parodic treatment of act 2 of Wagner's opera, out of which are generated the primitive personae of the *Wake* itself: Tristan, Isolde, and King Mark. Isolde received the nickname Issy, which Joyce shortened to Is and later symbolized by the "sigla ($\perp \wedge$)." I would suggest that, though Joyce adhered to the general outline of the opera, expanding it to include episodes from the romance versions, he retained throughout the *Work in Progress* years (1922–39) a sense of Issy/ Is/Isolde as the young daughter who, in fairly orthodox Freudian fashion, displaced her mother in his erotic imagination. It is not surprising, therefore, that the Isolde identity remains throughout the *Wake*, even in passages that have little to do with the Tristan myth, the dominant one for the young ALP. In short, I would maintain that the association of Lucia with the opera influenced one of Joyce's central themes and probably stimulated him to develop the major usurpation motif for this new book. The fifteen-year-old Lucia unwittingly sat for the extended portrait of the young, old Irish princess. Her incipient schizophrenia, which Joyce only gradually recognized as abnormal, shaped his portrait of the polyvalent seductress, if not of young womanhood in general. In later notes the signs for Issy are significantly multiple: ⊥, ⊢, and ⊣.

But the juvenile figure was not to be simply or solely a revised version of the Irish princess. Throughout the "Scribbledehobble" notebook, in which Joyce took notes under the headings of his early works and their subdivisions, we find fragmentary views of an adolescent figure whom Joyce clearly identified with his daughter. This is evident in the following sequence under the *Dubliners* heading "Eveline":

> her tongue her lipstick: she walked alone from school: told her friends pop walked zigzag: Man followed: books she read: her wit F.P. (figpie not fireplug): . . . pretty! what d'ye call it?: . . . bottoms of her feet: soles of her back: ate strawberries and got marks: not she!: presents her compts:"[11] . . . her letter, illustrated, don't tell him: . . . her journey Belfast-Dublin, change of porters (H.B.P.): . . . . (*James Joyce Archive, Notebook VI.A* 51)

The last note may be a reflection of Nora Joyce's ill-fated trip to Galway in April 1922, though there is no evidence in Ellmann that she took the children to Belfast. The childish remark about the porters could easily have been made by the fourteen-year-old Lucia. A parallel series occurs under the heading "Nausicaa," in which Lucia is mentioned by name:

> 2 girls adieu they both run 10 paces, stop: . . . she plays with suitors like Penelope: . . . turn in her eye rather taking: girl A walking pulls girls B's sleeve: Lucia girl's teaparty: W[oman] she said she must go and he asked her why and she said she must really and he asked but why must she and she said really and truly she must: . . . (*James Joyce Archive, Notebook VI.A* 151)

Here we find, along with clear references to Lucia's social behavior, an allusion to the cast in her eye. The observations on Lucia did not stop with the early notes. Though Joyce did not use most of this concrete data and did not produce so realistic a portrait of changeable girlhood and girlish behavior for his *Work in Progress,* in several of the early notebooks one detects evidence of his continued fascination with his daughter's behavior. In spring 1923, toward the end of Lucia's fifteenth year, while composing the Tristan piece, Joyce wrote the following, which appears in *Notebook* VI.B.3:

> Is washed hall/by standing wet/umbrella in corner [p. 51]:
>
> Is sang—Molly/Bawn, W is a/ charming girl I/ love, My Sweetheart/ when a Boy [p. 56].[12]
>
> Is has a dream—/it is interpreted/ by Jung [p. 63].[13]
>
> Joyce (d . . . god)/ Madame Fernandez [p. 74].
>
> Today she writes/ better [?] 'Yesterday'/ Is [Isolde] when she first/ counted 15 then 14 [p. 76].
>
> Is read paper/ like psalm/ Is had pity for/ poor devil in/ asbestos shirt in/ . . . ingroom in.[14] (85)

There is, of course, a risk that we may overread such entries, seeing Joyce as prescient when he was only preoccupied with the subject of madness. But perhaps we may be permitted a rather different sort of speculation based on four considerations: Joyce's apparent and perfectly natural association of Lucia with his heroine Issy, Lucia's deteriorating condition throughout the 1920s, the evidence for her essentially childlike nature provided by these documents, and the evolution of the Issy figure into the schizophrenic lookingglass girl.

Adaline Glasheen was the first to note that Issy is a multiple personality grounded partly in the work of Morton Prince's *The Dissociation of Personality* (1908) (Glasheen 89–96). The use of Prince's book is quite early, if we can judge from the appearance of the Boston motif in chapter I.5 in 1924. But the idea of dissociation must have occurred to Joyce earlier, perhaps when he studied the Tristan tale as reconstituted by Bedier, perhaps through his observation of his daughter. I would suggest that long before he could bring himself to face the problem of Lucia's disequalibriated personality, he felt the urge to dramatize his awareness of the access that it provided him to the secret recesses of the psyche. Far more than the double Isolde, princesses of Ireland and Britanny, rivals for the heart of a knight in Cornwall, who is himself the rival of an aging pantaloon of a King Mark, Lucia was a permanent reminder of the delicacy of mental balance and the fall into the irrational that shadowed Joyce's own existence through most of his adult life. His bitter comment to Miss Weaver in a letter dated 24 June 1921 is little more than a thin mask for a real concern for his own sanity and the validity of his creative endeavors:

> A batch of people in Zurich persuaded themselves that I was gradually going mad and actually endeavoured to induce me to enter a sanatorium where a certain Doctor Jung (the Swiss Tweedledum who is not to be confused with the Viennese Tweedledee, Dr. Freud) amuses himself at the expense (in every sense

of the word) of ladies and gentlemen who are troubled with bees in their bonnets. (*Letters I* 166)

It is too early to conclude on the basis of Lucia's deceptively simple documents the precise role she played in Joyce's fantasies, to say nothing of his last work. The preceding comments do scant justice to the questions these papers raise, the details added to our sense of the texture of Joyce's life, and especially of the crucial, and still rather hazy, Paris years. Important, strange, and private, the Lucia Joyce papers testify as through a scrim to a complex and anguished family background which may, after all, be closer to the norm than most of us are willing to admit.

Notes

This article originally appeared in *Joyce at Texas,* edited by Dave Oliphant and Thomas Zigal (Austin, Tex.: Humanities Research Center, University of Texas at Austin, 1983).

1. She was until her death (December 12, 1982) in the Grafton Geriatric Ward of St. Andrew's Hospital, Northampton.

2. Miss Lidderdale doubts there was a conversion: "She talked about it at one stage but she has never been baptized into the church and continues to go to Church of England services at the hospital" (letter from Jane Lidderdale to David Hayman).

3. Permission to print excerpts from the Lucia Joyce papers has been granted by Jane Lidderdale and D. D. C. Monro. I owe thanks to Richard Ellmann and Miss Lidderdale for assistance in locating these papers more precisely in relation to Lucia's life.

4. The article was indeed published in no. 4–5 of *Le Disque vert* as "Charlie et les gosses" and prefaced by Larbaud.

5. The echo of Stephen's reflections on his sister in "Wandering Rocks" is almost too resounding: "My eyes they say she has. . . . Quick, far and daring. Shadow of my mind" (*U* 243).

6. These papers are studded with references to gifts, marks of painfully needed affection. Lucia seems to equate sweets with ultimate satisfactions.

7. It may be noted that Beckett and Lucie Léon's brother, Alex Ponisovksy, are given relatively slight treatment, though they were among those who came closest to being suitors, to judge from the biography and the letters of Joyce.

8. She seems to be confusing him with George Antheil, another friend of the family and the actual composer of that piece.

9. Miss Lidderdale writes, "In the years I have known Lucia, she has referred only once to Ponisovsky. Her references to Samuel Beckett are not numerous but very varied as to her liking him or not" (Letter from Jane Lidderdale to David Hayman).

10. See the notes appended to current editions of the play.

11. French for "accounts."

12. Among the things Lucia says Joyce sang is "O Molly I can't say you're honest,

sure you've stolen the heart from my breast, I feel like a Bird [*sic*] that's astonished when the young vagabon [*sic*] steals its nest etc." (from "Real Life").

13. This item is curiously premonitory, but it probably refers back to Joyce's own experience with Jung rather than forward to Lucia's treatment by the psychiatrist in October 1934.

14. In light of Lucia's story, this allusion to a straitjacket is particularly poignant.

Works Cited

Delimata, Bozena. "Reminiscences of a Joyce Niece." *James Joyce Quarterly* 19.1 (Fall 1981): 45–62.

Glasheen, Adaline. "*Finnegans Wake* and the Girls from Boston, Mass." *Hudson Review* 7 (Spring 1954): 89–96.

Hayman, David. "A Meeting in the Park and a Meeting on the Bridge: Joyce and Beckett." *James Joyce Quarterly* 8.4 (Summer 1971): 372–84.

The James Joyce Archive. Notebook VI. A. Ed. Danis Rose. New York: Garland, 1978.

The James Joyce Archive. Notebook VI. B3. Ed. David Hayman. New York: Garland, 1978.

6. Major Addresses

Signs on a White Field

Hugh Kenner

"The mind of a grocer's assistant," Joyce said he had; and another thing he said of himself repeatedly was that from the Jesuits he'd learned the method of arranging things so that they could be comprehended. Given the defects of comprehension amid which we flounder it is open to us to wonder if the Jesuits lost hold of him too soon. It is also possible that what happened too soon was certain traditions of commentary getting hold of us. "The mind of a grocer's assistant" is a mind with a place for everything and everything in its place, a preference *Finnegans Wake* ascribes to Aristotle. Such a mind is also a mind for which, however multifarious the items it must order, the *principle* of ordering is quite simple, and we may easily bewilder ourselves by supposing that Joyce's schemes are more complicated than they are.

I want to try out the possibility that his idea of what goes on in life and should go on in fiction was so simple he understood it at twenty-two. I shall also hint at a corollary, that once we have at last really read *Dubliners* we shall find *Finnegans Wake* a great deal less strange. I'll begin with the fact that *Dubliners* commenced with an agreement to supply ten stories for a weekly paper. Ten stories is a lot of stories. Where to get ten plots?

Every Sunday in church they read the Gospel, and what is read is as often as not a short story: the account for instance of the two sisters at Bethany, whose names were Martha and Mary. Martha kept busy looking after the household and the guests; Mary listened to Jesus. Jesus told Mary she had chosen the better part.

It takes two or three minutes to read this brief narrative aloud; the source is St. Luke's gospel, chapter 10. In Joyce's day it was read in Latin, after which a homily was provided. The preacher would generally retell the story in English, and go on to explain how its elements were enacted in Dublin every day: there are people who fuss and fidget and people whose domain is the word, the mind, the spirit. We are to take this to heart.

And Joyce's first published fiction (August 1904: he was still in Dublin) was the unsettling little story called "The Sisters." The names of the sisters were Nannie and Eliza and they had a brother, a priest, now dead upstairs.

Reading the story today in *Dubliners,* we may think to wonder why Joyce called it "The Sisters," so much is its narrator preoccupied with the dead man. Then paying heed to the sisters, we may notice that though Eliza talks incessantly, Nannie, who's so hardworking she's "wore out," says nothing whatsoever, and this may prompt us to remember the sisters in St. Luke's narrative, one of whom kept conspicuously busy while Mary (who had "chosen the better part") preferred divine talk.

In St. John's gospel (chapter 11) we encounter these sisters again. They have lost their brother Lazarus, but since their guest is the Messiah the ending is happy: Jesus calls him back from the grave. (Dubliners are not Bible-readers, but the words of recall rang out from pulpits annually. "Come forth, Lazarus!" went a Dublin joke; but "he came fifth, and lost the job.") Joyce's story ends like the joke. Near the end all talk stops for everyone to listen. "I too listened; but there was no sound in the house." This brother lies in his coffin unresurrected.

"I am writing a series of epicleti—ten—for a paper," Joyce wrote to Con Curran of his plans at that stage, some time in mid-1904. With ten envisaged, it is no surprise if he turned to the New Testament for his prompt-book. Its themes were, by homiletic convention, reenacted all the time among Christian people: scales falling from eyes, faith moving mountains, assemblies in upper rooms; any preacher could tell you, and did tell every Sunday, how you'd recognize such things in the life around you. And we note that Joyce didn't say "stories," accounts of happenings; his word, "epicleti," pertains to his clarifications of what clergy took it upon themselves to clarify.

We may guess at what went wrong with Father Flynn. He grasped that God did not choose him—perhaps out of nonexistence? And, prompted by the enigma of the title, we may even divine the story's scriptural model.

We need not. But if we do it gives us two narratives to compare. Of Luke's Mary and Joyce's Eliza, the word-oriented women, we may note that whereas the Bethany Mary "sat at Jesus' feet, and heard his word," the Dublin Eliza chatters; as for the Dublin Nannie, the one who plays the biblical Martha's part and keeps busy, she is not silent because occupied but because gone deaf (and—the first version reads—"it would have been unseemly to have shouted at her"). There is no Messiah present of any description. And for counterpart to the center of St. John's story, when Jesus before he undertakes the miracle challenges the bereaved, "Believest thou this?," we have someone who (as the boy does not divine) some years ago lost all belief. Father Flynn was found "sitting up by himself in the dark in his confession-box, wide awake and laughing-like softly to himself": a Lazarus locked into eternal paralysis.

Had anyone in 1904 read "The Sisters" to its bottom, there would have been an outcry against the *Homestead* to rival the *Playboy* riots. But no one noticed, nor was it noticed either that the next story by "Stephen Daedalus" (10 September 1904) had for unwritten text "Follow me," words the gospels twelve times ascribe to Jesus. You'd follow Jesus to an ascetic life, but it's not to that life the sailor in "Eveline" has summoned an impressionable girl. What she has in mind is matrimony, meaning escape. What he has in mind . . . but we've no access to his mind.

Eveline Hill in the end does not follow this chap who calls himself "Frank": perhaps just as well for her if you ponder the probability of a house await for a bride in Buenos Ayres. When she doesn't follow he leaves anyway; and like the rich youth (Matthew 19) who also declined to follow, Eveline sorrows and will think for the rest of her life that it was by her own fault that she missed something grand.

In "After the Race," his next *Homestead* story (17 December 1904), "Stephen Daedalus" returned to the troubled Rich Young Man. Jimmy Doyle too at the end of his story is troubled, though not, like his scriptural prototype, on account of any injunction to distribute his heritage to the poor. No, he's remorseful after a meaningless night he has spent losing much of it at cards to other youths who are already rich. This is the least of the stories because most dependent on a prototype the others permit you to miss. Joyce said he meant to rewrite it but lost interest.

After that his connection with the *Homestead* lapsed; not that implicit blasphemy was discerned, but there were letters of complaint. Readers of "Our Weekly Story" were accustomed to a positive note. He wrote more stories, however, always about people reenacting some canonical story but not triumphantly. *What he thought people did was reenact*. In 1906 he even thought of a story about a man reenacting part of the *Odyssey*.

He'd also noticed that language keeps reenacting itself, not always successfully. When the priest puts the boy through the responses of the mass and the boy "patters," we may recall that "patter" derives from "paternoster," one of the responses of the mass. A patter is a decadent paternoster. Or instead of a failed recapitulation we may have the effort of a changeling. When Eveline at the harbor glimpses "the black mass of the boat" we may read over the phrase "black mass" without noticing, or we may notice it and try to fit it into a schema of some elaborateness, or we may be wise enough to reflect that, unlike "patter" and "paternoster," the black mass of the boat and the Black Mass of the devil's altar have nothing in common whatever save coincident sounds. One "mass" is from "massa," bulk; the other is from "Missa," sent; the Mass itself once punned: *Ite, missa est*. Joyce cherished such discontinuities, rhyming as they did with the discontinuities between Dublin lives and the examples they were supposed to be enacting. A failure of similar words to be related is an anticlimax, like the failure of Father Flynn to be Lazarus.

Let us restate our two themes before we go on. They are *reenactment* and *renaming*. The first says, what was said from every Dublin pulpit, that people's actions today fit into the contours of stories told long ago. The second says that words, chameleonlike, conceal identities—paternoster, patter—and conceal impostures likewise—black mass, black Mass. Note that the chameleon is not his background; he and it blend by illusion. Degeneration, imperfect recapitulation: all of Joyce lies between those poles.

On 8 December 1922, in Dublin, the Irregular firebrand Rory O'Connor was an Irish victim of an Irish firing-squad: one of four hostages the pro-Treaty government ordered shot in reprisal for another shooting. A man at whose wedding Rory O'Connor had been groomsman concurred in the, so to speak, fratricidal decision.

On 20 March 1923, in Paris, James Joyce commenced his new book in the middle, with a draft of "the 'Roderick O'Connor' fragment."

That was a different O'Connor, the last High King of Ireland, who surrendered to Henry II of England in 1175 back at the beginning of the infamous Seven Centuries. Still, it is difficult not to imagine some connection, though you'll search those pages of Joyce's scripture in vain for any trace of the 1922 Rory less ambiguous than his surname. Later Joyce flaunted Rory's first name, plainly spelled, on the very first page of his book—rory end to the regginbrow. But which Rory is that? For "Rory" is but a more phonetic way than "Roderick" of anglicizing the Irish *Ruaidhrí* (pronounced "ruri," *u* as in "rule," *i* as in "machine"), and the Rory O'Connor who was shot in 1922 would have been named for the unfortunate High King, in his own time Ruaidhrí O Conchobhair, who was embroiled in civil wars all through his aborted reign, saw even his son rise against him, and died, 1198, worn out, in a cloister. When he spoke his own name he said something like "Ruri O Conukher," and easing him into the history books as "Roderick O'Connor" was a piece of linguistic imperialism.

But what does it mean for that matter to say of the fragment Joyce drafted that it pertains to the last High King, though it seems to name him several times? As far as one can make out somebody after closing time (a pubkeeper?) is drinking up the leavings of every opened bottle in the place before he spins to his chair in a vertigo the words catch nicely—"one to do and one to dare, par by par, a peerless pair, ever here and over there, with his fol the dee oll the doo on the flure of his feats and the feels of his fumes in the wakes of his ears our wineman from Barleyhome he just slumped to throne." Well, when King Ruaidhrí submitted to Henry that was closing time on the kingship, so to speak, after which he spent years, a king in name only, finishing off the dregs.

The Wild Man from Borneo has just come to town . . .

—that nonsense song to be sure is a long way from the High King; but then so, in all but name, was his namesake Rory, whose best publicized exploit before he got himself executed was to seize the Four Courts in central Dublin with a gang of Irregulars and hold it against government bombardment for three days until 30 June '22, when the flames forced him out. That was the Civil War's beginning. "The Wild Man from Borneo," yes indeed.

And if you page backward in *Finnegans Wake* from the fragment in question, you keep encountering modern hubbubs, for example,

> . . . You can't impose on frayshouters like os. Every tub here spucks his own fat. Hang coersion anyhow! And smotthermock Gramm's laws! But we're a drippindhrue gayleague all at ones. In the buginning is the woid, in the muddle is the sounddance and thereinofter you're in the unbewised again, vund vulsyvolsy. (*FW* 378)

"Drippindhrue gayleague" looks like dripping hues/rues and gaiety and the Gaelic League but it seems to want to sound like *Tuigeann tú Gaedhealg* ("tigen tu gelg")—"Do you understand Irish?"; indeed you can't impose on frayshouters like us (free shouters? Free Staters? Shouter of the Fray?). The truculence beneath these sentences was still more explicit a few pages earlier:

> Guns.
> Keep backwards, please because there was no good to gundy running up agina. Guns. And it was written in big capital. Guns. Saying never underupt greatgrandgosterfosters! Guns. And whatever one did, they said, the fourlings, that on no accounts you were not to. Guns. (*FW* 368)

Truly, "the boomomouths from their dupest dupes were in envery and anononously blowing great," as you'd believe without so much as noticing the behemoths of the deepest deeps, and with all that spatting and gunfire it's possible to credit that the fate of Rory O'Connor among others is entangled in these tangled pages after all.

So a good first approach to *Finnegans Wake* is to remember that Joyce commenced work on it when years of Irish violence had just ended, and the Free State had just come into precarious being. If its confusion is "imitative form," Ireland had been providing a good deal of confusion to imitate, much of it emanating from disputes about how to read documents, such as the Treaty itself or de Valera's notorious "document number two" on which the book plays at least seven times, something Dev said was in effect the same as the Treaty and yet dear God not the same because the oath it implied was not an oath. "His own obsessive preoccupation with the meaning of words," writes F. S. L. Lyons, "led [de Valera] into intricacies of speech where deputies found it hard to follow him" (*Ireland since the Famine* [1973] 442), and there are even parts of *Finnegans Wake* that clear up a little if you imagine Dev writing them.

Back to O'Connor's name though: for it seems that in Ireland you cannot so much as bestow a name without making a statement. When they named the Civil War Rory for the High King they equipped him with a destiny, so the choice of destinies is no wider than the choice of names. Joyce found this convenient, since homonymous actors could interchange roles. When the huge James Laughlin, now elder statesman of avant-garde publishing, appeared silhouetted in his Paris doorway, Joyce heard "Lochlann," a Norseman, and announced, "We two last met on the battlefield at Clontarf." Like any proper author, Joyce had helped defeat this Dane of a publisher.

Such is the principle on which Rory O'Connor can play King Roderick O'Connor (or perhaps vice versa). By extension, the pub-keeper who is the King of the Inn can play either of them, or be played by them; and the father of a family can play King or Pub-keeper, since any family is a repertory company. To enact all of history, many thousands of roles, we can do with a surprisingly small cast. In 1977, five men and two women at Radio Éireann were enough to enact any scene out of Joyce that was asked for by a script with thirty or forty parts in it.

In *Finnegans Wake* the casting principle is chiefly onomastic; not just Laughlin/Lochlann or O'Connor/O'Connor but *any* pair of homonymns can interchange roles. This hushed-up fact of linguistic experience is the basis of what is called the pun. It bespeaks something evidently true, that the world has far more phenomena crying to be named than any language has phonemes, and the names get reused.

We have already seen Joyce in "Eveline" taking note of "mass," a bulk, from *massa*, and "mass," divine service, from *missa*. English speakers having found it unimportant to distinguish these (for seldom indeed would perplexity arise) they have ended up being, as people say, "the same word."

There's an Irish word, *curcagh*, a swamp, from which they named a city that gets written Cork, and a Spanish word, *alcorque*, from which they named a substance we call cork, and when Frank O'Connor on a visit to Joyce in Paris asked what that picture was and was told "Cork," he next asked what its frame was, and was told "cork" again. Being an old-fashioned story-teller for whom words have chiefly instrumental interest, O'Connor thought Joyce was going out of his mind.

Or consider the sign you can see today at the foot of the path to the summit of Howth where Poldy and Molly lay in that memorable light amid the rhododendrons; it enjoins tourists not to Disturb the Blooms. Since it was surely put up by an official who'd no notion of making a joke, common sense thinks it amusing provided you don't take it seriously; but Joyce would have taken it seriously. Common sense supposes such confusions rare. Joyce thought otherwise.

For he had scrutinized enough words to be convinced that potential confusion was their norm. The miracle, in his opinion, lay in how readers ever know which sense to collect, and one thing *Finnegans Wake* is about is the seemingly insuperable difficulty of reading anything at all. His books abound everywhere with sly examples: as when he has Molly Bloom reading in bed a book that actually exists under the title *Ruby: a Novel Founded on the Life of a Circus Girl.* Joyce improved on this by renaming it *Ruby, the Pride of the Ring,* a name which, if we found it in *Finnegans Wake,* we'd not know whether to refer to circuses or to jewelry. He would have enjoyed the way Coleridge in *Kubla Khan* made the earth breathe "in short thick pants," not to mention the seemingly arithmetical import of a 1980 head-line, "Pope Plans Talks to End Long Division."

Most puns are inadvertent; most go undetected thanks to context, which releases the appropriate meaning and hides the others. The word "Pope" creates for "Division" a context in church history, on which headline-writers feel safe in relying. It would be hard for even *The New Yorker* to prod us into finding "Pope Plans Talks to End Division" even faintly punny. But "Long" placed next to "Division" tugs it toward a classroom context the headline-writer ought perhaps to have noticed. We may guess that he'd spent so much of his day counting letters that the words were losing their meaning, and when words have lost meaning you may be very fluent with them, as fluent as the narrator of "Eumaeus," who tells us how Parnell "notoriously stuck to his guns to the last drop even when clothed in the mantle of adultery" (*U* 654). If the inadvertent pun results from a word bringing to one context its affinities for another, then the paragraphs of "Eumaeus" work with inadvertent puns on a Homeric scale, the scale on which we speak instead of mixed metaphor.

When Joyce finished "Eumaeus" in early 1921 he was drawing toward the spirit of the *Wake* he'd be starting two years later. A wake is a collective jollification. His *Wake* is a multiplicity of voices being misapprehended by a collectivity of ears. And such writing as offered precedent for "Eumaeus" is itself collective, resulting from a mass amnesia concerning normal ways for words to keep company. Among the partakers in this amnesia were the scribblers for Irish provincial newspapers who provided one model for the style of "Eumaeus," and "Eumaeus" in turn, where from end to end of every shapeless sentence the tropes wriggle in place like maggots, was one armature for the style of *Finnegans Wake.* Prune the Wakese from a Wakean sentence, even consult one of the author's unelaborated drafts, and you are apt to find a "Eumaeus" sentence, nerveless, meandering, only of interest when Joyce has later contrived to fill it with minute inappropriatenesses. You find, in short, a language that has died, but that like an unembalmed corpse is full of local life. The occasion calls for a wake.

So to get a vocabulary Joyce went back to his "black mass" principle and the mayhem that implies, for if any word can change places with any word that is like it, where can we hope to end? He might have asked a like question on being told from the pulpit that this or that pharisaic burgess—

William Martin Murphy for instance—was Christ in disguise. Such religiosity generated phantoms. And staring at words that have never existed before despite their availability to any pixilated typist, we permit them to prompt well-known locutions that aren't there at all, and the result of this we call "understanding," as priests call another result "religion." It is Joyce's fascination with this process that prods him toward utterly dead set-pieces of affectation, as spurious under analysis at the ballad of Finnegan's Wake itself. That ballad is unknown in Ireland save by transfusion from Irish America: not an Irish song but an American fake, like one of the uncanonical gospels.

In *Finnegans Wake,* for practical reasons needless to rehearse, the annotator's field of attention is apt to be the single word, at most the paragraph. Five decades' overview and commentary bespeak no consensus whatever about a controlling idea: almost as if the book didn't want to let you draw back far enough to see one. So while we can say of *Ulysses* that it is the Book of Bloom, or that it is a 1904 *Odyssey,* we can say nothing that fundamental of the *Wake.*

That the two books are conspicuously different is only part of the story. They are not *that* different. We are confident about *Ulysses* thanks to a tradition of commentary, which has supplied such fundamentals as the names of the eighteen episodes. That tradition in turn derives through loose apostolic succession from books whose authors Joyce prompted. Though he had the instincts of a Fenian conspirator, "conspiracy" is a misleading word to use. It is impossible to read with no idea *what* you are reading; no one in 1715 would have known what to make of Mr. Pope's *Iliad* who did not know it was translated from Homer, and numerous eighteenth-century poems would seem wholly chaotic did we not know what to expect of things we've been taught to call Pindaric Odes. Swift disoriented his readers by confusing the genre signals: critical tradition has taught us to call *Gulliver's Travels* and *A Modest Proposal* "satires," but new readers were led to think the former a travel book, the later a projector's pamphlet, and were increasingly vexed as they turned the pages and found these conventions getting less and less helpful, which was part of what Swift intended. And Joyce was Swift's Irish successor in subverting what an English tradition—this time "the novel"—leads readers to expect. Six decades later, *Ulysses* has in effect created its own genre, and if beginning readers seldom look into Gilbert or Budgen, advanced readers may not reflect how much is owed them, or what is lost through their not having had Wakean counterparts. Whatever Jacques Mercanton was to have written, war and Joyce's grave swallowed up.

That *Finnegans Wake* is a dream is one commonplace; and who is dreaming? An answer may be, the book itself, although Richard Ellmann writes of Joyce telling "a friend" (unidentified) that it was the dream of old Finn MacCool, "lying in death beside the river Liffey and watching the history of Ireland and the world—past and future—flow through his mind like flotsam on the river of life" (*JJI* 559).

That was likely one way he thought of it, but he also spoke to Mrs. Giedion-Welcker of "the story of this Chapelizod family," and these words ought to be weighed. The man whose seven years on his previous book had entailed so much care for its documentary aspect—deciding on a height and weight for Bloom, installing him in a house the Directory showed to be vacant—surely he was unlikely to have overnight let that order of things just slide? It seemed a natural assumption at one time that the characters of this night-book possessed, so to speak, daylight selves, recoverable, it was once thought, in chapter 4 of book 3, when the sleepers seem to be temporarily awake and out of bed. But this skeleton key proved unusable—3.4 is now thought to entail very deep sleep indeed—and commentators lost interest in an underlying "novel," indeed came to deem the very idea naive.

For in France, meanwhile, intellectuals were undergoing one of their bouts of scorched-earth radicalism, of the sort inaugurated by Descartes when he wiped all previous systems out of his mind as the first step toward a new one. By the time Claude Lévi-Strauss, Roland Barthes, and Jacques Derrida had reshaped the academy's canons of interpretation, bare dumb blind "text" lay dead for its readers to animate, readers so far as possible uninfluenced either by received (hence culture-bound) conventions—here Joyce would have approved—or by any hint of what the (equally culture-bound) author wanted—but here Joyce's assent would have been greatly qualified.

Though at present they shy away from close engagement, post-structuralists point to Joyce as a prime exhibit. Does not *Ulysses* itself enact the gradual encroachment of "textuality" upon representational narrative? True; and at present we generally hear that *Finnegans Wake* is pure "text," at the lowest estimate a sort of commentators' Rorschach, at the highest a massive vindication of post-structuralist theory. That's one quick way to make it uninteresting.

But by post-structuralist theory *all* books end to end are pure text, notably *Ulysses,* which however remains haunted by Leopold Bloom's remarkably substantial ghost, moving through a certain city in a certain year. Though the city in the book is a city of words, it corresponds so minutely to a city in Ireland that facts drawn from that city dovetail into the book even when the book does not mention them.

Fritz Senn has produced a minor but compelling example (*James Joyce Quarterly,* 19.2 [1982] 177–78). As the "Ithaca" episode opens, something close to sheer textuality is informing us that Stephen and Bloom on their way from the cabman's shelter discussed among other topics "the influence of gaslight or the light of arc and glowlamps on the growth of adjoining paraheliotropic trees." In the previous episode, in the cabman's shelter, Bloom and Stephen sit with the *Telegraph* spread out before them. That newspaper exists, and in its relevant issue, 16 June 1904, Mr. Senn found on page one, in the column that is before Bloom as he sits on Stephen's right, an article touching on artificial light and the growth of plants. So we can see what put one topic of conversation into Bloom's mind.

But (1) neither Bloom nor his mind has ever existed, except as a construct derived by us from *Ulysses;* that is not merely post-structuralist orthodoxy but received common sense about fiction. However, (2) the *Telegraph* article is not mentioned in *Ulysses,* so how does it put something into a mind that exists only as a derivation from *Ulysses?*

In planting something perhaps never to be discovered, perhaps for Fritz Senn to discover sixty years later, Joyce played an exhilarating Irish game. Excluded as he felt from the English consensus ("The language in which we are speaking is his before it is mine"), he could knowingly toy with what English empiricism said was the root assumption of that English invention, the novel, the assumption that physical stimuli prompt mental processes; could toy too with the bully assumption that English bourgeois reality is so normative we needn't pause over the mere texts that point our minds toward it. (That was Frank O'Connor's assumption.) So here's the stimulus *outside* the text, the response *inside* it. Joyce was teasing such plain readers as might some day come upon this Friday footprint; but let the prophets of bare textuality too explain if they can how it's possible.

So we may want to reconsider the proposition that *Finnegans Wake* is the first great book to have knowingly and explicitly locked extra-textual reality outside. Every once in a while a job of *Wake* annotation turns up sequences of stark extra-textual fact, as when actual Chapelizod houses turn up arrayed in obdurate sequence. When such substantialities poke through the fog, they are apt to get discounted for lack of a governing plot. Although we cannot say who mimes whom—whether, so to speak, a Bloom in this new universe imitates an Odysseus or vice versa—we can expect a here and a now to be present somewhere in the mime.

The book was begun, we know, just after the Troubles: Easter Rebellion, Black-and-Tan bloodshed, Civil War: a time when "executions" happened right and left. Oliver Gogarty lived to thank the swans for his narrow escape from being executed. Joyce's college friend Francis Sheehy-Skeffington had no swans on his side; he was trying to restrain looting and help the wounded when an insane Irish officer "executed" him the day after Easter Monday, 1916. Such executions were performed by bullet, though in less accelerated times their provenance was the scaffold. Tim Finnegan when he fell was climbing to a bricklayer's scaffold: "And people thinks you missed the scaffold. Of fell design" (*FW* 621). And a wake presupposes a corpse.

I'll follow a Yeatsian example in closing with rhetorical questions. May we be waking the corpse of someone executed during the Civil War? Not a firebrand like Rory O'Connor, but some man involved in war's peripheral business? Erskine Childers, whose uncle Hugh Culling Eardely Childers gave initials to the book's eponymous hero HCE, was another executed hostage of 1922. He was English and had thrown in his lot with the Republicans; the excuse for shooting him was that (contrary to a recent edict) he owned a revolver. The reason may have been that Arthur Griffith and Kevin O'Higgins thought him irksome. (Gogarty, by the way, thought shooting him was a perfectly good idea.) Childers was a skilled yachtsman; his boat ran arms in 1914 to his subsequent executioners.

An executed sailor, a foreigner; perhaps, in the *Wake,* Norwegian, metamorphosed into a pubkeeper? Let us try it.

Very briefly: he came to Dublin a seaman, married a tailor's daughter (perky, tiny), whom he'd met while ordering a suit from her father. (He needn't be a hunchback, despite the mixup with the story of the hunchback and the tailor.) With Anna, he settled down and opened a Chapelizod pub. There are two sons, a daughter. Some obscure misdemeanor involving girls and soldiers has done for him. (It need not make any sense. Skeffington's offense didn't, nor Childers's.) In a little place like Chapelizod the gossip is endless, likewise the misinformation.

One test is the finale, in which a plaintive woman's voice seems to be urging her husband to get up and go for a walk, then recedes into reminiscence, then drops into void whence, as if dying, it circles back to restart the book. These are by common consent among the most moving pages written by Joyce, and it is arguable that they gain even more poignancy if we imagine their words to be passing through the mind of the widow, the morning after the wake, trying not to become conscious of the stark fact that her man is no longer beside her: fantasizing even her own death in order to stay asleep, and dropping back into the busy sleep of the opening, to reenact the whole turbulence yet again.

Patrick Pearse had scheduled the Easter Rebellion for Easter Sunday, 23 April 1916: William Shakespeare's birthday, and also the tercentenary of his death. Though it got put off a day by mixed staffwork, Joyce would have been prompted to wonder: Was Shakespeare, dead and born on the one day, one more imitator of Jesus at Easter? Was Ireland to have been another? And was his own last book a rewriting of his first story, "The Sisters," the story of a resurrection that was not?

Note

This paper duplicates in some things the "Wake of Wakes" chapter in my book *A Colder Eye* (New York: Alfred Knopf, 1983; Penguin Books, 1984).

Ulysses and Its Audience

A. Walton Litz

This essay began as a meditation on the problem of writing yet one more time on *Ulysses*. I first encountered *Ulysses* thirty-five years ago, when—an unusual thing for the late 1940s—it was assigned as the final text in a Princeton undergraduate course on the English novel. I still remember the awful moment when I had to face a blank page in the typewriter and write something coherent about a work that had overwhelmed me with its greatness, but which I found bewildering at even the simplest levels of understanding. In the end I resorted to the Hanley *Word Index* and pro-duced a New Critical essay on a recurring motif—although at the time I was not self-conscious enough to know that I was being New Critical. I had noticed that Bloom's advertisement for the "House of Key(e)s" is linked with the Isle of Man and Home Rule, since the lower chamber of the Manx legislature is called the House of Keys. This led to the plight of Bloom and Stephen as a "keyless couple," each deprived of Home Rule; to the story of Reuben J. Dodd's son and the Isle of Man; to the crossed keys of the caretaker in "Hades"; to Phineas Fletcher's *Purple Island, or the Isle of Man;* and finally to the End of the World in "Circe," where the various parts of the motif are brought together as a kilted octopus *"whirls through the murk, head over heels, in the form of the Three Legs of Man"* (*U* 507). By the time I had finished I felt a bit more comfortable with *Ulysses;* at least I was inside the whale.

Since that first effort I have written on *Ulysses* more times than I care to recall, and each time the book has pressed me toward another perspective, another way of reading. As Bloom says in "Nausicaa," "Returning not the same" (*U* 377). Sometimes the changes have been prompted by new infor-mation—Richard Ellmann's biography, for example, or the explosion in our knowledge of how Joyce wrote *Ulysses*. More often I have been follow-ing, at a safe pace, the contours of literary study as it has altered radically over the past quarter-century. In thinking about these changes in my own view of *Ulysses,* and in the writings of other critics who have had more important things to say about Joyce's great work, I was struck by the dynamic and somewhat special relationship that has always existed between *Ulysses* and its more self-conscious readers.

This relationship has partly been a result of the book's own extreme self-consciousness about the act of reading. Many of the remarks of the char-acters can be taken as covert comments on "how to read," and I am not thinking only of the aesthetic discussions in which Stephen dominates, although these are useful. A number of Bloom's most banal remarks, like "Returning not the same," take on a pointed meaning when applied to the act of reading. Even more important are the changing forms of the episodes, which condition our ways of reading and prepare us for what is to come. When we turn from the strong, conventional narrative line of "Hades" to the opening pages of "Aeolus"—where the newspaper headlines fragment the primary narrative and we must read back and forth between text and captions—Joyce is educating us in a new and more complicated form of reading, with a different cadence and a different aim, so that when we reach the two-planed narrative of "Cyclops" or the succession of imitated styles in "Oxen of the Sun" we are immediately receptive to these methods. As the novel develops each chapter seems to end in a way that prepares us for the following chapter. "Nausicaa," for instance, which begins by restoring us to the familiar indirect speech and interior monologue of the earlier episodes, becomes more elliptical and "artificial" toward its close, until the final paragraphs with their imitative styles and three-part repetitions lead us smoothly into the opening of "Oxen of the Sun."

Yet the relationship between *Ulysses* and literary criticism extends far beyond the work's self-consciousness and reflexive form. In fact, it is difficult to think of *Ulysses* apart from the critical tradition, while it is not difficult to think of *Great Expectations* or *Four Quartets* in that way. Words-worth once said that every author, "as far as he is great and at the same time *original,* has had the task of *creating* the taste by which he is to be enjoyed" ("Essay, Supplementary to the Preface" [1815]), and Joyce is the supreme example of this Romantic and post-Romantic assumption that a great writer creates his own audience. For me, one of the most interesting developments in recent literary criticism has been the notion advanced by various reader-response critics that a "horizon" or common ground for our individual readings can be established by a recreation of the original audience for which the work was intended, or by a study of the traditional readings which have led to our present interpretations.[1] This reconstruction of an historical context in terms of reader-response has a great appeal for me, since I am always looking for ways to rescue historical scholarship; and it has given us a new approach to works from earlier and, we like to think, more stable literary periods.

But what of *Ulysses?* Did Joyce have an audience in mind, in any conventional sense of that term, while writing the book? What was the modernist audience of 1922 like, if it existed? To me these are very difficult questions. If you look in some detail at the responses that have survived from the years between the earliest reception of *Ulysses* and the best-informed responses of the 1930s, such as those by Edmund Wilson and Richard Blackmur, you get the strong impression that very few people read the book in its entirety, and fewer still read it in a fresh and independent way. The extreme difficulty of the work itself, combined with the difficulty of obtaining a personal copy, meant that from the very beginning readers were unusually dependent on the available accounts of *Ulysses,* especially the early essays by Pound and Eliot and Larbaud.

Thus we have the interesting case of a book that was canonized before it was published in full—canonized through the "spiritual" authority of Pound and Eliot, which is the only way in which any work ever enters the canon—but which had yet to find its audience. I have argued elsewhere that the direction of much later criticism was determined by Pound and Eliot, since it was Joyce's good fortune that his first readers were the two greatest poet-critics of his time ("Pound and Eliot on *Ulysses*" 5–18). However, Pound and Eliot did not form an ideal audience. To borrow Harold Bloom's terminology, Pound's difficulty was a lack of anxiety, Eliot's an excess of anxiety. Early on in the serial publication of *Ulysses* Pound began to resist its more experimental features, since he was determined to make *Ulysses* the culmination in English of a "realist" tradition that could be traced back to Flaubert and the Goncourt brothers. From "Sirens" onward he regretted the more and more radical departures from the world of *Portrait,* and virtually ignored the most important feature of the second half of *Ulysses:* the progression of styles.

Eliot, on the other hand, was simultaneously fascinated and deeply disturbed by the swirling energies of Joyce's amassing work. Writing in the *Egoist* in the summer of 1918, when he had seen only the opening chapters, Eliot found *Ulysses* "volatile and heady" but "terrifying"; and this anxiety is still there in the seldom quoted opening of that much-quoted 1923 review-essay, "*Ulysses,* Order, and Myth":

> I hold this book to be the most important expression which the present age has found; it is a book to which we are all indebted, and from which none of us can *escape.* . . . it has given me all the surprise, delight, and *terror* that I can require, and I will leave it at that.[2] (84 [italics mine])

In 1936 Eliot gave a lecture in Dublin, to the English Literary Society, that was never published (the manuscript is now at Harvard). The argument of the entire lecture is very like the later arguments about literary influence put forward by Walter Jackson Bate and Harold Bloom—Eliot even speaks of the special value of poetry that is *mis-read*. He says that sometimes the way in which literature from another time or place is misunderstood is the important thing, just as we may be deeply influenced in our personal lives by persons we understand very imperfectly. But of course Eliot's conclusion is the exact opposite of Bloom's: the need for humility and submission in the presence of the masters, not struggle and denial (one thinks of the last part of "East Coker," or of the Dantesque meeting with a ghostly other self in part two of "Little Gidding").

In this same lecture Eliot speaks of his fate—and by implication his good fortune—in having gone through his formative period (c. 1909–10) when Yeats was least powerful and most "local." The opposite was true in Eliot's relationship with Joyce. In a little-known piece on *"Ulysses* and *The Waste Land"* that appeared in *The Irish Times* exactly ten years ago (16 June 1972), Anthony Cronin recalled a conversation with Eliot from the late 1950s. Eliot told him that "as far back as 1918 he had been meditating 'a certain sort of poem about the contemporary world,' subsequently *The Waste Land*":

> Then *Ulysses* began to appear in *The Little Review*. Worse still, in one sense, a large part of the manuscript came into his hands as assistant editor of *The Egoist*. The effect on the further composition of the poem was, for the time being, ruinous. What he was tentatively attempting to do, with the usual false starts and despairs, had already been done, done superbly and, it seemed to him finally, in prose which, without being poetic in the older sense, had the intensity and texture of poetry. He abandoned his poem.
>
> Eventually Pound told him that "even if the thing has been done in prose it is necessary to do it in poetry also." This cheered him up and he decided to go on. (10)

Even after allowing for errors and exaggerations in the combined memories of Cronin and Eliot, this passage rings true to me. Eliot did not know how to handle *Ulysses,* and his considerable delay in producing *"Ulysses,* Order, and Myth"—a delay that vexed Joyce—was probably the result of indecision about how to read and present the work. It was not until Valery Larbaud's essay appeared, with its schematic information supplied by Joyce, that Eliot was able to process *Ulysses* into the world of *The Sacred Wood* and *The Waste Land,* to discover a source of order in the "mythic method." Already in 1922–23 the work was being shaped by its critical audience.

This intense interaction between *Ulysses* and its critics—and between interpretations—could be documented at any point in the sixty-year history of reading *Ulysses*. One thinks of the impact of Stuart Gilbert's 1930 study, which was partly engineered by Joyce to spike the early philistine charges of bolshevik formlessness; and even more of the impact of Gilbert's liberal but sanitized quotations from the novel, which became *Ulysses* to many readers. Or one thinks of the way in which the early criticism of *Finnegans Wake*—not, I am convinced, *Finnegans Wake* itself—produced some of the more feverish mythic and archetypal readings of *Ulysses* in the 1940s and early 1950s. But what I want to do in the rest of this essay is to focus on the more recent, more interesting, and I think more responsible readings of *Ulysses,* roughly from the mid-1950s to the present. I want to reflect on the ways in which criticism has revised the novel, and—perhaps more important—the ways in which *Ulysses,* because of its particular place in literary and cultural history, has set limits or "horizons" for our critical ambitions, especially for the contemporary urge to equate the critic with the artist and make criticism a form of primary creation.

One of the major issues in recent discussions of *Ulysses* has been the question of whether the work's form is essentially spatial or temporal. For the Romantics, a literary work was ideally a spatial image that fused the particular and the general into some organic whole. In a letter to Joseph Cottle of 7 March 1815 Coleridge said that the "common end of all *narrative,* nay, of *all* Poems is to convert a *series* into a *Whole:* to make those events, which in real or imagined History move on in a *strait* Line, assume to our Understandings a *circular* motion—the snake with its Tail in its mouth" (Coleridge 545). Early readers of *Ulysses,* moved by Pound's Modernistic restatement of this romantic assumption in his theory of the Image, sought to "convert a *series* into a *Whole*" and view *Ulysses* as a timeless Image. And this tendency was intensified by the more and more self-conscious critical theories of the 1940s and 1950s. One thinks of Joseph Frank's famous essay of 1945, "Spatial Form in Modern Literature," or of Northrop Frye's early criticism, where one of the givens is the belief that "the most natural thing for [a critic] to do is to freeze [the work of literature], to ignore its movement in time and look at it as a completed pattern of words, with all its parts existing simultaneously" (21). But with the 1960s and the decay of the New Criticism, emphasis shifted to the temporal nature of narrative, and to ways of describing reading as an act in time. And in spite of recent rear-guard maneuvers by the proponents of spatial form, a stress on sequential reader-response underlies most of the recent important work on *Ulysses.* I think it is symptomatic that one of the latest (and best) books on *Ulysses* was originally subtitled "A Linear Reading of the Novel" (Karen Lawrence).

This quarrel between proponents of Space and Time in the reading of *Ulysses* may sound like the sort of abstract, theoretical discussion—remote from the challenge of practical criticism—that has given recent literary criticism such a bizarre popular reputation. But it bears directly on some of the most important decisions we have to make in reading the novel, decisions about the nature and degree of Joyce's irony, for example, or about the way in which the Homeric frame is used. A "pure" spatial reading, if such a thing were possible, would dissolve historical time into the myth, as when Eliot discovered in the Russian Ballet performance of *Le sacre du printemps* "the continuity of the human predicament: primitive man on the dolorous steppes, modern man in the city with its despairing noises, the essential problem unchanging" (*The Dial* 71 [Oct. 1921]).[3] This is exactly that collapse of time and logical discourse that Yeats describes rather uneasily in the first (1925) edition of *A Vision,* where he is thinking of works like *The Waste Land* and *Ulysses:* "It is as though myth and fact, united until the exhaustion of the Renaissance, have now fallen so far apart that man understands for the first time the rigidity of fact, and calls up, by that very recognition, myth . . . which now but gropes its way out of the mind's dark but will shortly pursue and terrify" (212). *Ulysses* would then be like "those examples of medieval sculpture or book illustration in which figures from the Old and New Testaments, classical antiquity, and sometimes local history are all grouped together as part of one timeless complex of significance (Frank 209). A mainly temporal reading, by contrast, would leave much more room for historical ironies and the development of personality.

But in practice readers of *Ulysses* find it difficult to hold to these "pure" extremes, and are constantly being drawn toward more compromised readings. Even the most spatial readings tend to proceed chapter by chapter, and recent exponents of reader-response criticism have had to modify their theories to fit the novel's juxtapositions, overlappings, and deep perspectives. This is because *Ulysses* has both a powerful, conventional narrative drive—the juxtapositions in the early chapters remind one of Dickens—and a tendency toward spatiality which builds in the later chapters. Therefore all readers of *Ulysses* must have a double sense of the work: a sense of how we came to understand it in time, through a series of adjustments from chapter to chapter, as the novel educated us in how to read it; and a sense of the whole work as a timeless artifact. Joseph Frank's famous remark that works such as *Ulysses* cannot be read, only re-read, is a useful half-truth, but only a half-truth. In the case of this critical debate the very nature of *Ulysses* has set limits or horizons on the reach of theory.

Another example of the novel's control over the critic's lust for autonomy can be found in the application of post-structuralist criticism to *Ulysses*. I do not think it is an exaggeration to say that post-structuralist criticism regards language as a self-contained play of signifiers, and notions such as "character" or "the self" as fictions we create in order to give the "signs" an illusion of reality. From this perspective writing and reading are similar, and co-equal, acts of interpretation, and criticism is a fiction about other fictions. Such an approach seems well-suited to many modern works, and especially to what Martin Price has called "the symbolist novel," where "characters tend to dissolve into the elaborate verbal structure of the work, becoming nodes, as it were, of images or motifs; or they dissolve into aspects of one central character, dialectical forces within one situation or mind. The figure gives way to the ground, or at best there is a shimmering iridescence" (Price 292). This description of the modern symbolist novel seems right if applied to the later Virginia Woolf or to Beckett, but I find it inadequate to describe our complicated experience of *Ulysses*. The special quality of *Ulysses* is that it exhibits all the stigmata of the symbolist novel, as defined by Martin Price, and welcomes post-structuralist criticism; but at the same time, especially in the first half of the narrative, it shows a full and rather old-fashioned interest in character, such as we find in the great nineteenth-century commentators on Shakespeare. The way in which Stephen's character is built up, at least through the Shakespeare discussion in "Scylla and Charybdis," strikes me as very different from the way in which Boylan is constructed out of verbal bits in "Sirens," and these different methods interlock in the finished novel.

If this is true, then "character" in *Ulysses*—to focus on that term for a moment—cannot be fully understood either by partly mimetic critical notions based on nineteenth-century fiction and drama or by methods derived from structuralist and post-structuralist theory. Even W. J. Harvey, in one of the most sensible and pragmatic books yet written on *Character and the Novel* (1965), refuses to recognize this peculiar blend in *Ulysses*. Harvey finds himself forced by his rather primitive theory to choose between two kinds of characterization, mimetic and autonomous. In the mimetic frame, such words as "truth," "probability," "reality" refer to a natural order outside the work of literature. In the autonomous form of characterization, the same words (truth, probability, realism) can only relate to the internal terms of reference established by the work, its "internal morphology." To borrow an example from I. A. Richards: the mimetic theory will condemn Nahum Tate's happy-ending revision of *King Lear* because it is not true to nature, while the autonomous theory will condemn the happy ending because it is inconsistent with the internal structure of the play.

Harvey feels that he must make a choice between these two broad theories: he chooses the mimetic approach, and applies it with great success to a wide range of works. But the method breaks down in his treatment of Joyce, simply because both the mimetic and autonomous theories can be used as the basis for adequate—though partial—descriptions of what goes on in *Ulysses*. In fact, if we construct the broadest spectrum of critical opinion on "character" we can find passages in *Ulysses* to support every position, ranging from characters as unique essences to characters as mere folds in the time-structure of the novel. Joyce was too steeped in Aristotle, in Shakespeare, and in late-nineteenth-century criticism of Shakespeare to give up completely the notion of fictional characters as representations of permanent essences, manifestations of the inner whatness of the self. A modern behaviorist psychologist may believe that personality is merely a "repertoire of roles":

> There is nothing else. There is no "core" personality underneath the behavior and feelings; there is no "central" monolithic self which lies beneath the various external manifestations. . . . The "self" is a composite of many selves, each of them consisting of a set of self-perceptions, which are . . . specific to the expectations of one or another significant reference group. (Brim, quoted in Price 282)

This psychological jargon sounds very much like some contemporary critical jargon. But Stephen (and I think Joyce) takes a very different view of "roles." "Every life is many days, day after day. We walk through ourselves, meeting robbers, ghosts, giants, old men, young men, wives, widows, brothers-in-love. But always meeting ourselves" (*U* 213). "The boy of act one is the mature man of act five. All in all" (*U* 212). Or this echo of Hamlet's first soliloquy: "And as the mole on my right breast is where it was when I was born, though all my body has been woven of new stuff time after time, so through the ghost of the unquiet father the image of the unliving son looks forth" (*U* 194). It is this sense of individual *whatness* beneath all the variations of behavior and description that Stuart Gilbert describes in *James Joyce's "Ulysses,"* surely with Joyce's tacit approval:

> In most novels the reader's interest is aroused and his attention held by the presentation of dramatic situations, of problems deriving from conduct or character and the reactions of the fictitious personages among themselves. The personages of *Ulysses* are *not* fictitious and its true significance does not lie in problems of conduct or character. . . . All these people are as they must be; they act, we see, according to some *lex eterna,* an ineluctable condition of their very existence. . . . The law of their being is within them, it is a personal heritage, inalienable and autonomous. (21–22)

Most structuralist and post-structuralist critics would say that this notion of "individuality and rich psychological coherence" is a myth that runs counter to the "general ethos" of recent literary criticism (and recent literature), and they would point with some justice to the many instances in *Ulysses* where a nineteenth-century model for character will not hold. They might say that as the novel progresses the figures tend to lose their physical and psychological individuality; they become fields of force for the interplay of styles and themes. But in spite of the increasing artifice which marks the development of *Ulysses,* and the approach toward a theory of types such as that found in *Finnegans Wake,* Joyce's book of 16 June 1904 is supersaturated with the "felt life" of history and accumulated human experience. This is why the more humane term "book," which I have been using, seems more appropriate than the austere professional term "text." No work of literature with which I am familiar is more contingent upon a deep interest in human possibilities, past and present. That is why readers as different—and as intelligent—as Wilson and Empson and Kenner have been driven to speculate on what happens between the chapters, or after the close of the novel. Our overriding desire is to fill the empty spaces with the noisy business of life, not with the silence our theories may demand.

Let me sum up by saying what I have *not* been saying. I have not been saying that Joyce is a myriad-minded writer whose greatest work is too diverse, energetic, and "open" to be framed by a single critical perspective, although that is certainly true. Nor am I arguing that all literary works must be described in terms consonant with their original social and intellectual environments—the history of Shakespeare criticism would immediately disabuse us of that notion. I *am* saying that all works are more hospitable to some approaches than to others, and that this congeniality is historically determined. I believe we all feel, for example, that a Marxist approach is more illuminating when applied to Dickens than when applied to Spenser; or that deconstruction of an author whose viewpoint is radically ambiguous will be more successful than deconstruction of an author who holds strong ethical views about art as mimesis. To say something like "the act of interpretation is the real hero, not any one of the characters," would seem more appropriate to James's *The Sacred Fount* than to Trollope's *The Way We Live Now,* although it could help us to focus on some of the narrative peculiarities in Trollope's novel.

If, then, the historical setting of a work does indicate some sensible horizons for our reading—a community of relevant interests—the special place of *Ulysses* in literary and cultural history becomes crucial. For of all the great Modernist works, it is simultaneously most traditional and most avant-garde. When looked at closely, the "newness" of any Modernist work, whether in language or form or subject, can usually be seen as the result of traditional methods and values being placed under such stress that they fracture or collapse and are then reformed. This is especially true of *Ulysses,* which was the driving force in Modernism during the years of its growth and immediately after publication. Whether one thinks of the process of composition, or of the narrative development of the finished work, or of *Ulysses* as a spatial design, this mixture of the old and the new is always there. A traditional "story" is threaded through an increasingly discontinuous plot-structure that often resembles a cubist collage. Strong vestiges of an older belief in distinctive character and individual psychology are intermixed with techniques that fragment the "self" and dissolve personality into linguistic signs. Methods that reflect traditional assumptions about language and its mimetic powers are overlayed with methods that point forward to *Finnegans Wake* and the promises of post-Saussurean linguistics. From the perspective of sixty years we can see that the making of *Ulysses* coincided with one of those periods of accelerated cultural change that determine the shape of what is to come for some time. Otherwise we could find a better term for our recent past than "post-Modern." To me the greatest evidence of Joyce's genius was his ability to catch in *Ulysses* more of the dynamic energies of his age than we can find in the works of any of his contemporaries. Because no book of criticism can ever do justice to all these energies, no single "ideal" reading will ever appear. In fact, I would argue that attempts to do justice to everything in a work are always self-defeating, since they blunt the cutting-edge of practical criticism: ultimately

Frye's *Anatomy,* because it attempts to account for everything, will be of less use to a reader of *Ulysses* than S. L. Goldberg's narrow-minded and in some ways mean-spirited study, *The Classical Temper,* which cuts through the work with a Leavisite scalpel. What our sixty-year perspective on *Ulysses* offers is not a chance for magisterial syntheses, but a better understanding of the novel's place in history, and therefore a better understanding of the many ways in which it can be read. If the best criticism results from a constant and self-conscious adjustment between the horizons of our own cultural life and what we can recapture of a literary work's original horizons, then *Ulysses* gives us an unusual opportunity to define our present critical, literary, and social lives, since in it we find—appropriate to a book by a former disciple of Ibsen—both a history of the past and a history of the future.

Notes

1. I am thinking of the works of Hans Robert Jauss, and of the "Konstanz school" in general; see Hans Robert Jauss, *Toward an Aesthetic of Reception,* tr. Timothy Bahti. I am aware, however, of the liberties that Anglo-American readers have taken with Jauss's theories (see Brook Thomas, "Reading Wolfgang Iser or Responding to a Theory of Response," 54–65).

2. In *Selected Prose of T. S. Eliot,* ed. Frank Kermode, 175.

3. Quoted in Joseph Frank, "Spatial Form: Thirty Years After," in *Spatial Form in Narrative,* ed. Jeffrey Smitten and Ann Daghistany, 209.

Works Cited

Brim, Orville E., Jr. "Personality Development as Role-Learning." 1960. Quoted in Martin Price, "The Other Self" (below) 282.

Coleridge, S. T. *Collected Letters of Samuel Taylor Coleridge.* Ed. Earl Leslie Griggs. 6 vols. Oxford: Clarendon Press, 1959. Vol. 4 (1815–1819).

Eliot, T. S. "*Ulysses,* Order, and Myth." *The Egoist* 5 (June/July 1918). Rpt. in *Selected Prose of T. S. Eliot,* ed. Frank Kermode. London: Faber & Faber, 1975.

Frank, Joseph. "Spatial Form: Thirty Years After." In *Spatial Form in Narrative,* ed. Jeffrey Smitten and Ann Daghistany. Ithaca, N.Y.: Cornell University Press, 1981.

Frye, Northrop. *Fables of Identity.* New York: Harcourt, Brace & World, 1963.

Gilbert, Stuart. *James Joyce's "Ulysses."* New York: Vintage, 1952.

Jauss, Hans Robert. *Toward an Aesthetic of Reception.* Tr. Timothy Bahti. Minneapolis: University of Minnesota Press, 1982.

Lawrence, Karen. *The Odyssey of Style in "Ulysses."* Princeton University Press, 1982.

Litz, A. Walton. "Pound and Eliot on *Ulysses:* The Critical Tradition." In *"Ulysses": Fifty Years,* ed. Thomas F. Staley. Bloomington: Indiana University Press, 1974.

Price, Martin. "The Other Self: Thoughts About Character in the Novel." In *Imagined Worlds: Essays on Some English Novels and Novelists in Honour of John Butt,* ed. Maynard Mack and Ian Gregor. London: Methuen, 1968.

Thomas, Brook. "Reading Wolfgang Iser or Responding to a Theory of Response." *Comparative Literature Studies* 19 (Spring 1982): 54–65.

Yeats, Willliam Butler. *A Vision*. London: T. Werner Laurie, Ltd., 1925. Second Ed. London: Macmillan, 1937.

Notes on Contributors

DEREK ATTRIDGE holds a chair in English Studies at the University of Strathclyde, Glasgow, Scotland. He is the author of two books on English metrics, co-editor of *Post-structuralist Joyce: Essays from the French* (1984), and editor of the forthcoming *Cambridge Companion to Joyce Studies*. He is currently completing a book on questions of literary language with particular attention to Joyce.

MORRIS BEJA, professor of English and chair of the department at Ohio State University, is president of the James Joyce Foundation. He is the author of *Epiphany in the Modern Novel, Film and Literature,* and many articles on modern fiction. He has edited volumes of essays on Joyce, Virginia Woolf, and Samuel Beckett.

BERNARD BENSTOCK is professor of comparative literature and director of the Program in Literature and Society at the University of Tulsa. Past president of the James Joyce Foundation and member of the board of trustees, his most recent books are *James Joyce* and *Critical Essays on James Joyce.* He is the editor of a forthcoming volume entitled *James Joyce: The Augmented Ninth,* and with Shari Benstock is in the process of completing *Narrative Con/Texts in "Ulysses"* and *Narrative Con/Texts in "Finnegans Wake."*

SHELDON BRIVIC, associate professor of English at Temple University, is the author of *Joyce Between Freud and Jung* and *Joyce the Creator.* He has just finished a novel, *Stealing,* and is starting a Lacanian study called "The Subject of Joyce."

WILLIAM M. CHACE is professor of English and vice provost for academic planning and development at Stanford University. He is the author of *The Political Identities of Ezra Pound and T. S. Eliot* (1973), *Lionel Trilling: Criticism and Politics* (1980), editor of *James Joyce: A Collection of Critical Essays* (1974), and co-editor, with Peter Collier, of *An Introduction to Literature* (1985). He is now working on a study of the codes involved in literary criticism.

SEAMUS DEANE teaches at University College, Dublin. He has published both poetry (for example, *Rumours,* 1977, and *History Lessons,* 1983) and literary criticism (his *Celtic Revivals: Essays in Modern Irish Literature, 1880–1980* appeared in 1985). He is one of the directors of the series of Field Day pamphlets; his own pamphlets include *Civilians and Barbarians* (1983), and *Heroic Styles: The Tradition of an Idea* (1984).

MAUD ELLMANN is a lecturer at the University of Southampton; she has also been a visiting faculty member in the United States at Amherst College. She has published essays on modern literature, critical theory, and feminism. Her book on T. S. Eliot and Ezra Pound will soon be published.

RICHARD ELLMANN, professor of English at Emory University, is the author of *James Joyce* (2nd edition, 1982), *Ulysses on the Liffey,* and *The Consciousness of Joyce.* He has edited Stanislaus Joyce's *My Brother's Keeper,* volumes 2 and 3 of Joyce's *Letters,* and *Giacomo Joyce;* with Ellsworth Mason he edited *The Critical Writings of James Joyce.*

DANIEL FERRER is *maître de conférence* at the University of Besançon and currently *chargé de recherche* at the Centre National de la Recherche Scientifique-Paris. He has written on Virginia Woolf, William Faulkner, English and American painting, and literary theory. He is co-editor of *Post-structuralist Joyce,* co-author of *Genèses de Babel: la création de "Finnegans Wake"* (1985), and the author of several articles on Joyce.

ELLIOTT B. GOSE, JR., professor of English at the University of British Columbia, Vancouver, Canada, is the author of *Imagination Indulged: The Irrational in the Nineteenth-Century Novel; The Transformation Process in Joyce's "Ulysses";* and *The World of the Irish Wander Tale.*

MAURICE HARMON, M.R.I.A., is professor and director of a graduate program in Irish studies at University College, Dublin, and formerly was chairman of the International Association for the Study of Anglo-Irish Literature. He is the editor of *Irish University Review,* and the author of *Sean O'Faolain; Modern Irish Literature, 1800–1967;* the *J. M. Synge Centenary Papers; The Poetry of Thomas Kinsella; Select Bibliography for the Study of Anglo-Irish Literature; Richard Murphy;* and *Irish Poetry after Yeats.* With Roger McHugh he wrote *A Short History of Anglo-Irish Literature,* and he is now preparing a study of Austin Clarke.

DAVID HAYMAN, professor of comparative literature at the University of Wisconsin-Madison, has produced some forty articles and five books on Joyce, including *"Ulysses": The Mechanics of Meaning.* He has edited *A First-Draft Version of "Finnegans Wake"; In the Wake of the Wake;* and was editor of twenty-five volumes in the James Joyce Archive series. He is currently writing a series of manuscript studies illuminating the early development of the *Wake.*

SUZETTE A. HENKE, associate professor of English at the State University of New York at Binghamton, is the author of *Joyce's Moraculous Sindbook* (1978), and co-editor with Elaine Unkeless of *Women in Joyce* (1982). Her articles include studies of Woolf, Beckett, Nin, Richardson, Forster, Yeats, Farmer, and Cage. She is presently completing a book called *James Joyce and the Politics of Desire* and a study of autobiographical fiction by contemporary women writers.

PHILLIP F. HERRING, professor of English at the University of Wisconsin-Madison, is associate editor of *Contemporary Literature.* He has edited *Joyce's "Ulysses" Notesheets in the British Museum* and *Joyce's Notes and Early Drafts for "Ulysses".* His book *Joyce's Uncertainty Principle* is forthcoming from Princeton University Press, and he is beginning a book on closure in the modernist novel.

ELLEN CAROL JONES, a doctoral candidate in English language and literature at Cornell University, has published articles and reviews on Joyce and Woolf.

HUGH KENNER, Andrew W. Mellon Professor of Humanities at Johns Hopkins University, has been writing on Joyce and other subjects since 1947. At present he is working on *A Sinking Island* for Knopf; Joyceans and Yeatsians will be relieved to know that the island in question is England.

KAREN LAWRENCE is associate professor and chairperson of the English department at the University of Utah. She has written numerous articles on Joyce, and is the author of *The Odyssey of Style in "Ulysses."* The co-author of *The McGraw-Hill Guide to English Literature,* she is currently studying issues of gender, language, and authority in travel novels which involve a female protagonist's journey to a foreign country.

A. WALTON LITZ, professor of English at Princeton University, is a former Rhodes Scholar. In 1972 he was awarded the E. Harris Harbison Award for Gifted Teaching by the Danforth Foundation. He is the author of some fifty essays on modern literature and four books: *Introspective Voyager: The Poetic Development of Wallace Stevens; James Joyce; Jane Austen;* and *The Art of James Joyce.* His most recent publication, with Omar Pound, is *Ezra Pound and Dorothy Shakespear: Their Letters, 1909–1914.* He is currently preparing a new two-volume edition of the poems of William Carlos Williams.

J. B. LYONS, M.D., F.R.C.P.I., is consultant physician to Mercer's Hospital, Dublin, and St. Michael's Hospital, Dun Laoghaire, and Professor of the History of Medicine in the Royal College of Surgeons in Ireland. His books include *A Primer of Neurology, James Joyce and Medicine,* and *Oliver St. John Gogarty: The Man of Many Talents.*

ANN McCULLOUGH, O.P., associate professor of English at Edgewood College in Madison, Wisconsin, is currently revising for publication a manuscript called "B. W. Huebsch: Publisher to Modernism."

GIORGIO MELCHIORI, professor of English at Rome University, has edited, with G. Corsini, *James Joyce: Scritti Italiani,* a bilingual critical edition of Joyce's *Epiphanies,* and a symposium volume, *Joyce in Rome.* He is currently editing Joyce's minor works in Italian translation and preparing a revised text of *Ulysses* with full Italian commentary. He is also preparing for publication a bilingual Shakespeare, an edition of *2 Henry IV,* and, with V. Gabrieli, *The Book of Sir Thomas More.*

DAVID NORRIS, lecturer in English literature at Trinity College, Dublin, has written, lectured, and broadcast extensively in Europe, the Middle East, and America. He was principal organizer of the centennial Joyce symposium and chairman of the host committee. He is currently involved in the creation of a cultural center in memory of Joyce in a restored eighteenth-century building in central Dublin.

MARGOT NORRIS, professor of English at the University of Michigan, is the author of *The Decentered Universe of "Finnegans Wake"* and *Beasts of the Modern Imagination: Darwin, Nietzsche, Kafka, Ernst, and Lawrence.* She is currently working on a second book on Joyce, tentatively titled *Joyce and the Problem of Desire.*

RICHARD PEARCE teaches at Wheaton College in Massachusetts. He is the author of *Stages of the Clown: Perspectives on Modern Fiction from Dostoyevsky to Beckett; The Novel in Motion: An Approach to Modern Fiction;* and has edited *Critical*

Essays on Thomas Pynchon. Now he is working on a book called *Voices, Stories (W)holes: The Politics of Modern Narration* which focuses on Joyce, Woolf, and Faulkner.

JEAN-MICHEL RABATÉ, professor of English at the University of Dijon, has written *James Joyce: Portrait de l'Auteur en Autre Lecteur; Language, Sexuality and Ideology in Ezra Pound's Cantos;* and *La Beauté Amère: Fragments d'esthétiques: Barthes, Broch, Michima*. He has also edited a collection of essays on Beckett called *Beckett avant Beckett*.

BERYL SCHLOSSMAN is the author of *Joyce's Catholic Comedy of Language* and articles on Joyce, Montaigne, Augustine, Proust, and Benjamin. A Fulbright Scholar, she is currently completing a dissertation on Flaubert and Proust at Johns Hopkins University.

DAVID SEED teaches American and modern literature at Liverpool University, and is the author of articles on Henry James, T. S. Eliot, Isaac B. Singer, Henry Roth, and others. He has recently finished a critical study of Thomas Pynchon's fiction.

CAROL SHLOSS, first Fellow in the Humanities at Drexel University, is the author of *Flannery O'Connor's Dark Comedies* and *The Privilege of Perception: Photography and the American Writer*. She is currently working on a new book, *The Technologies of Modernism*.

ANDRÉ TOPIA, lecturer in English literature at the University of Paris X — Nanterre, has published articles on Joyce, Raymond Queneau, Samuel Beckett, Flann O'Brien, Virginia Woolf, and literary theory. He is currently preparing a book on parody and intertextuality in *Ulysses*.

ROBERT YOUNG, lecturer in English at the University of Southampton, England, has recently edited *Untying the Text: A Post-Structuralist Reader,* and is co-editor of the *Oxford Literary Review*.